Sowing
the
Mustard
Seed

Sowing the Mustard Seed

THE STRUGGLE FOR FREEDOM AND DEMOCRACY IN UGANDA

Yoweri Kaguta Museveni

Edited by
Elizabeth Kanyogonya and Kevin Shillington

MACMILLAN

Macmillan Education
Between Towns Road, Oxford OX4 3PP
A division of Macmillan Publishers Limited
Companies and representatives throughout the world

www.macmillan-africa.com

ISBN 0 333 68908 9

Maps drawn by Tek Art
Front cover photographs Manu Kanani, Camera Press, Kampala
Back cover photographs William Pike & Pippa Shillington
Other photographs courtesy of the author unless otherwise stated

Printed in Hong Kong

2006 2005 2004 2003 2002
10 9 8 7 6 5 4 3 2

THIS BOOK IS DEDICATED TO

my father, Amos Kaguta
my mother, Esteeri Kokundeka
my wife, Janet
and our children,
Muhoozi, Natasha, Patience and Diana

CONTENTS

CONTENTS

He told them another parable: 'The kingdom of heaven is like a
mustard seed, which a man took and planted in his field.
Though it is the smallest of all your seeds, yet when it grows, it is
the largest of garden plants and becomes a tree, so that the birds
of the air come and perch in its branches.'
Matthew 13: 31–2 (New International Version)

PREFACE

This book is the story of my own personal role in the struggle for freedom and democracy in Uganda over the past 30 years. The book has been a long time in gestation. I began writing it in Kampala in 1980, when I was Minister for Regional Co-operation in the government of Godfrey Binaisa, one of the interim governments set up after the overthrow of Idi Amin. Elections were to be held later that year. I hoped at the time that the armed phase of the struggle for freedom and democracy in Uganda would end and that we would now have our long-desired opportunity to reconstruct the old colonial state along democratic, non-sectarian lines. It turned out that my hopes were premature.

As I suspected, the elections were massively rigged and, with Milton Obote's return to power, it was clear to me that those of us who wished to see the proper reconstruction of a truly democratic Uganda would have to fight for it. We had warned the country that if the elections were rigged, we would take to the bush again, this time to wage a protracted armed struggle for the liberation of our country. Now that our suspicions had proved justified, a few comrades and I made the decision to begin that struggle.

It was to be a further five years before we finally overthrew the dictatorships of Milton Obote and Tito Okello and formed the government of the National Resistance Movement on 26 January 1986. I returned to the writing again in 1988, but the demands on the time of a President of a country like Uganda are very heavy, so it has taken a further eight years for the book to reach completion.

Although I have been President of Uganda for ten years, and have just successfully sought re-election for a further five years, I feel I should reiterate my position on leadership. This is that unless one's purpose in seeking it is to steal public funds, leadership, especially in an underdeveloped country like Uganda, is an endless sacrifice. Those seeking to provide honest leadership in such circumstances must work with inexperienced staff and inadequate funds and equipment. In addition, there is the ever-present danger of unprincipled divisions within society caused by an incomplete social metamorphosis.

I should emphasise from the beginning that I am not a professional politician in the sense that there are politicians in the West, and also here in Africa, whose life revolves around politics. For me, political leadership is a kind of national service, because the real livelihood of my people is keeping cattle. That is what has traditionally given us financial independence and security, provided, that is, that the regime in power does not interfere with us. Indeed, it is only when the regime disturbs our peace that we notice them at all. When I realised that unless we solved the national problems that beset Uganda in the 1960s, 1970s and 1980s, those problems would interfere with our livelihood, I decided I must, for the time being, accept the sacrifice as a service to my country.

Consequently, from 1965 onwards, but more especially since 1971, I accepted the mantle of leadership from my colleagues, knowing very well that, sacrifices notwithstanding, action had to be taken if Uganda's pitiable situation was to be reversed and transcended. When I started community work, I was only 22 years old, a student about to start university. I was nowhere near entering parliament or holding power, but I realised that my people were badly off and I decided to educate them. My involvement in politics, therefore, began with community leadership. Even as we launched the armed struggle against the brutal dictatorship of Idi Amin in 1971, I had no idea that the whole process would result in my eventual leadership of the country. During any of those 30 years, and especially since 1971, I could have been killed like my colleagues Martin Mwesiga, Mwesigwa Black, Valeriano Rwaheru, Abwooli Malibo, Raiti Omongin, and many others. Leadership, therefore, has been a tremendous sacrifice for many of us and was never a *sine qua non* for my original participation in the struggle.

To pursue the metaphor of the biblical quotation, before the 'mustard seed' of freedom and democracy could be sown in Uganda, the land first had to be cleared of the rocks and weeds of a corrupt system, which had given rise by the 1970s to sectarian dictatorship and violence. I believe that through our struggle in the 1980s the seed was finally sown and that it has fallen on fertile ground. The presidential and parliamentary elections of May and June 1996 showed that it has germinated and is growing well.

I relate this story in autobiographical form in order to inform the reader of my ideological development, from my youth to the present. I have written the book because I feel it is important for the people of Uganda, the people of Africa, and those in the wider world with an interest in Africa, to learn about the history of our struggle to liberate our country from dictatorship and to transform it into a democratic, modern, industrialised nation.

Yoweri Kaguta Museveni
Kampala
October 1996

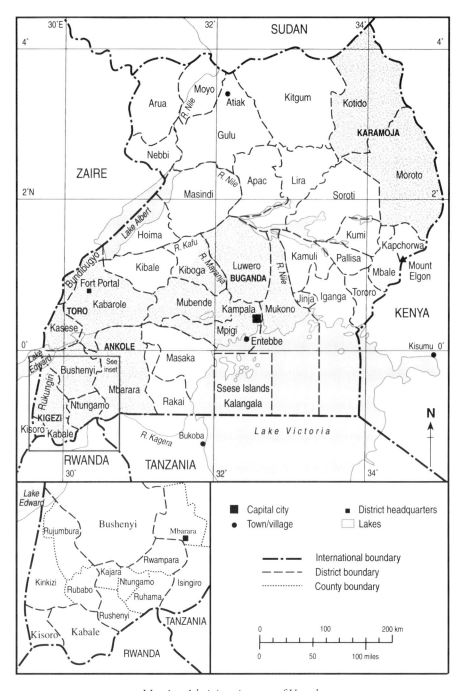

Map 1   *Administrative areas of Uganda*

Chapter 1

EARLY YEARS
[1944–58]

BACKGROUND AND EARLY CHILDHOOD

I was born among the Banyankore Bahima nomads of south-western Uganda in about the year 1944. I use the word 'about' because my parents were illiterate and so did not know the date. In such circumstances dates were associated with events. Parents would tell their children: 'You were born when such and such an event was taking place.' We who know how to read and write can now look back and use all sorts of sources to find out what was happening at the time: this may not always establish the exact date, but at least it will fix the year, and possibly even the month. In my case, my parents had two events for dating the approximate time of my birth. First of all, I was born during a mass vaccination of cattle against rinderpest and secondly, a king had just died. That was the Omugabe of Ankole, Kahaya II, who died in 1944. Another king was installed in 1945 and, according to my mother, I was born nearer to the death of the old king than the installation of the new one. That is how I settled on the year 1944. I was named Museveni after those Ugandans, known locally as 'Abaseveni', who served in the 7th Battalion of the King's African Rifles during the Second World War.

I was born at a place called Nyamambo, in the *muluka* (parish) of Nyaburiza in the *gombolola* (sub-county) of Ntungamo, in the county of Rwampara. My father, Amos Kaguta, was from the Basiita clan and my mother, Esteeri Kokundeka, was from the Beene-Rukaari branch of the aristocratic Bashambo clan. My mother's clan were the traditional rulers of the present-day *gombololas* of Kikagati, Ndeija, Rukoni, Ruhaama, Rweikiniro and most of Ntungamo. My ancestors originally lived in the old *gombolola* of Rubaare, in Kajara county. Having fallen out with the Bashambo rulers of the area (Beene-Kihondwa branch), they took refuge in the present-day county of Rujumbura which was being ruled by the Beene-Kirenzi, another branch of the Bashambo. Later they quarrelled with the Beene-Kirenzi and fled back to Kajara. When things cooled down in Rujumbura, they went back at the invitation of the rulers and were still there when the first Europeans came to Uganda in the late 19th century.

1

My paternal great-grandmother, Nyinanchwende, of the Banyabusaano clan, lived through that turbulent period when the British first came. She was a very important source of information about my family history. She was still alive when I was a young boy (she died when I was about 13) and she gave me a graphic account of how, in the early 1890s, she hid in a swamp, fleeing from marauding colonialists, with two of her younger sons, Kabuguma, my grandfather, and Kachuuya, his elder brother. They had with them a young male calf which nearly betrayed them by urinating on dry swamp grass (*ebigugu*), a fate she only averted by putting her hands on the *bigugu* so that she muffled the sound of the calf's urine. In the meantime, her husband, Kashanku, and their eldest son, Karacha, were withdrawing with the family's cattle. A boy standing very close to Karacha was shot from a distance by Nubian mercenaries under the leadership of the Europeans.

My great-grandfather Kashanku's father was Kyamukanga kya Mugurwa. Kyamukanga's father was Muhuta and his mother was Mugurwa, of the Bararira clan. This is my lineage as far as can be remembered by oral traditon.

When I was born to Amos Kaguta and Esteeri Kokundeka, two of my ancestors, Kabuguma and Karacha, had been dead only a few years. They had been rich peasants with large herds of cattle. My grandfather, Kabuguma, had about 200 cattle and Karacha, my great-uncle, had 700, which was a considerable number in those days. When they died, my father inherited 100 head of cattle, which put him in the ranks of rich peasants. Because of neglect, however, and the toll taken on the cattle by East Coast fever and other tick-borne diseases, my father's herd dwindled. By the 1950s, he only had about 50 head of cattle left.

The Banyankore have no traditional initiation rites. There was only one ceremony which I went through just after I was born. In our language this was called *okuta aha mugongo* and it was only for boys. When a boy was four days old, he would be placed on the back of a cow and given an imitation bow and arrow, as if to say: 'This is your cow, defend it.' It was superstitious, but people thought they were imparting warrior qualities into the child. This was a spiritual ceremony, which could be compared to baptising babies. When the child grew up, they would tell him: 'This is your cow, the one on whose back we put you.' Even now, we still have the offspring of the cow on whose back I was placed. I think the ceremony was supposed to indicate how lucky the child would be in life. If the cow died, then the child would be considered unlucky. If the cow prospered, they would say: 'This boy is going to be rich – his cow has prospered.' Mine have done very well, in spite of the many vicissitudes they have suffered! At one time when our cows died, because of my father moving to a tsetse-infested area, only one of my cow's progeny remained; but then it multiplied again and now there are many of them.

My tribe, however, are not prisoners of their superstitions. Their only other ceremony was associated with marriage. During pre-colonial times, the Banyankore had developed a regular army, so a young boy of about 15 would go into the army where he would spend many years. Originally there were militias, which were

2

called up whenever there was an attack, but at some stage the kings developed a system of regiments, more or less like the Zulus. At this time, the men would have spent much of their time in archery practice. When I was young, however, we only had arrows for bleeding cattle, whereas in the north of Uganda, for instance, they still use arrows for fighting.

When the British first came to Uganda at the end of the 19th century, there had been a very strong clan system among the Banyankore and the whole clan lived together. The group included their matrimonial allies and also some clients, the poorer peasants who looked after the cattle of the richer ones. So there were these three elements in a cattle settlement – the clan, their matrimonial allies and their dependants or clients (and, of course, the wives of all these men). A clan could occupy an area almost the size of a parish. This pactice of living together, however, was due mostly to insecurity. Clans were in constant warfare amongst themselves, usually over cattle and grazing rights. None of these clans was strong enough to defeat the other so they kept on with indecisive conflict, no one clan gaining the upper hand. When the British came with their superior technology and organisation, they imposed a new form of law and order. That was one of the good things which the colonialists brought to this area. Once people no longer had any need to live together for defence, the clans gradually dispersed. By the time of my childhood the clan system had largely broken down.

I was the first born of four among my mother's children, although one of them died young so only three of us survived. My sister was born in 1949. We do not know the actual day or month, but we are sure of the year because when she was born, the Anglican church was celebrating 50 years of being in Uganda, and she was named Violet Kajubiri, meaning 'born around the jubilee'. Then another boy was born in 1952 but he died from a trauma to his head because of poor maternity conditions. The fourth child, another boy, was born in 1960 and I shall write more about him later.

THE IMPORTANCE OF COWS

Cows were, and still are, central to Banyankore culture. All our cows have names and the names are descriptive, according to the animal's colour and the shape of its horns, but we also name them according to characteristics – some are fast-moving and others are slow-moving. The name not only identifies the cow, but indicates the name of its mother. So we say: 'the brown cow of the mother with the long horns', as the Arabs say 'Said bin Said', Said son of Said. In this way we can keep track of what has happened to such and such a cow – a form of record-keeping in what has traditionally been a non-literate society.

Our cows, with their large long horns, are remarkably gentle and even the bulls are placid. This is because of the way that we treat them. We do not regard them as existing only for commercial gain. They are like members of our families and we treat them very intimately. For instance, we have a brush called *enkuyo*, which we use to clean and massage the cow, a process we call *okuragaza*. This is done for most of the milking cows, but also for favourites amongst them. It is a form of communicating with them and they enjoy it very much. A cow will follow you everywhere if you massage it with that brush. I have a great personal feeling for my cows, especially the ones whose ancestors have been in our family for a very long time. They are like cousins and sisters to me. I think if I acquired other cows they would not mean as much to me. I do not have the same feeling for the exotic breeds from Europe, but perhaps over time they will become like adopted children and we shall like them.

In the days of my early childhood, my parents still lived a very traditional life and cattle were literally central to our whole lives. We lived in round huts made of wattle, young trees or branches (*emiganda*) and grass thatch, built within a cattle kraal. The animals were kept in the centre of a stockade which enclosed both the houses and the kraal.

For clothing, I wore the skin of a premature calf. This would often invite one of our more wild cows, called Kyasha kya Mbaaya, to chase me round and round mistaking me for a wild animal, an exercise which would promptly relieve me of the beautiful garment. The calf skin was only a cloak – otherwise children would go about naked. I had some clothes but my great-grandmother said that they were damaging me and sucking out my spirit and blood. She said: 'No, no! This is very dangerous', and she threw away my clothes. There was a struggle between my father, who was supposed to be a moderniser, and his grandmother who was a strong traditionalist. It was she who often clothed me in the calf skin although at that time it was no longer the common way of dressing. Even before the Europeans came, people were wearing textiles brought by long-distance travellers from the Swahili coast, carried by the Nyamwezi people of Tanzania. There was also bark cloth which was quite common here, although it was used mainly by the Baganda and Bakooki, and the people in the Bukoba area of Western Tanzania, the Bahaya. So the skin of a premature calf was really just for small children, not for adults. Traditionally, children – both boys and girls – were not supposed to hide anything, at least not until they reached puberty. That is why my great-grandmother used to complain: 'Why are you bandaging this fellow as if he has a wound? Let him be free!'

As part of this traditional way of living I had to wash in human urine as part of my toilet – I suppose this was meant to be some kind of protection against skin diseases. At times I had to drink cow urine mixed with milk, as this concoction was supposed to be a laxative (*kashumba*). If I fell ill, my great-grandmother would spit chewed tobacco into my mouth as medicine.

By the time I was born, the clan system had broken down to such an extent that we, my parents and I, were living alone in my father's kraal. Sometimes his brother's kraal would be joined with ours, but then they would quarrel and separate their kraals. My great-grandmother, Nyinanchwende, would live either with us – she had her own hut there – or with one of her other grandsons, though not with my father's brother. Since she was the mother of my grandfather, she had a wider catchment area than just my father's group. She had three sons, so she had two other blood lines apart from my grandfather's. She was very particular. She would only live with the head of each line. She would either come and stay with my father or she would stay with the head of one of the other two lines. Protocol was very strict on her side of the family. So within my family's kraal when I was growing up, there were either three huts if we were living with my uncle, or two or even one. My parents and their children all lived in one hut. It was not until I was 16 that I had my own hut – about the time I went to boarding school.

By the time I was in the sixth year of primary school, at the age of about 14, my bedding had evolved from cow hides (*ekyaahi*) to mats made of palm leaves, carpets made from swamp grass (*ebigugu*) and eventually mattresses and blankets. The idea of washing clothes and bathing with soap was accepted at that time but I still had to smear my body with cow ghee, which I resented very much because it smelled foul to me. This was not a sentiment shared by my father, who was sure I would bring bad luck upon the cows by not accepting enthusiastically the foul-smelling products of cows, including cow dung.

Infant labour was quite widespread among the Bahima and by the time a boy was four, he was already grazing calves. By the age of eight, he would start taking turns at grazing cattle. A child even as young as four had several regular jobs to do. One was to look after the calves which grazed near the kraal and not let them wander any further than about 200 yards. The main danger to the cattle came from certain birds called *esaasi* which eat the ticks on cattle. Eating the ticks was helpful, but they would also eat the flesh of the cows. So, looking after the calves really meant chasing away these birds. In those days there were no longer any wild animals because the population was already high.

A third job for a small boy would be, in the morning and in the evening, to ensure that the calves did not get out of the enclosures where they were kept so that they would not go and suckle the cows before they were milked. At the time of milking, you would allow the calf up to the cow to excite the cow's teats to yield milk. Then you would hold the calf back while its mother was being milked, some milk always being left for the calf. Another job was to collect water from the well in small gourds.

The toughest job, however, as I remember it, was clearing the cow dung from the kraal, especially during the rainy season. As a small child, you would carry small pieces of dung with your bare hands. As the only boy at that time, I was doing all these tasks. During the school holidays, I would graze the cattle daily without relief and combine this with drawing water from the deep well to the cattle's drinking trough. The water was carried in a heavy wooden bucket – no easy task for a young child. The three of us did all the chores: my father would look after the cows, and my mother and I would do all the other tasks together. When my sister was old enough, she had her own domestic tasks. The work was quite strenuous because we did not have any permanent help from outside. Normally my family might have expected to have been able to afford a dependant who was not a relative, a sort of client; but because the herd had been reduced to about 60 head by rinderpest in 1945, we had to do all the work ourselves, until later when the herd increased again.

CHRISTIANITY

One of my earliest childhood memories is of my own baptism which took place on 3 August 1947. Soon after I was born my parents converted to Christianity and when I was a young boy, they took me to be baptised. I was aware of what was going on though I could not have been more than three years old. In those days if you were still young when your parents converted from traditional religions to Christianity, you could be baptised without going through a catechism course, and so I benefited from that dispensation. My parents themselves had to go through the catechism course at the Anglican church which was manned by local priests, not missionaries.

Having converted to Christianity, my parents had to 'cleanse their marriage' (*okushemeza obushwere*) because their original marriage was considered 'pagan', which meant that it was non-Christian. The process of 'cleansing' entailed a re-wedding for people who had been married for a long time. Hence, I had the rare privilege of attending the wedding of my mother and father!

When it came to Christianity, my mother became a more serious Christian than my father, in terms of religious observances. My father remained a 'pagan', by which I mean that he maintained his traditional behaviour. He would smoke, drink traditional beer, curse, and later on, in 1955, he became a polygamist, taking a second wife with whom he had a further eight children. In substance, however, my father was more of a Christian than those who 'tear not their hearts but their clothes'. For example, he was enlightened enough to know that I should go to school. In fact, he moved his kraal from Kirigyime, four miles away from the school, to Kafunjo, two miles nearer the school so that I would have a shorter distance to walk. Even then, it was not all roses because we had to go to school through papyrus swamps walking barefoot, something that appals my children when I tell them about my early life.

Before my family became Christian, we did not eat any non-cattle products. The main staple of our diet was various types of milk – fresh milk, soured milk, and, once in a while, a kind of thick cream called *eshabwe* which we would eat with steamed bananas. We also ate cattle blood – we would bleed the cattle and bake the blood into a type of cake. In my culture at that time, eating non-cattle food was considered shameful. Sometimes you could eat solid food, but you would have to wait until it was out of your system before you were allowed to drink milk again. Mixing the two was supposed to be very bad for the cows! We would also eat veal once in a while, especially if the cows produced male calves. The eating of male calves was in effect a method of breeding control as only the best males would be preserved for breeding purposes. Adult cows would only be killed for a big ceremony, never for regular food.

My parents' conversion affected our lives in more ways than simply the religious. 'Christianisation' involved an element of modernisation and this demanded changes – changes which penetrated to the deepest aspects of our traditional culture. It even affected our eating habits, because keeping to traditional ways was considered 'pagan and ungodly' by Christian preachers. Later, I had some problems with the missionaries over that attitude – they were using Christianity to assault African traditions, even the good parts of our traditions. The message was that in order to be a good Christian you had to abandon tradition completely. As part of their attempt to appear as 'Christian' as possible, my parents had to learn new things and say that all our former ways were no good. As part of that 'modernisation', they changed into quasi-cultivators, and they also began to buy more of their food from cultivators. In fact, some degree of barter between herdsmen and cultivators had existed for a long time in our society.

I believe that it was good for my character formation that my father did not become over-Christianised, because the process of Christianisation sometimes meant pseudo-Europeanisation. As matters stood, the two worlds of the traditional and the Christian were forcefully represented in my family. My mother was a strong, born-again Christian and she influenced me a great deal. She was a teetotaller and belonged to the puritanical wing of the Anglican Church. I was more inclined to my mother's side because she was more disciplined, and this appealed to me. My father, on the other hand, stuck to his traditions although never forgetting to pray to God, the supreme creator, and to do justice to his fellow men. It was very good to have this dichotomous religious existence.

My father was a very kind person, except occasionally when he would drink and become rather violent. He was a person whom I could ask many questions – and if I did not ask, he would tell me. He would relate many stories to me as part of the traditional training. A boy child had to be with his father all the time – he was not allowed to remain in the hut in the morning but had to go out as soon as dawn broke. Then he would stay with his father while he was doing the milking, until he went out to the bush to look after his cows. At night it was the same. In my tribe, they do not like a boy who sits by the fire warming himself. They say: 'This one will come to nothing when he grows up.' He must be out doing some work.

Traditional Banyankore are confident, sometimes arrogant, no-nonsense people. The cattle-keeping Banyankore are devoted to their cows. My father will go to his grave without ever eating fish or chicken in any shape or form. When he became 'a Christian' in 1947, he took the revolutionary step of eating non-milk foods like beans, sweet potatoes and groundnuts for the first time, but there the revolution ended! Nevertheless, the traditional pride is an invaluable asset, if only it can be tempered with discarding scientifically irrational beliefs.

I am unable to understand why people in some parts of the world appear desperate to be accepted by whites. What I consider important is that the black man should have equal opportunities in all aspects of life. To hanker after sitting with a white man or marrying a white partner is nothing but an inferiority complex and sickness unless, in the case of marriage, there is genuine love between the couple. I should imagine that those educated people who retain aspects of their traditions which are compatible with life in modern society – those who shed off superstitions and other obscurantist misconceptions – are more balanced people. Those, however, who abandon their traditions lock, stock and barrel ought to be watched with care. I would not trust their sense of balance.

Education in our traditional society was an informal affair. Apart from daily training for the discipline of work, the mind was trained through story-telling. When my great-grandmother came to visit, she was a great source of stories. She told tremendous stories – very, very interesting. Parents posed riddles for the children to solve: suppose a problem was like this, how would you solve it? There would be games, at night after milking, and after eating or drinking milk. As late as midnight, people would sit by the fireside telling stories (including fictional ones), just to educate the children: what would happen to a bad person; or a greedy one; how cowards come to a bad end, and so on. This type of evening was called *okutarama*. All these stories had a moral theme to them and they were supposed to be character-building.

As well as story-telling, there would be traditional songs. Of course, in my family, these were frowned upon because we had become Christians, so we were not allowed to sing in the traditional way – we had to sing Christian hymns, except when my father was under the influence of drink. Then he would go back to his traditional ways. We would also have riddles to test the memory. For instance, someone would say: 'Each being has its own special intelligence or skills. What is it?' The answer would be: 'A bird can go in the air without support. That is its special skill.' Someone who did not know the answer would say so and the other person would say: 'Right, give me a cow', or 'Give me a heifer.' That was a sort of score and we would add up who had won at the end of the game. Another riddle was: 'How does water travel at night without being eaten by the hyena?' The person who was asked this riddle was supposed to ask himself: 'Why doesn't water fear hyenas while people have to go indoors at night?' These were tests of memory and they were well-known riddles from ancient times. Poetry recitation was also common, although not so much in my family. However, I did learn poems from the people around.

Despite the strengths of this traditional form of education and his own respect for our traditions, my father recognised the value of 'modernisation' and was very interested in the formal education which the Christian churches had to offer although he himself had not gone to school. To some extent, he had become disillusioned with cows because his herd had been much reduced by rinderpest, so perhaps he thought that depending on cows alone was not enough. He had also seen other families who had not been prosperous originally, but who had sent their children to school, and because of that had become chiefs, not through owning cows, but through education. Consequently, as early as 1951, he sent me to a Church of Uganda school. At that time, the present-day Church of Uganda was known as the 'Native Anglican Church'. These kind of 'church schools' were normally pre-primary institutions, funded entirely by the churches. They taught the alphabet and basic counting. We did not have any books or slates to write on and there was only one copy of an alphabet book from which we would copy the alphabet, writing it in the sand with our forefingers. So from the age of about six or seven I would walk the one mile to Muyogo Church School. For a few weeks I had also attended the Seventh Day Adventist school at Mushenyi.

It is interesting how these Europeans brought confusion here. I was not supposed to go to school in Mushenyi, even though it was much nearer home, because it was run by Seventh Day Adventists. To have gone to the Seventh Day Adventists would have been considered a very dangerous move by the Anglicans, but still I went because my father said: 'Why shouldn't you go to the more convenient one – they are all teaching the same things.' He was not a prisoner of religious beliefs.

PRIMARY SCHOOLING

When my father moved his kraal to Kafunjo, I started going to the goverment-aided Kyamate Primary School. Educational opportunities were still very limited in Uganda then and there were only four classes in Kyamate school although it expanded up to Primary Five in 1953. The boys and girls who were there before our time had to go to another school 25 miles away when they reached upper primary school, that is Primary Five and Six. In the whole county at that time, there was not a single school going up to Primary Six. Since I was considered too young, although I was then seven years old, I had to go to the girls' section, which only took pupils for the first year of primary school. This section was looked down upon by those in the boys' section and they called it *Kyenkobe* ('the place for monkeys'). At *Kyenkobe*, Primary One was divided into Classes A and B. Class B was some sort of pre-primary and Class A was the real Primary One.

My father had moved his kraal around March 1952 and I started at *Kyenkobe* in April. At the end of 1952 I finished Class One B, but instead of moving to Class A, I was moved to the boys' school at the beginning of 1953. This is where I met two of the boys who later on became my colleagues in the struggle: Martin Mwesiga and Eriya Tukahirwa Kategaya. In Primary One, and also in Primary Two, we would normally sit on the floor because there were no school benches for those classes. It was only in Primary Three that benches became available. In Primary Two we started writing in exercise books with nib pens and ink.

At the end of 1953 I finished Primary One and went on to Primary Two in 1954. In Primary Two I was doing very well academically, but I had one problem: I was continually losing my pens which would fall through the perforated cloth bag an aunt of mine had given me to carry my exercise books and pen. Whenever I lost my pen because of the multi-holed bag, the teacher would beat me, send me out of class or give me zero in subjects where I had used pencil instead of pen and ink. I would then be afraid to tell my father that I had lost my pen, although surely this was not my fault. As a consequence of this harassment and lack of facilities, I no longer enjoyed going to school although I had been intensely keen at the beginning. In later life I was able to realise how harmful some of the old-fashioned teachers could be to the children because of their poor teaching methods. The parents were also partly responsible for not helping their children to love studies.

One can thus see how easily children from peasant families can be discouraged from continuing with education because of small problems caused by the failures of unenlightened parents and unprofessional teachers. It was very easy to detect the source of my problems in Primary Two: a bag which had been eaten by cockroaches and was thus full of holes! But who was there to do anything about it? Neither my parents nor my teachers could do anything. Instead, I was being harassed by both! Blessed be the day when all Ugandan children will have enlightened parents who can sympathise with them, as well as professional teachers who are capable of finding out the root of a particular child's problems. Fortunately, I managed to pass the exams and continue to Primary Three, in spite of the teacher giving me a number of zeros for writing in pencil.

With the learning itself I did not have any particular problems in primary school because I had a good memory and found it easy to recall what I had learned – about God, history, geography, and so on – it was all very interesting. We were taught in the vernacular up to Primary Four. The teachers taught all the subjects, including English, in our own language. We were fairly fluent in English by Primary Four because we had learned first to construct sentences, then vocabulary and composition, joining sentences into a story.

While I was in Primary Four, in 1956, I had an attack of continuous hiccups and had to be taken to Ishaka Seventh Day Adventist Hospital. The attack was not very serious or painful, and it only lasted a few days. The doctors never discovered what had caused it. My parents sent me to the hospital mainly because they were worried rather than because of real need. I stayed at the hospital with my mother for several weeks and, as a result, missed much of the first term of school.

The only other significant problem I had at primary school was in 1958 when I was in Primary Six and I insulted the class teacher by raising my thumb and baring my teeth at him (we call this *okuhema* and *okuha mutinzi*). I think I had just been naughty – talking in class, or something like that – and when he told me to go out of the class, I raised my thumb and bared my teeth at him. Unfortunately, another teacher, whom I did not know was at the back of the class, saw me and told him. We were always abusing the teachers like that when they were not aware, so it was just bad luck that I was caught. As a form of punishment, the class teacher treated me very badly, making me work half-naked cutting a lot of papyrus reeds from the swamp. Although I did not tell my father, I was worried that he might hear of it from someone else because I knew that he would come and fight the teacher. They were quite a wild group, our people, and very protective towards their children. Parents were in the habit of fighting teachers who beat their children and the wrangle could have led to my missing my Primary Leaving Examinations which were due that year.

Chapter 2

YOUTH AND POLITICS
[1958–66]

SECONDARY EDUCATION

At the end of 1958, I successfully completed my Primary Six and in early 1959 I entered Mbarara High School for two years of junior secondary school. This was my first experience as a boarding student and it was also the first time I was away from home. The main problem at Mbarara High School was hunger because we were underfed. Ordinarily, children in Ugandan villages are often undersized due to malnutrition and also because of infection by parasites such as worms. In many Ugandan homes in those days, however, you would at least have a full stomach even though much of the food was not necessarily particularly nutritious. In Mbarara High School, on the other hand, there was neither the quantity nor the quality and one felt hungry all the time. I entered the school weighing 82 pounds (37 kg) and left after two years weighing 65 pounds (29.5 kg), in spite of the fact that I was 15 years old. The trouble was that we were too young to be assertive and complain, so we just had to accept it. The headmaster and deputy headmaster were former army officers, Major Edward Cleaver and Major Bothwick, who was a Scotsman. They were good men really and I do not know why they were not feeding us properly, perhaps it was lack of money. The other teachers were all Ugandans.

In 1960 I went to Ntare Senior Secondary School and there the food was much better. We had a very good headmaster called William Crichton, also a Scotsman. He was very conscious of the importance of feeding the children properly. He had been an administrator in the Sudan colonial service with a master's degree in education and sometimes he would teach English. His school was well liked by the pupils and there were never any riots there. At Ntare almost all the teachers were white – there was only one African teacher out of about 20 members of staff. I came to enjoy the arts subjects, but I also liked biology because it was well taught. In some science subjects, such as chemistry, the teachers would teach badly, introducing new subjects without explaining their genesis, and expecting pupils to 'cram' things without understanding them. They would say: 'The symbol for sodium is Na' and when I asked, 'Why? Why not say "So", if it is sodium?', they replied: 'You must just take it as it is.' It was only much later on that I came to learn that the symbols were taken from Latin and Greek and were internationally recognised. It was quite incredible the way some teachers were turning children against their studies, and so unnecessarily! Their attitude was: 'If you want to pass your exam and get a good job, you must take it as it is and memorise it.' They were threatening us – and threats have nothing to do with real learning and understanding.

I had a similar problem with French. We were taught that French has masculine and feminine words. But how do you know whether something is masculine or feminine? What is the logic? Is there no law, no guide? They said: 'No, no. You must just learn it and memorise the gender of evey single word.' In this case there was more justification for such a prescription, but I thought I did not have time to waste with things for which I could not see the logic and I gave up on French as well. I always wanted to understand things logically, to know how you proceeded from A to B. In 1962, however, an African-American teacher called Howard came to teach at the school. He gave us some understanding of chemistry. He said: 'This is the atom – it has a nucleus which has neutron, protons and electrons forming an orbit and it is they which determine the valence of an element.' We then understood that the valence of an element was determined by the arrangement of the electrons in its orbit. If Mr Howard had stayed on, I would have gained a lot of interest in chemistry, but he had to go away after a short while because he was in the Peace Corps, together with two other white Americans.

Ntare School was very different from many other secondary schools at that time. It had been founded in 1956 and was not based on religion, like other older schools in the country which were predominantly Catholic, Protestant or Muslim. Boys came to Ntare School from all over the country and the school developed a character of its own where one was free to make friends regardless of religious denomination, tribe or social class. The headmaster, Mr Crichton, was a very liberal-minded man and he encouraged many children who would have been expelled for rebelliousness in other schools. Instead, he would counsel them. He even allowed us to go for walks outside the school premises, while other schools were like prison camps. By letting us be free to go out in our spare time, he helped us develop a sense of personal responsibility and self-discipline.

For A-level, I took English, History and Economics as my subjects. We were not taught much African history and the literature was mostly European – Tennyson, Yeats and, of course, Shakespeare: we learnt many of the famous speeches. Although this kind of education was irrelevant to our situation, it was useful since all societies are basically the same. Reading *The Merchant of Venice*, as we did in Senior Three, we could see the conflict in the old society, where the new merchant class was being looked at as ravenous and greedy. It was clear that Shakespeare was denigrating Shylock as an undesirable character for wanting his pound of flesh; but capitalism is exactly like that. Even if we did not appreciate all these implications at the time, the stories were interesting and we could see later how they applied when we learned more about societies.

What interested me most in history was the formation of states in Europe – particularly in Italy and Germany during the 19th century. I understood more when I went to university and learned about the evolution of capitalism, and the whole idea of markets. I was also fascinated by the French Revolution, and bourgeois opposition to the taxes imposed by the feudal order because it interfered with trade – which was also the reason that the Prussian Junkers wanted a unified government. Therefore, although there was often little direct African relevance in our curriculum at that time, I did not feel that our education suffered because of it. Subsequently, one can read other more relevant books, once one has learnt the skills, the discipline, and especially the habit of reading – and that we did learn at Ntare School.

As far as sport was concerned, I was active in cricket and football. In later years I played in the school's first teams for both sports. I had become quite good at football by the time I left Ntare School.

In 1962 I became a born-again Christian (*mulokole*) and I remained one until 1966. There were some missionaries from the Anglican centre who came to preach at the school every Sunday. After the service we had Scripture Union meetings in the course of which I got to know the Bible very well. What interested and appealed to me most was the personal discipline. The missionaries' preaching would also appeal to our sense of self-interest: 'If you want to succeed, you should avoid trouble, drinking, going after girls, and so on.' It was the moral teaching which appealed to me – the idea that you should not squander your life. Apart from the puritanical discipline, there was the Christian fellowship where we helped one another through advice and sharing problems. However, there were also public confessions. The idea was that if you confessed the sin publicly, you would be too embarrassed to commit the same sin again. Public confessions did not appeal to me much, even though the self-discipline did. I broke with the born-again Christians in 1966, partly because of these public confessions, and their exposing of one's personal life.

Later on when I thought more about it, I thought it was rather stupid. If the matter is between oneself and God, then that is where it should remain. The other source of disagreement with these Christians was political, because some of the European Scripture Union leaders appeared to want to use religion subtly to induce a kind of meekness in the face of oppression. Meekness meant obeying authority. Some of them would tell us that we should not get involved in politics because it was 'worldly'. True Christians were supposed to aim at 'heavenly life' and to ignore worldly things which are temporary and passing. They would quote the Bible out of context, for instance, from Matthew – when somebody hits you on one cheek, you should turn the other cheek; when someone asks you to walk one mile, walk two. Then I said to myself: 'This is very, very dangerous.' They would say: 'Your kingdom is not here – your kingdom is in heaven. Don't complain. Don't worry about your life here.' At this point they would bring in the story from the New Testament about a rich man and a poor one called Lazarus. The rich man was living in comfort while the poor man was begging at his gate. Now, when they went to heaven, Lazarus was in the bosom of Abraham and the rich man was in hell. The rich man was shouting: 'Please Lazarus, give me some water to quench my thirst because I am burning here in hell.' It seemed to me that they were preaching that if you are poor here on earth, don't worry because you will be rewarded in heaven. To my way of thinking, this was very, very dangerous. It was misleading people – telling them not to worry about their own welfare, and to transfer all this to God. So that is how I eventually broke with them.

The missionaries also condemned violence, in all circumstances, as a means of liberation. In order to fight injustice, one had to pray and leave the rest to God. My differences with these people came to a head in 1965 during a Scripture Union conference at Busoga College, Mwiri, in Eastern Uganda. I introduced a motion to denounce Ian Smith's Unilateral Declaration of Independence (UDI) in Rhodesia and my motion was dubbed 'political' and 'worldly' and was, therefore, disallowed. Their leaders were full of obscurantist ideas and they overlooked altogether the moral issues of the Rhodesian situation, as if they were conscious agents for subduing the fight for justice. I believe they were honest men, but they were imprisoned by their beliefs. Because of their stance on these issues, I decided in 1966 to withdraw from the Scripture Union, fully confident that it would not affect my relationship with God. Since then, I have remained a non-denominational, God-fearing man. I believe that God is not a Muslim, a Protestant, a Catholic or a Jew. He is above all these petty differences created by groups that are not always independent of pecuniary interests.

POLITICAL AWAKENING

I was secretary of the debating society when I was in Senior Three, and bearing in mind that this was an A-level school, for a boy in Senior Three, one year before taking O-levels, to be elected secretary from the whole school was quite significant. I had been active in the debating society from the very beginning. Even in Senior One and Two I had begun challenging the older boys in Senior Six, and that was why I was elected secretary of the society. The subjects we debated were nearly always political. This was the height of the Cold War, when current issues included the Congo crisis, Ugandan independence, and Ian Smith's UDI. In my capacity as one of the leaders of the debating society, I promoted debate among the schools of Ankole and Toro.

In my later years at secondary school, I started to become politically active in a more general way. As far as national politics were concerned, from 1960 until I left university in 1970, I was a DP (Democratic Party) sympathiser. This political affiliation was based upon nothing more than historic sectarian grounds – in 1956 the Bahima chiefs and the Catholic leaders in Ankole had made an alliance against the Protestants. Since my parents were DPs, I also became a DP sympathiser, a 'youth winger'.

I did not have a party card – you did not need a card in order to be considered a member. Political parties were not organised to the extent that we went around the country canvassing people to buy party cards; rather, we simply press-ganged people emotionally. The so-called party workers never had time to go down to the grassroots to do organisational work. Instead they created hysteria by setting people against each other, polarising them along the lines of their tribal or religious identity – there was nothing about ideology or policies. If people are divided into identity blocs, as was happening under the UPC (Uganda Peoples Congress) government, this often translates into actual local oppression – people lose their jobs because they belong to the wrong group, and so on. Even in the rural communities you would hear that a chief had been dismissed because he was a DP supporter – which in my home area meant that he was either a Catholic or a cattle-keeper – but this was also true at the national level. Even now the question of policies never comes into discussions of party politics. The argument is simply: 'You are black, therefore you are in this party; you are white, therefore you are in the other party; you are a Protestant or Catholic, therefore you two cannot belong together in the same party.' If someone takes a position on an issue, it is after he or she has already been press-ganged into an identity group. The person then argues this position from the point of view of identity, and not from the merits of the issue at hand.

We, in our small debating group, were following political developments closely all the time – not just in the newspapers and the radio, but also through talking to local politicians, who were linked with the national politicians. At that time the UPC had split into two factions and we were talking to the wing which was not happy with Obote, as well as with the DP. Because the headmaster did not restrict our movements, we were able to go out in the evenings. All that was required was that we should attend lessons and be there at lights-out, which would be at about 10.00 p.m. Otherwise we were free to move outside the school premises, so it was easy for us to keep in touch with what was going on in politics.

We were also informed in our political opinions by reading magazines such as the *East African Reporter*, which used to carry articles on East African political matters, and even the *Uganda Argus*, the local national newspaper owned by Lonrho. It was independent of the government and was critical at times.

The core of this group – Martin Mwesiga, Mwesigwa Black, Valeriano Rwaheru, Eriya Kategaya and I – gradually evolved into a political cell of nationalist-minded young people opposed to the sectarian political atmosphere prevalent in those days. I would say that the group coalesced rather than that it was deliberately constituted. These four friends of mine in particular played a vital role in the political struggles that lay ahead.

I had been with Martin Mwesiga since primary school days in 1953. He was quite outstanding in school work and was the head prefect at Ntare School. He came from a cattle-keeping background like myself, but his father had been a sub-county chief in Ankole, which put him in a slightly different social group from ours. People who became chiefs tended more towards Christianity than ordinary peasants. He was very gentle and mild-mannered, with a quiet sense of humour, but also very determined and courageous, which is how he had managed to join us. When we had political debates within our group, he put forward a lot of ideas but he was not as effervescent as I was. I had not known Mwesigwa Black for as long as I had known Martin. We had met at Mbarara High School. Mwesigwa was nicknamed 'Black' because he was very dark-skinned, but his real first name was William. Like Martin, he was quiet and mild-mannered. He was also from a cattle-keeping background and his parents were born-again Christians. By contrast, Valeriano Rwaheru was from a farming background, short and stocky, and he was a Roman Catholic. He too was quiet but noticeably courageous in the skirmishes to come. He was, therefore, a very valuable person to have around in difficult times. All three of these men were to lose their lives in the 1970s, in the struggle against Amin. Eriya Kategaya, whom I have known since our first year in primary school, is the only one of the four who is still alive today. His origins are in a mixed background of cattle-keepers and cultivators. He is quiet and reserved, but enormously courageous, as he was to prove in his clandestine work in the years ahead.

One of the fundamental elements which influenced our group in those days at Ntare School was revulsion at the sectarian politics in Ankole (which comprised the administrative areas of Bushenyi, Mbarara and Ntungamo Districts). The so-called Protestant faction was aligned with the UPC and the Catholic and Bahima factions with the DP. These factions were formed by opportunists seeking public offices they could use to accumulate wealth. In fact, Ankole was a microcosm of the sad story of political sectarianism in the whole of Uganda. Therefore, our small group's stand against sectarianism and opportunism at that early stage in our lives, and also in Uganda's political history, was really quite remarkable. We started fighting these political ills around 1965. Prior to that, members of the group had been influenced by the sectarian political parties, like everybody else.

After the group had coalesced around progressive new thinking, we started to be attracted by the talk of an East African federation. Influenced by the European history we were studying in upper secondary school, we saw how Italy and Germany, as late as 1870, had transformed themselves from weak principalities – more or less like the sheikdoms of the Middle East – into powerful states. At that time, however, we did not recognise that the Western imperialist, capitalist pattern had emerged with the unification of Germany. Nevertheless, the example of previously feudal principalities uniting and forming powerful modern states to challenge France, Britain and Russia, appealed to our growing pan-Africanist outlook.

I saw that Africa – or at any rate East Africa – would benefit if such unity could be achieved.

As I followed the debate on the East African federation, I started to develop an admiration for Julius Nyerere, who stood firm in favour of the federation, as did Tom Mboya in Kenya and Grace Ibingira in Uganda. I also developed a dislike for Milton Obote – although, since at that time I was a DP supporter, I did not approve of him anyway. He was a crucial element in frustrating the federation idea by giving the impression that Nyerere sought to dominate East Africa. The real reason that Obote did not want an East African union was because he was not going to be the head of it, since he was a weaker politician than Nyerere and Kenyatta. Therefore, it appeared better for him to say that he did not want a small matter such as an East African union – he would rather support Nkrumah's notion of a union of the whole of Africa, an impractical idea which Obote knew would never happen. There was also talk of the British and the Americans being behind the federation idea so that, on the one hand, they would neutralise the Zanzibar revolution by absorbing it into a wider entity and, on the other, frustrate Kwame Nkrumah's dream of uniting the whole of Africa. There is now evidence to show that the frustration of these ventures had the backing of American and British imperialism.

Nkrumah's view that a continental government should be created immediately was not realistic because, apart from the lack of the necessary infrastructure, in the short run, it would have been easier to achieve unity using regional groupings rather than attempting to unite the whole continent. In the event, however, Obote joined reactionaries using such arguments to frustrate efforts at African unity, while at the same time pretending to be Nkrumahists. In the case of an East African union which was feasible, opportunists such as Obote, who were also political dwarfs, feared its realisation because they wanted to remain big fish in small ponds.

The ultimate failure to create an East African federation was a serious blow to the African liberation movement. Here were peoples who were homogenous in many ways, who had similar political and economic institutions, and who could have formed a political unit which would have given the region a wider resource base and made the union viable. The frustration of the realisation of the East African federation was no less than a treasonable act. I hope our generation of leaders will not make the same mistakes. When Julius Nyerere advocated this unity in the 1960s, he won my admiration.

On the local scene, our group at different times briefly sympathised with Kakonge's and Ibingira's factions of the UPC, although they were quite antagonistic towards each other. The Kakonge faction was radical and socialist-inclined, while the Ibingira faction represented the conservative, pro-capitalist wing of the party. This was because our own ideological formation was still incomplete. Although we had a strong antipathy towards Obote's unprincipled ways, we did not yet have a coherent counter-perception. One of Obote's most unscrupulous actions was to have misled the traditionalists in Buganda and then, after some years, to have made an about-turn over the same issues: such actions have cost the country a lot of blood.

Because of our revulsion at these political deceptions, we had a vague admiration for political actors whom we regarded as more principled. In our minds, this meant somebody who would tell you exactly what he thought and who was not a hypocrite. This, of course, was not sufficient because it is possible for honest people, firmly convinced of their beliefs, to be not only misguided but actually dangerous because of their misconceptions. We were searching for principled politics, which we thought meant honesty and selflessness, although we did not yet have clearly formed ideas about achieving such politics. We were, however, staunchly anti-Obote. On 22 February 1966, the day that he arrested five members of his cabinet, three of us, Martin Mwesiga, Eriya Kategaya and myself, went to see James Kahigiriza, who was then the Chief Minister of Ankole, to enquire about the possibility of going into exile in order to launch an armed struggle. Kahigiriza discouraged us, saying that we should give Obote enough time to fall by his own mistakes. We saw him again a few weeks later and he gave us the example of Nkrumah, who had been overthrown in Ghana by a military *coup* two days after Obote's abrogation of the Ugandan constitution. Kahigiriza advised us that Nkrumah's example showed that all dictators were bound to fall in due course. Inwardly we were not convinced. We knew that dictators had to be actively opposed and that they would not just fall off by themselves like ripe mangoes. Later I went to Gayaza High School with Mwesiga to contact one of Grace Ibingira's sisters in order to find out whether she knew of any plans afoot to resist Obote's dictatorship. She, however, did not know of any such plan. We came to the conclusion that the old guards had no conception of defending people's rights and we resolved to strike out on our own.

For the time being, we decided against exile since we realised we needed more time to study. I have come to understand that lack of knowledge is a major factor in many of the mistakes that have occurred in Africa since the 1960s, so it is fortunate that at that time we began to turn our minds to university. We deliberately chose not to go to Makerere. Because of our group's involvement in politics, we all put down Dar es Salaam as first choice for university. In this we were influenced by Julius Nyerere's distinctly more positive and progressive leadership. We thought, and rightly, that there was more political information in Dar es Salaam, especially since all the African liberation movements were based there. I, for one, had decided that if I could not get into Dar es Salaam University, I would go away and do other things rather than go to Makerere.

COMMUNITY WORK IN ANKOLE

Before setting off for university, however, we had some teaching work of our own to do. It was Mwesigwa Black who suggested that I join with him in doing something to help eliminate nomadism among the Bahima sub-group of the Banyankore people. Because of their nomadic way of life, many Bahima children did not go to school and modern ideas about animal husbandry, hygiene and health did not percolate through to them. They did not believe in supplementing their pastoralist activities by cultivating food or cash crops. Their quality of life, therefore, deteriorated in all fields: nutrition, education, health, science and technology, literature and art, community cohesion, fertility and social progress in general.

The problems were not entirely of their own making. When the colonialists came, they had interfered with the socio-economic systems they found in place. The production, for instance, of the rich and nutritious finger millet, a staple food in Ankole, went into steep decline. The colonialists called on the 'natives' to shift from food to cash crops such as coffee and cotton. They did nothing to build up the cattle industry, as it would have competed with that of the white farmers in Kenya. It was partly through this neglect that the cattle in Ankole were decimated by tsetse fly and tick-borne diseases such as East Coast fever. Because the Bahima in Ankole were dependent on cattle, they became impoverished and large numbers of them dispersed all over Uganda to the areas of Masaka, Mpigi, Mubende, Luwero, Busoga, Bukedi, Teso, Lango and Acholi. Some of them even crossed into Tanzania. Wherever they went they faced exploitation and persecution. They worked for little or no pay or were branded as 'foreigners' and told to go back to their homelands. They lived as serfs all over the country, in spite of being extremely diligent cattle-keepers.

The local collaborator chiefs in Ankole, although mostly Bahima, were busy protecting their own interests and did not mobilise these poor people to reorient their lives in order to survive in new situations. To a limited extent, a small group of the cultivating Banyankore somehow benefited from the situation by growing the then prized cash crops, especially coffee, but not cotton. The Banyankore roasted the experimental cotton seed to show that cotton could not grow in Ankole, a trick the colonialists fell for. Nevertheless, the quality of life deteriorated in Ankole although there were superficial trappings of 'development', for example the introduction of woven cloth to replace cow hides and bark cloth, the elimination of mass killer diseases such as smallpox and some literacy and education for a small fraction of the population.

At the end of 1966 and during the early part of 1967, Mwesigwa Black and I decided to lead a peasant struggle against these injustices. We walked from kraal to kraal in the present Kazo and Nyabushozi counties of Mbarara District urging peasants to refuse to vacate their land. We encouraged them to till and fence it, in spite of obstructions by the UPC district administration.

The problem with the cattle-keepers of Ankole was not that they did not know how to look after cattle – it was that they lacked education. If their cows died, they thought it was just bad luck, or that they had 'bad bones'. So our task was to educate them about modern cattle-keeping methods. We would approach the most influential man in the neighbourhood and explain to him what we were trying to do. We would spend the night in the area and the next day the influential man would gather the people in his area and we would talk to them about fencing their land and treating their cows with modern medicines.

When they said: 'How can we afford to pay for the fencing of our pasture?', we would ask them: 'How many cattle do you lose in a year from wandering away and getting lost because your land is not fenced?' They would then begin to understand that if they fenced their land they would not lose their cattle. So they began to see that it would be worth their while to sell a few cows to pay for the fencing in the knowledge that they would benefit from more cows in the long run. We used the same argument when they said that they could not afford to buy modern medicines when their cows became sick. We pointed out the numbers they were losing each year from preventable diseases and showed them that this would no longer be the case if they bought modern drugs. The number of cows in the area began to increase and the people could then see the reasoning behind our arguments.

Because of the use of ancient cattle-keeping practices, not only were cattle dying from preventable diseases, but children were not going to school. If people did not fence their land, in order to prevent their cattle roaming into other people's homes and gardens, they had to keep the children at home to restrain the cows – to act as a human fence. Another reform resulting from our campaign was the elimination of the ancient and labour-consuming practice of the daily removal of cow dung from cattle enclosures – a task of which I was only too well aware from my own childhood! This had been necessary because in the past, cattle had to be kept within strong enclosures to discourage cattle-raiders and wild animals. So by introducing a simple technique such as perimeter fencing, we were able to solve the problem of the cows having to be continuously looked after; and also the cleaning out of the stockade was no longer a continuous chore. In addition, the cows fertilised the land with their cow dung. This simple reform saved much time and labour and freed most children to go to school. The other reform was the elimination of the cruel practice of coaxing cows which had lost their calves to accept being milked by a decoy, using the skin of the dead calf to simulate a live and suckling calf. This was called *okukamwa obwasi*. It was necessitated by the high calf mortality rate and the resulting shortage of milk to feed families. As the mortality rates have fallen, this barbaric practice has also declined.

High rates of cattle mortality have now virtually been eliminated and this has resulted in the growth of herds. The elimination of nomadism has cut down on labour wastage, and led to a reduction in infant labour, so that more children now attend school. The Bahima have also started growing food crops, thereby not only leaving more milk for calves, but also greatly improving the nutritional levels of their society. In the past, cows were milked dry so that families could get enough milk. This involved milking a cow twice per milking (*okushubya*) which meant four rounds per day. Now a cow is milked once in the morning and once in the evening, thereby leaving the rest of the milk for the calves. Peasants are also beginning to realise that, with the use of modern drugs and cattle-keeping methods, they can control their own economic and social destinies and not continue to depend on fate and the elements, as they have done for generations past. Because they now grow food, they consume less milk and sell the surplus. This has greatly increased their cash incomes.

Our modest efforts of urging and assisting the pastoralists of north Ankole to settle down and modernise certain aspects of their otherwise archaic, rough and inadequate lives brought these dramatic results in spite of the fact that we were opposed by a local government motivated by inter-caste hostility, and a central government motivated by corruption and a general anti-people stance.

It was possible to register communally owned land and have it fenced, at the village level, for instance. This policy of public ownership would have been beneficial if it had been pursued at that time. The UPC elements in positions of power, however, wanted to prevent the peasants from gaining legal control over their pieces of land. The peasants in the area filled in forms (the legal requirement for land being leased to them), but the authorities would not allow them to complete the process. The hope of the UPC reactionaries was that the peasants would be forced to migrate out of the areas so that the people in power could grab it for their own use or give it to their cronies. Following our intensive mobilisation campaign, however, the peasants settled on the land and, to a large extent, abandoned their nomadic way of life.

The peasants responded positively to our education programme and followed our advice. The job was left incomplete, however, because as a result of this mild modernisation, the cattle population increased dramatically without the quality of the breeds and pastures improving correspondingly. This strained the capacity of the soil because the cattle population to acreage ratio had been gravely upset. In the interests of the growing population, good animal husbandry and soil conservation, it would have been better to use this area for dairy farming as dairy cows give high milk yields and require less grazing land. However, these were problems for the future.

Today, the two counties of Kazo and Nyabushozi have the largest concentration of cattle in the country. The cattle are mostly owned by peasants and the cattle population in the area is about one million. At present the cattle population in the whole of Uganda is about four million, which means that these two counties together have one quarter of the total. Moreover, the area now has a population of 140 000 settled peasants. Much of this development came about because of the struggle we started in the 1960s.

Chapter 3

DAR ES SALAAM UNIVERSITY
[1967–70]

At the time when I started my university course, the government paid all the costs and one could study anywhere within East Africa. That was how I was able to choose Dar es Salaam. At that time the East African Community was becoming a reality. It was possible, for instance, to deposit your savings at a post office in Uganda and withdraw the money in Dar es Salaam.

Attending Dar es Salaam University was my first opportunity to travel outside Uganda. We travelled first by boat from Port Bell in Kampala, across Lake Victoria to Mwanza and from there by train to Dar es Salaam. I found it very interesting looking at the water and seeing the different peoples along the railway line. I remember seeing a lot of mangoes in the Tabora area, but the journey itself was not particularly eventful. When we arrived in Dar es Salaam, I was not alone as a number of us from Ntare School had been travelling in a group.

Martin Mwesiga was one of the few colleagues and friends I had known since our schooldays at Kyamate Primary in the early 1950s. He was slightly older than me and had been two years ahead of me at school, but this gap had been narrowed because I skipped the third year of junior secondary school. He was now starting his second year in Law at Dar es Salaam and it was he who showed us the way from the station to the university. Eriya Kategaya and Mwesiga qualified as lawyers at the University of Dar es Salaam while Mwesigwa Black gained a Bachelor of Commerce degree at the University of Nairobi. Valeriano Rwaheru, who had also been a colleague of ours at Ntare, qualified as an engineer, also at the University of Nairobi, while I graduated with a Bachelor of Arts degree in Political Science.

The university accommodation was very comfortable, with two people to a room. The rooms were big and well-ventilated. Tanzania had not had a university until independence so the halls of residence were still new, and there were many new buildings with good facilities. The hall in which I stayed first was called 'Biafra' because it was set apart from the other halls of residence, and this was the time of the Biafran war.

As far as the Biafran situation was concerned, we were first carried away by President Nyerere's position of support for Biafra. But later on, after listening to a delegation of Biafrans who came to address us, I developed some doubts about their position – particularly whether the Igbo politicians should really have gone to the extent of seceding from Nigeria. One of their delegates was Michael Mopara, a minister in the Nigerian Eastern Region. We asked the delegates a few questions which they failed to answer. One question was: 'Assuming the government in Lagos was corrupt, why didn't you use Biafra, or the Eastern Region, as a base to liberate the whole country? Why did you have to break away? Is it that you want to be big fishes in small ponds?' Their answer did not impress us because they showed some prejudices against northerners, such as: 'You know these Hausas are primitive ...' That kind of attitude began to give me some doubts about their whole stance. If they had really been supporting a move for change, the Eastern Region, where they already had a big force and a population of about 12 million, would have been a good starting point for a country-wide liberation.

At Dar es Salaam University we found a very good political and intellectual atmosphere with a lot of modernist revolutionary thinkers such as Walter Rodney, and other lecturers from Europe. We became exposed to new ideas and this gave us a very good chance to become familiar with pan-Africanist and anti-colonialist ideas, the most dramatic of which was the exposure to the role imperialism had played in distorting socio-economic development in Africa. This played a large part in focusing our own political outlook as far as internal and external issues were concerned. We had previously had a vague nationalist feeling but it now took definite shape because it was backed by a coherent ideological outlook.

We became aware that the greatest danger to the welfare of Africans was imperialism in its modern manifestation of unbalanced, non-reciprocal foreign capital penetration, resulting in one-sided expatriation of dividends. This had led to a continuous net outflow of resources from the backward regions of the world to advanced Western Europe, North America and Japan. We discovered that by the 15th century, the initial unbalanced world development of science and technology in the world had resulted in European predators starting the process of enslaving the peoples of Africa, Asia and Latin America. They had relied on the monopoly of gunpowder and the process had gone through various stages: the slave trade, the looting of precious raw materials, and eventually, colonisation and effective occupation of the whole continent which completely distorted the development of Africa.

For the degree course we started off with three subjects in the first year, then continued with two for the second and third years. I began with Law, together with Economics and Political Science. At Dar es Salaam they had a unique way of teaching it as a subject, rather than as a profession. After the first year I dropped Law because I did not find the way they were teaching it very useful. We had to spend a lot of time on case law and, of course, it was heavily loaded towards

European culture. I remember a particular case called *Amkeyo vs Regina.* Amkeyo was a man in Kenya who had stolen a cow, slaughtered it, eaten it and buried its skin in his hut. Now, according to the British laws of evidence, and their concept of marriage, a wife cannot give evidence against her husband because, before the law, they are one person. So how can a man give evidence against himself?

Nobody knew where the cow skin was – there was some suspicion that Amkeyo had eaten the cow, but there was no proof. Later on Amkeyo quarrelled with his wife and she reported him to the police who came and dug up the missing skin of the cow from his hut. I don't know who advised Amkeyo about this British law, but when he went to court, he argued that his wife was not a competent witness to give evidence against him since they were one person! However, the British judge said: 'No. Natives do not really marry so they cannot benefit from this law. This law cannot be used by people like you. It is only for people who really marry – yours is only woman purchase!' So the judge allowed the wife to testify against her husband because, according to him, she was not really his wife. When I read that case, I thought we were wasting time learning a lot of rubbish. It was just like acting – like being on a stage! In any case, the law of two people 'being one' to me was an absurd one – the fact that if I committed a crime, my wife could not report me! What they should have taught us was principles of modern law as Part A of such a course, and Part B could have been the application of those principles to our society. That would have been a better approach, but these lecturers were stuck on European case law.

As far as the other subjects were concerned, there was a lot of nonsense in Political Science as well. I disliked constructing models: 'Let us assume this, let us assume that, and so on.' My question was: 'But why do you assume? Why don't you study reality? Why do you waste so much time constructing models when you have reality?' We used to have a number of conflicts with the lecturers who were mainly from Europe and America. There were a few African lecturers but they were heavily Western-influenced.

We had access to a large number of books and we attended seminars and lectures about imperialism, liberation, the evolution of society, the material and metaphysical world, and disengagement from colonially controlled economic structures. We thought it was important to start a new course and indeed we agitated until it was introduced. It was called 'Development Studies' and it was for the study of the laws that govern society. We had learnt that society does not develop accidentally, but that it does so following certain laws. We were of the view that a scholar should learn these laws, and that is how the course was started. The course eventually became mandatory for every student at the university – whatever other subjects he or she was studying. Some of us were so excited about this new world outlook, but also frustrated at the way things were, that we decided to form a student's organisation which would focus and help organise the work of ideological consciousness-raising among the students about the current situation in Africa – and examining how it had come about.

UNIVERSITY STUDENTS' AFRICAN
REVOLUTIONARY FRONT

Around September 1967, we met with a small group of students and formed the University Students' African Revolutionary Front (USARF). Our membership was pan-African, consisting of students from Uganda, including people like Eriya Kategaya, James Wapakhabulo and Martin Mwesiga; from Kenya, Zambia, Malawi, Zimbabwe; and a few from Ethiopia. John Garang from Sudan, who came in 1968 to do some postgraduate work, was also a very active member. He was always telling us about their problems in southern Sudan. At that time he was a junior member of the Anyanya movement; he later went on to lead the Sudan People's Liberation Front.

The purpose of USARF was to form a study group, as a parallel to the official lectures which we regarded as obscurantist. We decided to set up our own self-help education programme. There was an element of rebellion in this because every Sunday, when others were going to church, we would sit conspicuously somewhere where they could see us, studying our own laws of social evolution and inviting lecturers such as Walter Rodney whom we thought would be helpful to us. Rodney was not one of my formal lecturers because he was teaching History. He was simply a part-time lecturer to our informal group. This was during the time he was writing *How Europe Underdeveloped Africa*. He was a very influential person for our group but I had a disagreement with him concerning his attitude to God – he took the Marxist line that there is no God and I could not agree with this. I saw it as beyond our scope – in the panorama of all the things that are knowable, how can one know that there is no God? I took the view that we should stick to the things that we know. That was the only issue over which I disagreed with Walter Rodney.

We also invited other revolutionaries from other parts of the world – people like Stokeley Carmichael (now Kwame Toure) whom we invited specifically from the United States, and Cherry Duggan, later Prime Minister of Guyana, but at that time in the opposition, who was on his way to attend the independence celebrations of Mauritius in March 1968. We used to find out who was passing through the area and invite them to come and give us lectures at the university. We would advertise the lectures among the student body and, as a result, our group gained a lot of publicity.

I was elected chairman of USARF for the whole time I was at the university. It took a while for our ideas to become accepted as most of the lecturers were conservative. Our group caused trouble by challenging the lecturers whose views of the social sciences we saw as distorted. We felt they were not telling us the truth. Our agitation, however, resulted in another student and myself becoming the first students to be elected onto the University Council, the university's policy-making body.

USARF also challenged the university branch of the TANU Youth League which had been taken over by opportunists who merely wanted to please the politicians in town. In so doing, they had made the TANU Youth League on campus unpopular among the students. Their transparent opportunism did not escape the notice of the general student body which saw them as career seekers – people who were praising the TANU party and government so that when they finished college they would be able to get lucrative jobs. Our approach was different. We were determined to support TANU, but we were also willing to criticise it. That appealed to the students because even those who did not agree with us realised that at least we were honest. Our balanced approach earned us respect from both the student body and the TANU government.

Because of this, the TANU Youth League reported us to Nyerere alleging that we were preaching a dangerous anti-TANU line. Influenced by these reports, Nyerere came to the university in 1969 to counteract us. Before he came, we called a meeting to discuss strategy. Some thought we should not ask questions because if we did, it would confirm what the Youth League had been telling Nyerere and he would be hostile towards us. But I said: 'No, that is not correct. If you keep quiet, that will make Nyerere more suspicious. It will confirm that we are really subversive, and not bona fide critics. So let's ask him in the presence of everybody the things we have been saying in private.' The questions had to be submitted to the vice-chancellor in advance and by the time I convinced my colleagues that we should submit a question, it was rather late. Since we were a thorn in their flesh, I think the lecturers wanted us to have a collision with Nyerere so that he would put us down in front of everybody to expose us.

So I was very surprised, after Nyerere's initial speech, to hear the Vice-Chancellor call: 'The first questioner is Yoweri Museveni.' My question was about *ujamaa* – I was attacking the concept of *ujamaa* saying that it was simply primitive communalism and could not be used as a modern ideology for management. In reply Nyerere spoke for about half an hour and he made the students laugh. He did not really answer my question, but nor did he 'put me down', as the lecturers may have hoped, and at least he realised that we were not subversive – indeed I think he respected us.

My problem with the concept of *ujamaa* was that Nyerere was using his tribe as a model for the rest of Tanzania. But his tribe was one of the underdeveloped ones, with no social differentiation. So my criticism was: 'First of all, what you are saying is not true for the whole of Africa because in some areas like Buganda we had classes: a peasant class and a feudal class. So you cannot say that there was this idyllic African society where everyone was a friend of everyone else, and which was spoilt by colonialism.' I knew that there was exploitation in pre-colonial Africa and that much of the damage to Africa was done by the chiefs, for instance, in their collaboration during the slave trade. So I did not like the idea of painting a false image of an ideal African society which was messed up by the Europeans as such a picture would camouflage present-day exploitation. Nyerere came back to the university a second time, but this time we did not attend the meeting. I understand that after the meeting he was heard to ask where we were.

By the time we left the university, quite a tradition of radical thinking had developed. This new, more enlightened atmosphere forced into retreat the very backward ideas which the university students had started to foment. In 1966, for instance, before we arrived, there had been a student rebellion against national service and the resulting confrontation between the students and the government had led to the closure of the university for about a year. At that time, university students had regarded themselves as an emerging elite but they seemed to be dedicated almost solely to bargaining for privilege and position.

For our part, we distanced ourselves from the search for privileges which many student leaders fall prey to. They are attracted by such temptations as overseas trips and running around with the most beautiful girls on campus in an undisciplined and purposeless manner. Minor distractions of that kind are what constitute 'privileges' in an unpoliticised student community, but such deviations undermine the credibility of a potential leader.

CONTACTS WITH FRELIMO

Instead of going to Europe to attend international students' conferences, where recruitment into foreign intelligence services sometimes took place, in December 1968 I organised a trip for seven students, including myself, to visit the liberated zones of northern Mozambique. The others were Owen Tshabangu and Emmanuel Dube from Zimbabwe, Andrew Shija and Msoma from Tanzania, Kapote Mwakasungura from Malawi, and John Kawanga from Uganda. Kawanga had also been with us at Ntare School.

We had first met with Frelimo (Front for the Liberation of Mozambique) during 1967, my first year at the university. We went to their offices and told them that we wanted to help them publicise their materials and raise funds for them. Mondlane was very interested in us. Frelimo, and in fact all the liberation movements, had a very difficult time then because the local reactionaries were attacking them. The line of attack was: 'They are spending too much time out of their own country. They are not fighting, they are just consuming money here in the bars, running around with European girls.'

There was a double-pronged attack by racists and imperialists against the liberation movements. On the one hand, by working through people like Houphouet-Boigny of Côte d'Ivoire and Kamuzu Banda of Malawi, they took the line that the liberation struggle could not succeed because the whites were too strong. The liberation fighters were just hot-heads who could not make any impact and they were making the whites more adamant by fighting them. The message was that the enterprise was not feasible and that the fighters should not even try.

The other line of attack was from people who were pretending to be great sympathisers of the liberation movements but who claimed that they were frustrated by the lack of seriousnesss on the part of the leaders of the liberation movements.

These people would condemn the leaders individually as no-good people who were squandering Africa's money. By undermining the leaders and saying they were all useless, they were, in a subtle manner, linking up with the likes of Houphouet-Boigny: 'If all the liberation leaders are useless, why give them money? Why give them arms?' The next stage in that argument would be: 'Maybe Houphouet-Boigny is right, after all.' Even some of the communist regimes were reasoning like the officials in the town. The Cubans believed in action by the leader, following the example of Castro: the leader of the liberation movement had to be in the battlefield; if he was not in the battlefield, he was not serious. Therefore, it was a very bad time indeed for the freedom-fighters and when we approached Frelimo, Mondlane was very happy because nobody had ever approached him offering that kind of support.

We helped them by organising sensitisation meetings – such small-scale events had not been happening before – and we invited Mondlane to speak at the university to create more awareness and counteract hostile propaganda. Some of us could not, at that time, comprehend why people should write things they did not take the trouble to understand. We wondered why they did not go and witness the real situation for themselves so that they could criticise from an informed position rather than from prejudiced ignorance.

Countries such as Tanzania and Zambia were the only bases for the liberation movements, and if the local population was hostile, the local officials would also use that as an excuse to become hostile too. It was through these countries that the few arms and little money coming from outside would be handled. Therefore, it was important to create a friendly atmosphere for the freedom-fighters and that is why Mondlane was very happy with us. He was a very intelligent, very pleasant man, and easy to talk to. I believe that Frelimo would never have suffered the problems it did if he had lived. He was a real freedom-fighter. He was criticised by the reactionaries, pathetic enemies of their own interests, for having married a white woman. But he had married his wife 13 years before he even thought of joining the struggle! So what should he have done? Should he have divorced his wife in order to prove that he was a 'real African'?

Implicit in that kind of criticism was the idea that all whites are enemies. This was really an enemy strategy, to imply that the struggle was a racist one, and not a struggle for justice. Within this racist polarisation were the African exploiters who argued that a black exploiter is preferable to a white one – also a very dangerous line to take. If a white man is helping you, why should you throw away his support? Some would argue: 'Ah, but whites are not genuine.' That, I would argue, is not your problem. You should give him an assignment, initially one which is not too sensitive, to test whether or not he is genuine. Why should his motives concern you if you can get the results you want from him?

That is why I said in 1968: 'Let us go and see for ourselves. Why are we arguing? They say they have a liberated zone, so let's go there and see it.' Some of my friends did not support me in this because they had been affected by the hostile propaganda. Some of them said: 'Mondlane will eliminate you' and when I asked them why, they replied: 'The man is a CIA agent.' I countered: 'But why should he eliminate us, even if he is a CIA agent who is masquerading as a freedom-fighter? It is in his interests to show us that he is fighting so that he can continue his work as an agent. If we go there and he kills us, then everybody will know that he is no good.' I could not see how Mondlane could have eliminated us, even if he had been a CIA agent. So I insisted that we should go but some of my friends were still uncertain and so they dropped out. There were supposed to have been ten of us but in the end only seven went.

We went to the border in Frelimo trucks – Mondlane did not come with us himself but he sent some people to accompany us to a small town near the border where we met Chipande, then Frelimo Deputy Secretary of Defence. (Samora Machel was the Secretary of Defence. Chipande has been Minister of Defence since Mozambique became independent.) We crossed the River Ruvuma in boats and started walking on the other side. For our part, we were very impressed by Frelimo's progress. By 1968–9 they controlled huge areas of their country and were inflicting heavy losses against the Portuguese. We found that Frelimo had evolved a good system of organising the population in branches and neighbour-hood committees similar to those we were later to introduce in Uganda as Resistance Councils and Committees.

In the liberated zone, Frelimo had zones of operation under commanders, who in turn were responsible to the chairman of that zone. The soldiers were local Makonde people but the commanders were all from the south of the country. We found that one group within Frelimo was led by an ignorant chief and was anti-white and anti-Mondlane. This group was fomenting tribalism arguing that since Mondlane was from the south of the country, he was 'using' the northerners. This idea was supported by some officials in Tanzania who thought that the people from the south were not serious because the fighting was being done by the north-erners. Because of the location of the struggle, the fighting had started in the Makonde area. They put forward a 'solution' that the north should secede from the rest of Mozambique and join Tanzania. One of the Tanzanian ministers came from a tribe near the Makonde area and he was very, very dangerous. So our going to the liberated zones exposed all these reactionaries and weakened the bureaucrats who were obstructing Frelimo.

When we were in Mozambique, the dissident group murdered a man called Samuel Kankhomba who was following behind us to organise an ambush against the Portuguese for us to witness. He was murdered on the Tanzanian side because the dissidents were in collusion with some Tanzanian officials, who took no action against the murderers. There were some bombing raids by the Portuguese while we were there but we were not frightened because conventional bombing is useless in those circumstances in the bush, unless the attacks are accompanied by infantry. The chances of hitting any of the guerrillas were remote. While we were there, we were given a little basic military training in drills and manoeuvres, although not with weapons. We were to receive real military training from Frelimo after Mozambique's independence in 1975.

The biggest test for the Frelimo leaders and combatants was hunger, since food production had suffered because of the war. The other major problem, as for any group fighting for freedom in Africa was tribalism. Because of our backward, pre-industrial economies, there are no pan-national social forces which can ensure horizontal linkages. The only organised groups are either tribes or religious factions. These are easily exploited by foreign forces and local opportunists to bring about the divisions which exacerbate the weaknesses of African societies. Mozambique was no exception. The war had started in 1964 in the Cabo Delgado Province, a predominantly Makonde area. Immediately, the opportunists sought to use this predominance of the Makonde people in order to overthrow Mondlane's leadership.

It is really pathetic to see the abundance in Africa of people who are ready to be used by Africa's enemies to fight against the vital interests of all Africans, including the interests of the opportunists themselves. An ignorant tribal chief, Kavandame, himself from the Makonde area, would say: 'Look at my age: am I to die in the bush? Go and take a big town so that if I am to die, I shall die in a city.' In saying such things, he was directly opposed to the Frelimo strategy of a protracted war which would wear down the enemy. A 'quick war' was not possible and would only give the enemy an advantage because the enemy had superior material capacity in terms of tanks, planes, and so on, which could be used to decimate the liberation forces if they exposed themselves to that concentrated power.

Our visit showed us that Frelimo's strategy was paying off and that the liberation movement was doing a good job against the Portuguese. When we went back to Tanzania, we described to the press everything we had experienced and witnessed. Our contact with Frelimo was invaluable, both in our own education and in our future struggles.

CONTACTS WITH OTHER GROUPS

Our role in the student movement had three effects: it radicalised and deepened the ideological content of our thinking; it made us quite well known on the African scene, especially in liberation movement circles; and it reinforced our pan-Africanist views and enabled us to make pan-Africanist contacts such as President Nyerere.

Because we were politically active, our group attracted the attention of various communist regimes which were very keen to attract students to their side in the Cold War, which was at its height at that time. But we in USARF opposed such inducements as foreign trips because we saw them as a form of corruption. These expenses-paid trips were meant to woo students, but nothing positive would be achieved by them, indeed the trips could actually take away the revolutionary zeal of the students. On one occasion, I had a small contretemps with the North

Koreans, who used to organise conferences and tours for students and journalists mainly to drum up support for their cause against the South Koreans and the Americans. They arranged a journalists' conference in 1969 to which they invited me. I said I would accept the invitation only if they would also give me some military training while I was in North Korea. The North Korean ambassador in Dar es Salaam agreed, I think as a way of persuading me to go.

When I got to Korea, I found that nobody there had any idea about my military training. They were more interested in mobilising delegates in their polemical war with China, at that time undergoing its 'Cultural Revolution'. However, I pestered them so much that eventually a colonel was detailed to give me a short course in weapon-handling, using a rifle and a pistol. I was taught how to load, unload and clean the weapons, and given a little target practice. It was the first time I had ever handled a weapon and at that stage I was not a very good shot, although later on I improved. Using such tactics, we kept on poaching knowledge about warfare and thus, from such humble beginnings, was the National Resistance Army created.

We had already grasped the fact that Obote was intent on exercising dictatorial powers over the people of Uganda through the sectarian control of military power. He deepened the northern monopoly of the army, a process that had been started by the British colonialists. The sole purpose of this was to sidetrack the political process, since it had proved inconvenient for his purposes, and to rely on a sectarian army to keep himself in power. But Obote was laying the ground for his own eventual downfall through military *coups*. We had understood Obote's schemes as early as 1966 and that is why we set out to break this monopoly by acquiring the necessary military skills. The appropriate time had not yet arrived, but it was drawing nearer.

THE PRESIDENT'S OFFICE, 1970

I finished university in March 1970 and returned to Uganda to look for a job. By then most members of our group had left university and gone out to work. Mwesiga and Kategaya were in the Attorney-General's chambers in Kampala, Mwesigwa was at the University of Nairobi as an assistant lecturer, and Rwaheru was an engineer with East African Railways. I went to the Foreign Service Commission for a job interview.

I was interviewed by a large panel and the following day the chairman of the commission called me back to see him in his office on his own. He seemed to think that I was a bright fellow and he said to me: 'Why don't you work in the President's Office? The President needs some young people around him.' This man (Abdalla Anyuru) had been in the Uganda National Congress, the predecessor of the UPC. There were some people who were trying to work with Obote to try and help him do better. So I was recruited into the Foreign Service and appointed to work as a research assistant in the President's Office. My office was on the first floor of Parliament Buildings. The work was quite interesting and it entailed carrying out political and economic research in magazines, journals and other publications, and compiling data. But any work, however good or useful, would eventually come to nothing because Obote's only ideology was and is power and I recognised that in him. I saw him quite regularly, among other places at the Uganda Club which was a sort of parliamentary club. He would often stay there late into the night, drinking beer with his cronies.

Because Obote's ideology was power, he provoked divisions even within his own party. In every district there would be several wings of the UPC – the Muwanga faction, the Ibingira faction, the Kakonge faction, and so on. All these people were constantly reporting each other to Obote. Whenever people were united, Obote was worried. In the end, this kind of system was bound to collapse. I thought so at the time, but in the meantime, apart from the office work, I continued with the community mobilisation work I had started in the late 1960s. I had bought some land at my present home in Rwakitura, Nyabushozi county, and I started acquiring some cattle.

Some people from Mbarara District Administration had told the Vice-President, John Babiiha, who was also the Minister of Animal Industries, that I was encouraging peasants to grab land and settle on it. I went to his office to see him and said to him: 'You are the one who told us that we must adopt practices appropriate to the modern world. But when we apply to the government for land titles, the people in the Land Office refuse to process our applications. So should we listen to you or to the Land Office?' He said: 'Oh, the Land Office has been misled. You go ahead with your work.'

Thus, in order to develop our community programme, we found that it was not harmful to create alliances with politicians at the national level. We had no problem with the DP, but it was also useful to have some people in the UPC, if it could help us in our work. We soon learnt to use the system. The politicians were always manoeuvring for power and if one was serious, it was always possible to work on them, even using their own interests and selfishness, to promote our programme. A man like Obote would be very happy if we initiated a community programme provided we associated it with him so that he could claim it as his own.

Amin, however, was in a different category altogether and that is why during his regime we had to take up arms. With Amin, you could not make even limited progress using the system because he was a killer. Obote would not send people to kill someone in order to take his house – Amin would. In the next chapter I shall digress a little from my narrative to consider the historical and political background to the armed struggle which we started in 1971 after Idi Amin assumed power.

Chapter 4

A BRIEF HISTORICAL REVIEW

THE AFRICAN BACKGROUND

When the European exploiters first set foot in Africa in the 15th century, the natural process of growth and advancement towards higher forms of civilization was interrupted and distorted. This affected both the economies and the people of Africa. The dominant exploitative relations in production, distribution and exchange were imperialist/capitalist ones which have always worked to the detriment of the African people.

The processes of economic, industrial, agricultural, social, cultural and political advancement were stunted and there was regression in many areas. The West was, meanwhile, making gigantic strides forward in technology and many other fields. In manufacturing and technology, the levels which had been attained in Africa, for instance in extracting iron from its ore and shaping it into various tools such as hoes, spears and arrows, were not consolidated. Africa even lost self-sufficiency in the elementary technological fields of fire-making and ironmongery, and now depends on the importation of even the humble hoe and other basic implements.

The worst blow, however, fell on the people themselves: approximately 50 million Africans were torn from their motherland and taken to the Americas to act as unwilling instruments in laying the foundations of Western capitalism. Capitalism was built on the bones of African slaves. They were coerced into playing an important role in emancipating Europeans and North Americans from poverty and underdevelopment. From this time the trade between Africa and Europe, which had existed in various forms for many centuries, was transformed to Africa's disadvantage. Unequal exchange became a characteristic of international commerce, with Africa always at a disadvantage. African wealth, from human beings to crops and precious minerals, was exchanged for worthless articles like trinkets, mirrors and beads. As a result, Europe and North America are now in the Nuclear and Space Ages, while we are still in the hand-hoe era.

Africa has the highest infant mortality rates, the lowest levels of calorie intake, the lowest average life expectancy, and the lowest number of doctors and other skilled personnel per head of population. Substantively, we have regressed from the late Iron Age levels we had attained just before the Europeans arrived. This is the general African context in which Uganda finds itself. Although at the time of independence in 1962, according to people like Milton Obote, there was 'prosperity', Uganda was a microcosm of the general African condition of underdevelopment. The limited education which created a small middle class of professionals, the commerce which created the retail trader, and the cash crops of the small farmer did not transform this basic reality. If these pseudo-modern economic activities were of any benefit at all to the African people, this was purely incidental and secondary. They could not, and did not, bring the African to the Western standard of living and development.

Even in the heyday of so-called economic prosperity, Uganda was still very backward: millions were walking barefoot, underfed and suffering from worms, and without adequate medical services; and their mental world was still dominated by superstitions – to mention only a few of the woes that afflicted and still afflict the Ugandan and his fellow African. Economic and social structures lacked the ingredients to usher in the basic changes which could have transformed a primitive social order into a modern, civilised one. These basic ingredients are: an independent technological base, coupled with managerial and entrepreneurial skills.

UPC AND KY – MARRIAGE OF CONVENIENCE

Uganda became independent on 9 October 1962. The Prime Minister, Apolo Milton Obote, had formed a government with the help of the Kabaka Yekka ('King Alone') Party, the regional non-democratic movement in Buganda, central Uganda. I hesitate to call Kabaka Yekka (KY) a movement of or for Buganda because nearly 38 per cent of the people who live in Buganda are not Baganda. Moreover, a large element of the Catholics, who are an important proportion of the Baganda, did not approve of the KY role in Buganda politics, which at that time was dominated by the Protestant elite.

The UPC, which had no base in Buganda, was a Protestant-based party while the Democratic Party (DP) was largely a party for Roman Catholics. The UPC and KY teamed up to form the first post-independence government through an unprincipled marriage of convenience. This was not a true alliance but an attempt by both groups to use each other. The result was the intrigue and counter-intrigue which had been inherent in the original alliance itself.

The alliance consisted of a series of mutual pacts between the UPC and KY, one of which was that KY would have the exclusive right to field all candidates in Buganda, competing against the DP. The UPC would field candidates elsewhere, but not in Buganda. The two parties would then join forces at the national level. The two also worked out how they were to share power if the alliance won the elections. The 1962 Constitution gave powers to the Buganda parliament (the Lukiiko) to decide whether Buganda's 22 representatives to the National Assembly were to be directly elected by the people, as was the case in the rest of the country, or nominated by the Lukiiko. Elections to the Lukiiko were held in early 1962 and KY defeated the DP. During elections to the National Assembly later that year, the Lukiiko decided that Buganda's representatives to the national parliament should be nominated, and not elected as elsewhere in the country. This left the DP without any representatives from Buganda since all the nominated members were from KY. The UPC won 38 seats, against 24 seats for the DP. Combined with the 22 seats from Buganda, the UPC-KY alliance formed the government and the DP went into opposition. The basis of political affiliation at the very beginning of Uganda's independence was, therefore, opportunistic and sectarian, with divisions along religious and tribal lines. These divisions clouded the real issues and prevented the electorate from distinguishing between important issues and trivial ones.

The interests and needs of the people were, therefore, not made a focal point because opportunistic, ideologically and politically backward politicians had so fragmented society that common interests were lost sight of. The peasant in Lango, northern Uganda, did not regard the peasant in Buganda as his ally: he was persuaded to believe that the Baganda were 'arrogant' while the Baganda were told that the Langi were 'primitive and cruel'. This atomisation of the masses into sectarian groups served the interests of the politicians who divided and ruled the people. Sectarianism gave them an automatic and cheap, exploitative political base. It was what philosophers call 'ideological obscurantism', which means obscuring the truth in order to serve the interests of a clique.

Political awareness among the masses was anathema to this type of politician. Samwiri Mugwisa, a UPC government minister in Obote's second administration, once admonished people in Mukono saying: 'You women! Why do you bother with politics? You should concentrate on growing potatoes and sending your children to school and forget about politics!'

Although I had been too young to vote at the time of independence (the voting age then was 21) because of the sectarian politics in the country, as I explained earlier, I sympathised with the DP. My parents were DP supporters by virtue of belonging to the Bahima sub-group of the Banyankore people. Although most Bahima are Protestants, in the mid-1950s and early 1960s, most had allied themselves with Catholics because of the caste, ethnic and religion-based politics in Ankole, which was also being practised in other parts of the country.

UPC officials were thoroughly unscrupulous and used all kinds of crude methods such as double voting, hooliganism and demogoguery to win votes and entrench themselves in power. I remember a speech by one Silvanus Baguma, a UPC campaigner at Nyamitanga in Mbarara in 1963, in which he said that once an African government had taken power, it would never give it up. He added that DP supporters were therefore wasting their time because the UPC would never relinquish power – whether people voted for it or not. Seventeen years later, during the farcical elections of December 1980, UPC campaigners took up the same theme of 'we shall win power whether you vote for us or not.' The DP, on the other hand, used less crude methods. The party was more popular than the UPC in 1980 and would have won if the elections had been free and fair. However, the DP's ideological base was the same cheap opportunistic sectarianism, using the Catholic religion in the same way that the UPC was using the Protestant one.

THE 1966 CRISIS

The UPC came to shape most of the subsequent history of independent Uganda. By 1965 the KY had been dropped from the coalition and some opportunist KY members of parliament had joined the UPC. By 1970, when Obote declared Uganda a one-party state, the opposition had been whittled down to only eight members and fissures soon started appearing within the UPC itself. The first to fall was John Kakonge whose political inclination was towards the left. He had nation-wide popularity within the party, as its Secretary-General since 1960, and it is widely believed that he would have been returned to leadership at the party elections in Gulu in 1964 had the elections been democratic. Incapable of practising democracy within itself, the UPC could hardly have been expected to nurture it in the country at large.

In 1964, the UPC was split between Kakonge on the one hand and Obote, in alliance with Grace Ibingira, on the other. The two factions claimed they had ideological differences, with Kakonge on the left of the party and Obote and Ibingira on the right. It is true that there had been some leftist talk in the Kakonge wing – he was ousted from the post of Secretary-General and replaced with Ibingira at Gulu in 1964 – but personal ambition cannot be ruled out as a motivating factor in all these manoeuvres, as well as the usual problems caused by ideological underdevelopment.

In 1966, the UPC divided itself further, with Obote this time claiming to be on the progressive wing of the party, while Ibingira was now of the conservative wing, claiming that Obote was 'pro-communist'! There were some real issues at stake this time, for example the army. The armed forces were becoming more and more sectarian. There was no attempt to ensure that soldiers were recruited from all parts of Uganda so that the character and composition of the nation would be reflected in the army. The Obote-Ibingira alliance had not been based on any matter of principle and once the common obstacle against whom they had united, John Kakonge, had been removed, they had no strong reason to remain together. The split was now characterised as 'Bantu' versus 'Nilotic', but even this latest grouping did not last.

The UPC had first been split between 'left' and 'right'; then it was 'Nilotic' versus 'Bantu'; and finally the Nilotic faction splintered itself and the party still further. These perpetual fissures showed up the contradictions within the UPC, because if it had been a properly constituted and operated political organisation, with at least one common purpose, a way of handling and containing differences would have been sought and found. The only consistent objective, however, especially in Obote's case, was to stay in power, regardless of the cost to the party and the country. The divisions also showed that the party's ideological position was false and dangerous to the country. Its members defined and fought each other as enemies and, therefore, had little time left to tackle the country's problems of backwardness and underdevelopment.

These UPC fissures culminated in the arrest and subsequent detention of Grace Ibingira and four other ministers (B.K. Kirya, Dr B.S. Lumu, M.M. Ngobi and G.B. Magezi) in February 1966 after a motion in Parliament which accused Obote and Amin, among others, of being implicated in the theft of gold, ivory and coffee from the Congo (now Zaire). This theft had been carried out under the guise of helping the Congolese nationalists who were fighting Moise Tshombe, the Belgian puppet ruler.

Apart from the detention of the principal accusers, there was also interference with witnesses. After Obote's fall David Oyite Ojok, who had been one of his supporters in 1966, admitted to me in February 1971, at Lake Hotel in Bukoba, Tanzania, that Obote's group had to 'work very hard' on one Kisembo, then a captain in the army. He added that if this Kisembo had been located, he could have given the evidence he had been dissuaded from giving in 1966. This could have been used to discredit Amin at the time of his seizure of power.

Whether or not the allegations against Obote and Amin were true, Parliament had voted that a Commission of Inquiry be set up and that Idi Amin, who was then deputy army commander, be suspended while investigations were carried out. The Prime Minister, Obote, arbitrarily reversed this near-unanimous vote of Parliament and took no action against Amin. As if these illegal actions were not enough, in addition to arresting his cabinet colleagues and protecting Amin and himself from inquiry into the gold affair, on 22 February 1966, Obote suspended the Independence Constitution and openly adopted dictatorial powers, including those of detention without trial. The following day, Amin, who had been deputy to Brigadier Shaban Opolot, was promoted to be Army Chief of Staff. The Lukiiko tried to resist these moves by calling upon the central government to remove itself from Buganda soil, but all this did was to give Obote the chance for a final showdown with the Kabaka. On 24 May 1966, the army, led by none other than Idi Amin, attacked the Kabaka's palace and forced him to flee into exile.

THE ARMY UNDER OBOTE

In all these crimes and intrigues, Obote had relied on the army, which was tribally biased, thanks to the colonial policy of recruitment. The bulk of the former colonial force, which had been expanded from one battalion to a force of 8500 by the time of Amin's *coup* in 1971, had been recruited from the northern peoples of Acholi, Lango and West Nile. Obote's own figures after his overthrow were: 4300 Acholis and 1300 Langi out of a total of 8500, most of the balance being made up by West Nilers, who were Amin's people.

Obote has tried to cover up one additional crime against the people of Uganda by citing the colonial policy of biasing recruitment into the army in favour of the northern peoples. They were supposedly more 'martial' and 'warlike', while the southerners, from the centre and west and most of the east of the country, were 'soft' because they ate a staple diet of *matooke* (green bananas), compared to the northern staple diet of millet which is supposed to be more hardy! These are bankrupt and false ideas which can only be accepted and bandied about by ideologically bankrupt politicians.

The pre-colonial history of Uganda shows that, on the contrary, the more advanced social formations had evolved in the southern and western areas of what is now Uganda. That is not to say that the peoples of the northern part of the country had not made significant progress. Nevertheless, advanced social formations had evolved in such areas as Buganda, Bunyoro and Ankole as well as Karagwe, Biharamulo, Ngara, Kigoma, Ukelewe, together with Bukoba in Tanzania, and Rwanda, which are closely related in terms of culture, language and tradition. These areas were part of the pre-colonial interlacustrine states of the Bantu civilisation. It goes without saying that sophisticated social, political and economic systems, such as those established in Rwanda or Buganda, could not have evolved without complementary military systems.

Although the art and practice of warfare in these areas was still backward compared to the Zulu system – which had achieved some revolutionary gains in the form of the short stabbing spear as opposed to the long throwing spear that was still characteristic of Ugandan states – significant achievements had nevertheless been attained, notably a large militia, a navy in the case of Buganda, and regular armies in Rwanda, Ankole and Bunyoro. It is, therefore, an incontrovertible historical fact that the southern peoples of Uganda had a martial tradition of no mean proportions. In fact, the colonial rulers feared that tradition and set out to undermine both it and the higher forms of social organisation that had evolved in the south; and they invented lies to cover up their intentions. It was infinitely more inexcusable, however, that the so-called independence politicians continued perpetuating such falsehoods.

To return to the point at hand: the military recruitment policy which Obote, as Prime Minister, had inherited from the British in 1962, but which he could have changed. Instead, he expanded it and sought to benefit from it for his personal ambition and sectarian aims. Having consolidated the practice of tribally biased recruitment and promotion, he proceeded to use the army against Parliament, against the constitution and against the people of Uganda. He even used it against his own political party. It was this tribal, sectarian and unpoliticised army that eventually overthrew him and intensified the country's political crisis.

Having overthrown the constitution, Obote became a real dictator and used his illegally acquired powers to cover up his crimes. Many prominent Ugandans were subjected to detention without trial, that hallmark of Africa's political underdevelopment. Among those detained were: William Wilberforce Nadiope, former

Vice-President of Uganda, Grace Ibingira, Minister of State in the Prime Minister's Office, Dr B.S. Lumu, Minister of Health, George Magezi, Minister of State, Paul Ssemogerere, Benedicto Kiwanuka, President of the DP, Badru Kakungulu, leader of the Muslim community, Major Barnabas Katabarwa, a senior army officer, Dani Wadada Nabudere, and many other prominent Ugandans.

Obote also covered up massacres by the army and police such as the ones at Nakulabye in 1964 and at Kisubi, Luwero and Lubiri in 1966. There were other killings all over Buganda after the Kabaka was overthrown. The army unleashed a savage slaughter of Baganda in which people were loaded onto army trucks and simply disposed of. Such crimes would not have been tolerated in a properly functioning democracy. Moreover it would have been easy to discover the culprits, but Obote said that he wanted to 'teach the Baganda a lesson'. National institutions such as the army, the churches, the university, the police, the judiciary and the civil service had been interfered with and were, therefore, easy to influence and manipulate.

Having been given the wrong foundation by the colonialists, the so-called army was not even a proper army, but just a colonial levy of riflemen with a low level of education and literacy. Instead of taking the first opportunity to correct these anomalies, Obote reinforced them. Unlike Julius Nyerere of Tanzania, who built a strong national army from the former colonial force, Obote intensified the Ugandan army's tribal character and even failed to tackle the problem of low educational standards and make technical improvements such as acquiring suitable arms and armaments to improve the quality of the armed forces as a whole. No coherent policy study was carried out and most of the officers were either ignoramuses like Amin or political favourites who were professional failures.

On top of all this, the army became virtually a wing of the UPC with army officers sometimes wearing UPC colours. The few educated soldiers – men like Tom Angutuko, Barnabas Katabarwa, Sarapio Kakuhikire, Gus Karugaba, Eridadi Senkoto and Ongodia – were either weeded out or suppressed. Although the Amin-Obote clique had initially had a general northern bias, by 1970 the army had degenerated further into specific tribal cliques to the extent that a junior officer refused to salute a superior unless he belonged to the same tribe. A soldier would use all sorts of tricks, including removing his military cap and pocketing it, in order to avoid saluting an officer from a 'bad' tribe.

To compound these problems, the official army languages of Swahili and English were replaced by indigenous languages not understood by everyone; there were secret recruitment exercises in which northerners would travel on lorries to other parts of Uganda following recruiting teams, so that they would fill up the quotas intended for recruits from other parts of the country. The northern factions eventually fought it out and Amin emerged as victor, in the process murdering thousands of soldiers and civilians, mainly from Lango and Acholi. The main political problem in Uganda at that time, therefore, was the army, which effectively prevented the country from attaining democracy.

Obote and Amin's factional infighting practically ruined the country and by the end of Amin's rule in 1979 an estimated 500 000 Ugandans were to die at the hands of Amin and his henchmen. The list of deaths is endless. Among them were: Brigadier Hussein, Colonel Arach, Colonel Langoya, Sarapio Kakuhikire, Barnabas Katabarwa, Valentino Ochima, Michael Ondoga, all army officers; Hassan and Festo Wawuyo, both policemen; ex-ministers Basil Bataringaya, James Ochola, Joshua Wakholi and Alex Ojera; other prominent politicians such as Alex Latim, Sarapio Obonyo, Martin Okello, Nekemia Bananuka, Felix Tibayungwa, Joseph Bitwaari, Dr Sembeguya, Ali Kisekka, Ben Kiwanuka, Joseph Kiwanuka, Francis Walugembe and Shaban Nkutu; civil servants Frank Kalimuzo, Abdalla Anyuru, Yuda Katundu and Erifazi Laki; and church leaders such as Archbishop Janani Luwum. This was the high price Uganda paid for a corrupt, mismanaged and sectarian army.

From the very beginning, therefore, the general principles which lay behind the eventual aims of our group were clear: we should mobilise the people into a popular organisation, even if at the beginning we did not know exactly how we would do this, at least as far as the civilians were concerned. We were certain, however, that there was a need to recruit a truly national force. Later on, during the second phase of fighting, we evolved the idea of using local committees based within the population – a popular force producing a popular, national army which would be more difficult to manipulate than a tribally biased force. Even though the tribal force eventually turned against Obote, it was only after it had been manipulated by him and others, and had caused a great deal of havoc in the country.

RELIGION AND POLITICS

Because politicians at the time of independence were politically and ideologically bankrupt, their reliance on divide-and-rule tactics included using religion in secular matters such as winning political votes. All the independence political parties were involved in these practices – with the DP allied to Roman Catholics, the UPC to Protestants and KY to Protestants in Buganda. Obote, however, took it further than most. He interfered particularly with the Church of Uganda (the former Anglican Church) by heightening any anti-Baganda sentiments among the non-Baganda Protestant clergy. This interference caused numerous splits in the Church which went on into the Amin era.

There were endogenous factors within the Church itself which could have caused such fissures, but government interference exacerbated the problems. Interference in religious affairs was, however, most marked in the Islamic religion. Obote went to the extent of setting up a UPC Muslim organisation known as NAAM (National Association for the Advancement of Muslims) to rival the traditional Muslim community leadership of Prince Badru Kakungulu. Muslims in Uganda had to choose between the two rival mosques of Kibuli and Wandegeya. This interference in Muslim affairs even played a role in the anti-Obote *coup*. Just before he ousted Obote, Amin had switched from NAAM-UPC Muslims to Kakungulu's group, which had no love for Obote.

Groups like these provided a popular backing for Amin's *coup*, especially in Buganda. If such constituencies of opposition against Obote had not been created, Amin's *coup*, assuming that it took place at all, would have been opposed by the whole country. Obote had, however, destroyed any sense of national consensus on almost all issues. Because there was no better alternative, most Ugandans welcomed the *coup*. Obote seemed to have been surprised that people in Uganda celebrated his downfall but this was inevitable, considering the number of groups in society he had antagonised: the DP and KY supporters, the religious communities, the various UPC factions estranged since 1962, the Muslims, and UPC leftists like Nabudere and Chango Machyo.

This grouping of alienated forces created a broad anti-Obote front and Amin benefited from it. We, who were working underground in 1971 and 1972, soon discovered how dangerous it was for us as there were plenty of informers around. Our political opposition to Amin, because it was on matters of principle, was misunderstood by many to mean that we were pro-Obote. Consequently, other anti-Obote forces also opposed us until quite late in the struggle against Amin. In Ankole, for instance, during 1971 and 1972, I had to be careful of both DP supporters and supporters of Kahigiriza's faction of the UPC called *omufunguro* – meaning a diluted UPC. It was only after 1972, when the tide began turning against Amin, that we started gaining some ground, but even then people continued supporting him for fear of Obote coming back.

Obote's interference in the civil service followed similar patterns to his interference in military and religious affairs. First of all, he imposed Abdalla Anyuru as chairman of the Public Service Commission, contrary to the 1962 Constitution which provided for a non-partisan civil service. At the same time, in the local administration chiefs were deposed because they were pro-DP or pro-KY, for example in Ankole where Edward Rutehenda, Yonasani Rwakanuma and John Machwa, who were county chiefs, were removed from office.

I am not suggesting that national institutions such as the army or the university should have remained aloof from national affairs, but they should have been made to justify their existence by serving society within the context in which they were created. Obote attempted to use national bodies for the benefit of the UPC and since there was no democracy within the UPC itself, their manipulation could only serve very narrow interests.

MONARCHIES, FEUDALISM AND IMPERIALISM

By 1970 Obote had declared Uganda a one-party state. He had detained hundreds of political opponents and other innocent people, carried out provocative acts of interference in national institutions for partisan and personal purposes, overthrown the constitution and traditional monarchies in the regions of Buganda,

Ankole, Bunyoro and Toro where some of them, especially in Buganda and Toro, were very popular. He allowed a tribally biased army and police force to massacre people, especially in Buganda in May 1966, but also in other places, for example in Bwongyera in Kajara, Ankole. (The latter were killed while they were at prayer in a mosque because of allegations that they had not supported a certain Islamic UPC faction.) Nobody was arrested and nobody was tried for any of these murders.

The alleged overthrow of feudalism in Uganda by Obote in 1966 led various countries, especially leftist ones, to regard him as a lonely revolutionary who was heroically battling against the all-powerful feudal forces in Uganda, especially in Buganda! In fact, the misunderstanding of this aspect of the political crisis in Uganda, throughout the independence period, contributed to the country's ever-deepening crisis. Some African leaders were victims of this distortion and continued supporting Obote long after he had stopped serving any useful purpose for the people of Uganda.

The crucial question to consider in this connection is whether feudalism was the principal framework within which production, distribution and exchange were carried out in the Uganda of the 1960s. In fact, the nascent feudal states in Africa had collapsed when they were confronted by colonialism, the instrument of Europe's capitalism. The Europeans used the existing feudal structures to establish colonialism in Uganda, with some of the feudal lords working as collaborators. They worked as junior partners until 1928 when the heavy dues imposed on the peasants became an impediment to colonial interests. The latter sought to use the peasantry to produce more cash crops and other raw materials for their metropolitan industries. Hence, the economic power of the feudalists was broken by the *Nvujjo* and *Busuulu* Land Laws of 1928 which abolished the most important feudal privileges and left only nominal ones. Rent on land was restricted to an annual flat rate of six shillings, irrespective of the size of the land. Landlords could no longer evict peasants from their land. This power was reserved for the Governor.

This law ended the feudal lords' power and many of them sold their lands, thus fragmenting the original 8000 square miles (20 720 sq km) of land given to the 1000 collaborator families of the 1900 Agreement. These families found their original land holdings no longer profitable and they sought new opportunities like further education or joining the peasants in the production of cash crops. Moreover, these 1000 collaborators were not necessarily the traditional feudal landlords of pre-colonial days. Many of the pre-colonial nobles had followed the Kabalega-Mwanga line of strongly resisting colonial rule and had been deposed along with their sovereigns. Those who turned their backs on national independence were rewarded with land grants and chieftaincies, while others were recruited from Christian converts. In fact, the page boys of the old palaces became the new lords, provided they accepted colonial rule and worked for it. In Ankole people like Nuwa Mbaguta, the first *Enganzi* of Ankole, were collaborators in the most basic sense of the word.

By 1966, therefore, the dominant economic interests in Uganda were imperialist rather than feudal. Those feudal interests which were left were remnants from former systems and manifested themselves more in society's superstructure than in its economic base. Among the feudal remnants in the economy were the *mailo* land system in Buganda, which had survived the 1928 so-called reforms, and the *obushumba* (serfdom) system in Ankole. In this case, a person without any cattle of his own would work for a cattle-owner in exchange for food and other forms of non-monetary payment. However, such economic feudal manifestations were secondary to the dominant imperialist concerns of the production of cash crops and mineral exports.

Therefore, by defining feudalism rather than imperialism as the main problem in 1960s Uganda, Obote was creating artificial divisions among the people, and his added use of force eliminated any possibility of a national consensus. He thus actually served imperialism by emphasising internal differences while neglecting to address the contradictions between the country's national interests on the one hand, and those of imperialism on the other. Without national unity, the different petty bourgeois factions (traditionalists, parvenus and religionists) were all competing for what were in effect imperialist favours. This relegated the evolution of a national strategy for disengaging from imperialism to the back burner. In fact, people like Obote did not comprehend the workings of imperialism in the neo-colonial phase.

This problem continued until the NRM came to power in 1986. Up to then, Uganda's leaders had not been able to handle correctly the relatively simple problem of building national unity. My brief experience with the UNLF (Uganda National Liberation Front) administration, in which I occupied senior positions (as Minister of Defence and later Vice-Chairman of the Military Commission which succeeded Godfrey Binaisa's administration), showed me that it is easy to create unity among the people provided one has no personal ambitions of self-advancement, one is not corrupt and one is ideologically clear and politically perceptive. Unfortunately, many opportunities were lost under the Lule and Binaisa administrations. All these errors I have mentioned – sectarian politics, the rigging of elections, detentions without trial, dividing the army and the religious institutions, and promotions not based on merit or experience – created artificial divisions among the people and made it possible for Idi Amin to seize power and keep it for eight years. We have now begun to tackle these problems, but it is particularly tragic that they could have been avoided if the country had started off with the right leaders.

In 1970, when I returned from university and joined the President's Office as a research assistant, I briefly joined the UPC in the hope of bringing about reform from within. This was because the Democratic Party, with which I had originally sympathised and from which one might have expected a core of opposition to Obote to emerge, had lacked a dynamic leadership and that was long before Obote had banned the party.

44

The DP was led by conservative men who had limited perspectives both in terms of ideology and modes of struggle. They expected gentlemanly behaviour from people like Obote and when it was not forthcoming, they threw up their arms in defeat and resignation crying: 'What can we do? These people are cheats; they are unprincipled!' Each one of them would then abandon the struggle and concentrate on personal survival. In terms of ideology, they confined themselves to colonial and neo-colonial ideas. These so-called leaders did not have an overall view of the evolution of society from the primitive forms of the past to the complicated structures of the present and the future. They did not take note of the positive and negative aspects in all these systems and try to work out a proper synthesis for our country in its present age. Some DP leaders were not even convinced of the desirability of African rule itself. They would cite the political bankruptcy of the independence generation of African leaders to justify delaying African independence. They did not see that it was the failure of those particular politicians in specific situations, combined with foreign manipulation, rather than the failure of the concept of African independence which was the problem. The style of the DP leaders was, however, always gentlemanly and civilised. Because they generally had independent means of living, they were less openly materialistic than the UPC leaders.

The UPC was largely composed of *lumpen bourgeoisie*, or what in Ghana were known as 'verandah boys'. They had no independent means and were not prepared to work patiently. The UPC leadership were generally an uncouth breed, anxious to get rich as quickly as possible using the state apparatus and regarding their own crude style of operation, as exemplified by Obote, as the virtue of 'political shrewdness'. Ideologically, they were bankrupt and they were certainly unequal to the task of national emancipation. By the late 1960s, the UPC had managed to stifle the DP completely and some of us, who were already striking an independent posture in student and community affairs, joined the UPC in the hope of injecting a progressive spirit into it. That slim hope, however, was shattered by Amin's violent seizure of power in January 1971 – an event which was to prove a turning point, not only in my own political life, but ultimately in the lives of all Ugandans.

Chapter 5

FIGHTING AMIN (1)
[1971–2]

AMIN'S *COUP*

On 25 January 1971 – a day that will live in infamy in the history of our country – I left my house (number 35 in Kireka Housing Estate, a suburb of Kampala) to go to work. It was a Monday and as I was walking towards the bus stop, I noticed that there were no other people going in my direction. People were just standing around on the verandahs of their houses and someone shouted after me to ask where I was going. I said that I was going to work, but he told me that I should not proceed towards town as there had been some problems during the night. Apparently a clash had occurred between two groups of soldiers involving an armoured personnel carrier around Nakawa township, which is between Kireka, where I lived, and the centre of Kampala. Nothing much happened during the day, except for a number of soldiers moving about. Then at about 5.00 p.m. there was a radio announcement, read out by an army captain, that Obote had been overthrown and that General Idi Amin, the army commander, had taken over the government of Uganda.

News of Amin's *coup* met with mixed reactions on the streets of Kampala. Some were ecstatic, and demonstrated their joy on the streets. Others who joined them felt it served Obote right. Those happiest with the *coup* were mainly the Baganda, who blamed Obote rather than Amin for all their woes. Others, such as DP supporters, were also happy, but they did not go to demonstrate. Their attitude was: 'It had to end this way. We are not surprised.' During the day I met with a few colleagues and we tried to analyse the situation to see what should be done.

Amin had first come to our attention in February 1966 when he was named in the near unanimous vote in Parliament which had accused him of misappropriating the proceeds of the sale of ivory and gold from Zaire. Following the subsequent showdown, in which Obote arrested five members of his own cabinet and suspended the constitution, Amin was promoted to army commander. Amin soon went on to demonstrate the nature of his leadership when he used heavy artillery against the Kabaka's palace in May 1966. By 1969 Obote's highly dangerous policies of tribal manipulation were beginning to rebound on him, as Amin and Felix Onama, the Minister of Defence, turned against him. On 19 December 1969 there was an assassination attempt on Obote as he was leaving a UPC conference in Kampala. Amin was present, wearing the UPC colours – that is the way the army behaved in those days – and when Obote was shot, it seems Amin just ran away and hid himself.

By the end of 1970 a number of investigations were pending against Amin, for corruption and misuse of defence funds, as well as for complicity in the murder of his second in command, Brigadier Okoya and his wife in January 1970. Okoya had publicly accused Amin of cowardice for his behaviour on the occasion of the assassination attempt on Obote the previous month.

Thus Amin's *coup* of January 1971 was the climax of a crisis that had been building up since 1961, when a marriage of convenience had been struck between Obote's UPC and Mutesa's KY parties. Over the whole of that period, the only politician who had taken anything like a principled position on any issue was Benedicto Kiwanuka, the leader of the Democratic Party. Ben, as he was popularly known, was ideologically right-wing, but he was politically principled, which was admirable, whether or not one agreed with his ideas. Although a Muganda himself, Kiwanuka had opposed the demands by the Buganda Lukiiko for an excessive degree of autonomy for Buganda.

Another principled politician of the period was John Kakonge who had been UPC Secretary-General, but he seems either to have been weak-kneed, politically inept, or both, because he had allowed himself to be cowed by Obote's blandishments and intrigues. The whole of the 1960s decade in Uganda's political life was a period of intrigue, culminating in Obote virtually abandoning power to Amin. These intrigues among politicians had so weakened mass movements such as DP and UPC that Amin just picked up the mantle of power from a political leadership emasculated by its own ideological narrowness and its unprincipled conduct of state and political affairs.

What then should I and my colleagues do? By January 1971 our loose political association, composed of people like Eriya Kategaya, Martin Mwesiga and Mwesigwa Black, was little more than a study group and not yet an activist one. We had contacts with progressive politicians such as Dani Wadada Nabudere, Kintu-Musoke, Jaberi Bidandi-Ssali, Kirunda Kivejinja and Raiti Omongin. They were leftists who had been expelled from the UPC in 1964 for having belonged to the Kakonge wing of the party. Some of us also belonged to the Uganda Vietnam Solidarity Committee, which Nabudere had formed as a support and protest group to oppose the American war of aggression against the Vietnamese people.

At that stage within our group, I was considered an initiator rather than necessarily the leader. I argued strongly that we should regard Amin's *coup* as an opportunity. There would be no scope to work within an Amin 'system' in the way that we had within Obote's. We would, therefore, ultimately have to fight Amin and, in destroying him, we had the opportunity to dismantle the colonial state and rebuild it on a proper popular national basis. I told them, therefore, that I wanted to leave the country immediately to make contacts outside, for I feared that Obote, who had been abroad at a Commonwealth conference at the time of the *coup*, would be misrepresenting the true situation in Uganda.

INTO TANZANIA

That afternoon Richard Kaijuka, who also lived at Kireka and who later became a minister in the NRM government, gave me some money, and I left Kampala that night for Mbarara. There I was joined by four comrades, Erifazi Laki, the *saza* chief of Rwampara county, Ankole, Yuda Katundu, Abbas Kibazo and Zubairi Bakari from Kampala. We crossed into Tanzania at Murongo Ferry on 27 January. We travelled in Laki's Volkswagen through Kayanga where we spent the night and then on up to Bukoba on the shores of Lake Victoria. At Bukoba we were received by the regional authorities who were somewhat sceptical about our intentions, but after they had contacted Dar es Salaam, we were summoned to go to the Tanzanian capital. We had left Laki's car at Kayanga in Karagwe district, and from Bukoba to Dar es Salaam we travelled in a station-wagon Landrover with one civilian escort. We spent the night of 28 January at Kahama, after a bad meal at Lusahunga, stayed the next night at Chalinze and finally reached Dar es Salaam at 8.00 a.m. the following morning.

We were driven to CID headquarters which was located in the present Central Police Station. After brief questioning, the Director of Intelligence, Emilio Mzena, came and drove us at high speed to a Msasani beach house which had belonged to the former Secretary-General of TANU, Oscar Kambona. There we found Akena Adoko, who had been director of Obote's intelligence system, and Sam Odaka, who had been Foreign Minister in the deposed government. Adoko and Odaka were crestfallen and they must have been only too aware that they had, to a large extent, been responsible for the tragedy that had befallen Uganda. They had been among the many ministers and colleagues of Obote busily flattering him at the Uganda Club in Kampala, singing *Tukutendereza* ('Praise to the Lord!') to him.

I took one look at these men, listened to the few completely inappropriate remarks they made regarding our country's situation and concluded that they were not equal to the task before us. Akena Adoko suggested that I should go back to Uganda and get some money from Mukombe Mpambara, who was one of the UPC diehards in those days, but since I did not see how it would further the country's interests, I refused.

I told Adoko and Odaka that people in Uganda were jubilant, and that the Israelis and the British appeared to be behind the *coup*. Adoko had been responsible for the infiltration of so many state organs by the intelligence services of foreign countries, and now here he was mourning a situation of his own creation.

There had been no appropriate politicisation to maintain a nationalist orientation. As a result, foreign agents such as Baruch Barlev, a military attaché at the Israeli Embassy, and Mike Davis from Britain, had quite open roles in the post-*coup* period. It was clear that Amin was the darling of the British, who were the first to recognise his government and promise him support. Anyone who thought that a buffoon like Amin was a good leader for Uganda was clearly an enemy of our country.

After a cup of tea and some biscuits, we were driven to State House, Dar es Salaam, where we found Milton Obote and briefed him on the situation. He was crestfallen although he perked up when he saw us. He appeared pleased that we had come although he later came to resent me very bitterly when I started telling him a few home truths. Right from the beginning, he had little hope of being restored to power by purely Ugandan efforts because he must have known that many Ugandans detested him. He banked mainly on the Tanzanians intervening militarily, in collaboration with countries like Somalia and Sudan which had taken a public stand against Amin's government.

After a short while, President Nyerere came in. He, too, was pleased to see us and after a brief chat with Obote, he called me out to the balcony. He remembered me from my university days and it appears that he had observed with interest the activities and principles of USARF. The fact that I was known to Nyerere in this way helped establish respect for our analysis of the Ugandan crisis. Even if, for his own political reasons, he did not always go along with everything we proposed, credibility with 'Mwalimu' was to be of crucial importance in the years ahead. On this occasion he told me that he would not recognise Amin's regime and that he would stand firmly on the side of the Ugandan people and help them fight to regain their rights. I was very encouraged by his combative mood and his determination to help Ugandans emancipate themselves. Nyerere approved of our ideas and he hoped that we would link up with Obote and find a way of working together. The main way in which he backed Obote was by funding his activities but he also helped us a little so that we would not completely run out of money.

After staying in Dar es Salaam for a few days, during which there was some diplomatic activity in the course of which some countries – Somalia, Sudan, Egypt and Guinea – stood firmly on our side, our party left the capital for Bukoba. Laki, Katundu, Kibazo and Bakari returned to Uganda, re-entering through Mutukula. I stayed on in Bukoba for a while until Rashid Kawawa, who was then Vice-President of Tanzania, arrived. I had a discussion with him, trying to convince him, after which we decided that I should go back to Uganda and try to start an underground movement.

EARLY CLANDESTINE CONTACTS IN UGANDA

Before I left Bukoba to re-enter Uganda, Lt Col. David Oyite Ojok arrived, having escaped from Parliament Buildings in Kampala which had been surrounded by Amin's soldiers. Oyite Ojok had been the army quarter-master general. After splitting with Amin, Obote had used Ojok to create his own faction in the army. Ojok himself was quite a courageous individual. The problem with African leaders, including soldiers, is not a matter of personality but arises from their view of the world and of politics. Although Ojok had some good personal attributes, his way of thinking was very different from ours. Later on we were to encounter important differences over strategy, but for the moment I had a brief general discussion with Ojok, together with Mr Kawawa and other Tanzanian officials. Ojok then went on to Dar es Salaam while I made my plans to go back to Uganda.

When I was ready, Mr Karumanga, then Bukoba's district security officer, drove me to Mutukula. I had disguised myself and went safely through the police checkpoint. My only disguise was the wearing of a hat. The main thing about disguise is to break one's normal profile. By wearing something as simple as a hat, it is not easy for police to recognise you, unless they have prior information. I would later use different disguises, sometimes appearing as a Muslim or posing as a student. Apart from physical disguise, it is crucial in clandestine work to have correct identity papers and not be outrageously different from your normal personality or knowledge, because you must always be prepared to bear out the disguised identity under interrogation.

I took a taxi from Masaka to Kampala and arrived at Nsambya just in time for the seven o'clock curfew. I stayed with my friend, colleague and co-fighter, Martin Mwesiga, about whom I shall write more later. We reviewed the situation before us and I briefed him about discussions with the Tanzanians, Obote and the rest. The following day, Mwesiga informed other colleagues that I had returned and they all came to see me. They were Mwesigwa Black, by then an economist, Ruhakana Rugunda, a student leader in the National Students' Union at Makerere University at the time, and Dani Wadada Nabudere, who had a law practice in Mbale and whom Amin had just appointed chairman of East African Railways.

In our discussions two lines of thought emerged: should we wage an armed struggle against Amin and work clandestinely with only a few of our comrades infiltrated into Amin's government as listening posts; or should we refrain from active underground work and instead work from inside the government with a view to participating in the elections which Amin had promised in the near future? The first line of action was supported by Martin Mwesiga, Mwesigwa Black, Rugunda and myself while the second was advocated by Nabudere. This difference in the type of strategy we should adopt caused a split between us although we remained in contact. I stayed with Mwesiga for one more day and then moved to Mwesigwa Black's home near Naguru. The following day I left Kampala and spent the night at Nganwa Hostel in Mbarara. Word got round that I had been sighted in town and a group of people, some of whom I knew, started hunting for me.

At that time the political situation in Ankole, and indeed the whole of Uganda, was very difficult for underground workers like ourselves. Because of the confusion that Obote had sown in the country, creating and perpetuating factional and sectarian politics, Amin's takeover had been popular in the whole country, not so much because people liked Amin but because many had resented Obote bitterly, especially in Buganda after his overthrow of the Kabaka. Since the public was not properly informed, anyone who opposed Amin was thought to be an Obote supporter and this created problems for us in many areas including Ankole, Buganda and Busoga. In Ankole, all the former DP supporters and the Kahigiriza faction of the UPC welcomed the take-over and regarded us as enemies or at least as very misguided. Operating in some of these areas was, therefore, very dangerous.

I hired a taxi from Mbarara to Kinoni, 14 miles (22 km) on the Kabale Road and left a message for Laki. I then went back to Mbarara, changing taxis several times on the way to avoid detection. While in Mbarara, I saw Nekemiya Bananuka who was Secretary-General of Ankole. I made contact with Apita, Assistant District Commissioner, and another man who was a bank manager, to inform them that we were preparing to fight Amin and that they should get ready to help. After this I took a taxi to Kaberebere where I waited for a truck which dropped me at Kikagati and I crossed the Kagera River at Murongo. I spent the night in Karagwe before proceeding to Bukoba.

We stayed for a while at Bukoba Lake Hotel together with Fred Bananuka and Oyite Ojok who had recently returned from Dar es Salaam. I also met Lt Col. Tito Okello who had left Uganda earlier. Our view of people like Tito Okello was that some of them were good men individually. Tito was less educated than Ojok, and an older type of colonial soldier. Ojok was the type who had finished O-level education and been brought into the army just after independence, but who had also been trained under the old colonial conditions. The O-level-educated soldiers thought they were better than the Tito type, but their concepts and views were really the same on basic issues.

During my stay in Bukoba I made trips with Ojok to the Ugandan border trying to make contacts with the people inside the country. We went to Murongo to wait for a Lt Silver, for whom I had earlier left a message in Mbarara, but he failed to turn up. After waiting fruitlessly for some time, Ojok said that he knew a policeman at Kikagati who might be of some help. I borrowed a bicycle and took the ferry to look for him. On the other side, I cycled up to Kikagati Police Station and managed to trace the man and give him the note Ojok had written him in his own language, Luo. When he read it, he looked very uncomfortable and worried.

Although I had not discussed the message in detail with Ojok, I understood that it was to introduce me to this policeman so that I could act as a go-between. I had already proved that I could cross into Uganda and come back, whereas Ojok was too well-known to have been able to go himself. I understood that this note was to establish a link so that the policeman would know that I could be trusted. The message was also probably telling him to contact other people, to inform them that the idea of resistance had not been abandoned. Soon afterwards a fresh platoon of the Armed Special Force arrived from Mbarara and took up positions. Among them I noticed one Babiiha who had been a year behind me at school. I realised I was taking a very big risk because my fate now depended on whether this man would recognise me, and if he did, whether he knew that I had gone underground and was, therefore, wanted by the authorities. To make matters even more uncertain for me, Ojok's contact started speaking in Luo to the leader of the new arrivals. Perhaps Ojok wanted to know his opinion on how matters stood. They went apart from the others so that I could not hear what they were saying and I decided not to wait for the outcome of their discussions. Instead, I left a message that Ojok's policeman should come over to the river at 4.00 p.m. if he had anything to tell me. I rode off on my bicycle, but the man never turned up.

I did not like working with these colonial types of policemen. We were contemptuous of them because they did not base their contribution to the struggle on conviction. They based their contribution on salaries and that is what made me very uncomfortable working with them. Our own people would not have acted like that – they would have told me clearly when to go and when to come and not left me in suspense, exposed to unnecessary risks.

MATTERS OF POLICY

After staying in Bukoba for a while, I started to become rather restless because matters were stagnating so I decided to write a memorandum to President Nyerere. In this I suggested that either the armies of Tanzania, Somalia, Sudan and other African countries opposed to Amin should invade Uganda, topple Amin and restore Obote to power, on condition that he mend his ways; or, failing that, a broad-based united front comprising all valid and genuine political opinions in Uganda, with or without Obote at its head, should be formed to lead an armed struggle against Amin. I made it clear that the UPC alone could not wage a successful struggle against the Amin regime. The memorandum caused tremendous excitement although it was very mild according to my view. Some Tanzanian bureaucrats thought I was being very disloyal to what they called 'the Ugandan authorities', meaning Obote and his group, which consisted of Sam Odaka, Akena Adoko and several others.

Some of the Tanzanians thought we were spies sent by Amin, but I was not in the least concerned by such lies. I told the local officials in Bukoba that I wanted to go to Dar es Salaam and they organised for Ojok, Fred Bananuka and myself to travel there by bus. On our arrival, we were given rooms in Rex Hotel, while the Obote group were being put up in government lodges – Rex Hotel was good enough for us, the poorer sector of the liberation struggle!

Obote had apparently left for Sudan and Odaka assumed leadership while he was away. In the meantime a debate developed between us and the Obote group and clear differences began to emerge. Those who said that they were loyal to Obote treated us as enemies and held certain views which we knew to be wrong and dangerous. At that time I was alone in Dar es Salaam discussing with the Obote group, but we had a few supporters at the university – some Ugandan students who had not yet completed their degrees, among them Amanya Mushenga, who was later to become our Minister of Education.

Differences developed over two major points in this debate. The first was whether we should have a well-structured organisation or whether we should fight for an individual. Our unalterable position was that we were only prepared to shed our blood for the sake of principles and for the sake of the organisation and never for the sake of an individual. We went further and said that not only did we believe in fighting for an organisation rather than for an individual, but that the organisation should be a united front of all genuine political opinions in Uganda.

The second point of dispute was whether we should be prepared to fight a conventional or a guerrilla war. The Obote group argued for a conventional war, that is, a head-on collision because they said Amin was weak and would run away at the first sound of gunfire. They also argued that a prolonged fight would provoke Amin into killing a lot of innocent people. We, on the other hand, argued that since Amin already had the state apparatus in his grip, he was, in the short run, superior to us. We argued that the only feasible road to victory was for us to start from our present position of weakness and work up to one of strength. We added that the idea of using inferior forces to confront Amin's army in a decisive show-down would be a strategic blunder.

We advocated instead a guerrilla war of pinpricks against the enemy, tiring him and only going on to the conventional stage when we had marshalled enough forces in material, men and experience to overwhelm him. It was within our means to start fighting using the available resources and to build up our strength gradually. Within this conventional versus guerrilla war debate, there was another one on whether we should concentrate on an internal or external struggle. It was our view that the main preparations should take place within the country while we engaged in subsidiary activities outside, that is, that the external front should only be used as a catalyst to support the internal front.

In addition to these two fundamental differences, there was also the question of whether or not the army should be politicised. Obote's people were against political education in the army because they argued that politics would be divisive. We tried to explain to them that we were not talking about partisan party politics, but rather, the understanding of politics in general. Our idea was that we would equip each soldier with a political knowledge of Uganda and the politics of the world in general, so that the soldier would be able to understand what he or she was fighting for. Obote's people, however, remained unconvinced.

A debate also arose as to whether the struggle should be launched from outside Uganda or from within the country. We argued that if there were to be any external inputs, they should only be at the preparatory stages. This was in order to avoid the charge that Uganda had been invaded by outside forces which, in fact, is what happened in September 1972. This misconception distorted the whole perspective of the struggle, thereby giving the impression that there was no popular internal resistance against Amin. It appeared that the opposition against Amin was being plotted and orchestrated by outside forces like Tanzania.

THE FRONT FOR NATIONAL SALVATION

The Front for National Salvation (Fronasa) was formed in 1971 in Dar es Salaam by those of us based in exile in Tanzania who were opposed to Amin but who were not ready to work with Obote unless he changed his ways fundamentally. Through the early part of 1971, we tried to find common ground with Obote, but we disagreed in very fundamental ways. Hence, we had to form a separate organisation. By that time, some members of our original group had begun to trickle in. Among those involved in the formation of Fronasa were Raiti Omongin, Martin Mwesiga, James Wapakhabulo and myself in Dar es Salaam, and Mwesigwa Black and Valeriano Rwaheru in Nairobi. Raiti Omongin was an old UPC supporter who thought he was a communist – I think he had even been to China! Omongin had recruited some boys into Obote's group but problems had developed in their camp near Morogoro in northern Tanzania. The Tanzanians had had to separate Omongin's group from the rest. The members of our group inside Uganda were Eriya Kategaya, Ruhakana Rugunda, Ikuya Magode, Maumbe Mukhwana, Abbas Kibazo, Haruna Kibuye and Haruna Bakari and Akena p'Ojok. We formed the pioneer committee of the front, which was conceived as an alliance of different ideologies and organisations and the pioneer committee was a nucleus to which other organisations could rally. Initiatives would be taken mainly by those of us who were outside Uganda, one of us then travelling to Uganda to brief the members there.

In 1971 alone I travelled in and out of Uganda five times: in February, April, June, September and December. Each time I would stay for about a week, mostly in Kampala. The first time I came into Uganda in February 1971, I stayed with Martin Mwesiga at Nsambya and later with Mwesigwa Black at Naguru-Katale. Sometimes I would stay with Abbas Kibazo at Kibuli and at other times with Eriya Kategaya who was then living at Mulago and later on moved to a house near Makerere. (All three places are suburbs of Kampala.)

The main purpose of such visits was to discuss future plans, to recruit civilians for training abroad and, later on, to infiltrate arms into the country. The main effort of the movement in those days was to win limited external support to enable us to carry out some military training and also to buy arms. We needed an introduction to the science of arms which in those days was a mystery to us. The monopoly of arms had been used by Obote and Amin to stifle the development of democracy in Uganda, and in order to break this stranglehold, we had to end that monopoly.

EARLY PREPARATIONS FOR THE STRUGGLE

Some African forces were willing to help us in our search for arms, in modest ways, but only if we remained under Obote's aegis. Yet we knew that Obote was a liability in Uganda because of the many mistakes he had committed during his tenure of power. In spite of his record, Obote had somehow built up a reputation outside the country as an enlightened African nationalist politician. Yet Obote's strategy was always wrong because he feared the involvement of the masses in the struggle, preferring instead to seek quick solutions such as using non-Ugandan forces to try and oust Amin, or invasions like the abortive one of 1972. For our part, we preferred a people-centred, protracted armed struggle of the kind we eventually used in Luwero in the early 1980s.

In August 1971, we brought some boys into Uganda and positioned them on Mt Elgon without any arms, in the hope of buying some later; but the boys were not sufficiently disciplined and soon gave themselves away. A boy called Wafula went to the market in Bumbo where he was arrested and made to talk about his activities. Amin's soldiers then arrested the rest of the group, including Raiti Omongin, and took them to Makindye Maximum Security Prison in Kampala. Without knowing that the Omongin group had been arrested, I came to join them in the camp. I went through Mbale to Bumbo with Magode Ikuya and Abwooli Malibo. We were, however, stopped and questioned by a Special Branch man who suspected us of wrongdoing. We told him that we were students carrying out some research on the mountain. He believed our story and it was he who told us that some suspicious people had been arrested in the area a few days previously. Then we knew we were in trouble. We went up and spent the night at the forest camp in order to complete our deception and came back the following day to report to the Special Branch man. Fortunately, he was not there and we proceeded to Nabumali, where we separated. I left for Kampala, and Ikuya and Malibo headed for Mbale.

We knew on this occasion that, apart from the indiscipline of the boys caused by inadequate ideological and military preparation, the implementation of the plan was all wrong. We had introduced them hurriedly into the mountain forests without preparing the people in the area to act as a cover for them. This had come about because of pressure from some Tanzanian ministers. The Tanzanians wanted to get rid of the Omongin group, which could not get on with Obote's group, and they put us under pressure to take them inside Uganda. They said: 'Museveni, you have been saying you like to work from within Uganda – take these people and work with them from there.' We tried to argue against it but the Tanzanians insisted, saying they would supply us with arms later. With hindsight, we should have refused until we were ready, as we did later on, after the 1972 debacle.

In the circumstances, the correct thing to do would have been to infiltrate cadres into parts of the country where they could have easily blended in with the population. Some of the bureaucrats we were working with, however, wanted quick results and we, too, were over-anxious not to annoy our Tanzanian supporters. We needed to demonstrate that we could 'do something', so that we would qualify for more support. Revolutionaries should be very careful of such mistakes. This particular error resulted in setbacks for us and for some time we even lost the support we had acquired. In subsequent years we learnt to stick to our own strategy: any support we received had to be given in order to implement our accepted strategy. When we adhered to that principle, victory was assured.

During 1971, I tried to procure arms from all kinds of sources. I even took a trip to the rebel-held territory of eastern Zaire, in an attempt to buy guns from the Mulele supporters there. I travelled with a man called Richard through Kigoma to Burundi, and across Lake Tanganyika to a place called Fizi, in Zaire, near Uvirra. We climbed the steep mountains in cold temperatures until we came to the 'headquarters' of 'General' Shaban Maulana. By the time we got to Maulana's camp we were very hungry but, unfortunately, some of the foods they consider delicacies in Zaire, such as snails and monkey meat, are taboo to many Ugandans. As a special guest of Shaban Maulana, I was given a bowl of snails which I declined. I simply ate some honey with a little rice that we had brought with us, but the rice was soon finished and, in order to stay alive, I had to make a tactical compromise and taste a little of the monkey meat.

As it turned out, our trip was futile: these people had no arms to sell and I started on the treacherous trip back to Kigoma through Burundi. Our boat almost capsized when we were crossing Lake Tanganyika. The oarsmen sang songs, calling on their ancestral spirits to protect us. In spite of the medicine we had taken to 'bewitch' the wind before starting off, the wind was not impressed. It almost sent us to the bottom of one of the deepest lakes in the world. There was danger too from another quarter. We had to watch out for Greek fishing boats which were licensed to fish in Lake Tanganyika. They were known to ram dug-out canoes on sight, assuming them to be local 'poachers', fishing in their licensed waters.

After many trials, Frelimo and the Tanzanians decided to give us some arms. This decision was taken around April 1972. By that time we had trained a few batches of fighters inside the Frelimo liberated territory and we had also been joined by some boys who were deserting Obote's camp.

The training we received from Frelimo was basic, the kind given in armies all over the world – the only difference in the case of Frelimo being the tactical orientation. First we were trained as an individual – how to handle weapons, how to aim a rifle, how to take cover, advancing under fire, fieldcraft and so on. In Portuguese these are called *actes individuel*. We were taught mostly in Swahili, but I learnt some of the drill commands in Portuguese. Once the individual has been trained, then he is trained to act in a group, including section battle drills, platoon battle drills, in attack, in defence, and so on. Finally, the two are combined and one is taught how to use individual and group skills to achieve military success.

In conventional warfare an army is already formed, but with revolutionary freedom-fighters, one starts with nothing. The problem is how to build a small force while you fight. The freedom-fighter must be trained to appreciate that reality. The trouble with the Oyite Ojoks was that they only knew how to use forces that had already been created, and they could not understand how it was possible to build up a force in the course of fighting. In practice this means that freedom-fighters must sometimes spend a great deal of time running away, which may look cowardly to a general in an air-conditioned room, but for the fighter on the ground represents survival. In revolutionary warfare, the mere fact of an insurgent surviving and not being eliminated is in itself a success. This, therefore, means that the tactics are different: the guerrilla concentrates on withdrawal and surprise attack, using his forces sparingly, while in regular armies soldiers make deliberate direct attacks and hold captured territory.

When eventually, in April 1972, President Nyerere decided to provide us with arms, a greater element of certainty came into our work and there were fewer risks for some of us. Fronasa had not been able to reach a compromise with Obote on any major points, and the Tanzanians maintained their aid to Obote, but now they supported us too, on the side, since they realised that we could make a valuable contribution. We utilised their support to train a number of political cadres, mainly with Frelimo in the liberated areas of Mozambique. We were thus slowly able to infiltrate trained political cadres back into Uganda to create bases, secret camps where, in some places, arms and ammunition were stored and from which the local population could be contacted.

We began infiltrating arms into Uganda around May 1972, some to Kabale, some to Atiak and some to Kampala. Those in Kabale were kept by James Karambuzi and Joseph Bitwaari, who were publicly executed by Amin in 1973. The ones in Kampala were kept by Haruna Kibuye, and those in Atiak by Akena p'Ojok. We also developed cells in Toro, Mbarara, Mbale and Jinja.

A cell was initially composed of one or two people, with the anticipation of growth, the original contact forming the nucleus. The cell would then establish a base. The bases were not always physical ones out in the bush – sometimes they were within the population. A cadre would come into an area after establishing links with at least one supporter who could protect him. By getting legal personal identification and work documents, he would assume a cover which would enable him to explain his presence in the area, in case he was questioned. After carrying out careful observations, he would start talking with other people to try to enlist their support.

One of our bases was in Kigezi where we were working with Joseph Bitwaari and James Karambuzi; another was in the Kikagati area where we had bought some land as a cover for our operations; there was another base in Mwenge, in the Toro area, where we were operating with Abwooli Malibo and some boys from Kabarole. We also had one in Kampala where intellectuals such as Eriya Kategeya liaised with the workers' cell (*abawejjere*) of Haruna Kibuye, Zubairi Bakari and Abbas Kibazo.

This cell in Kampala was particularly important for two reasons: they were able to gather intelligence against the reactionary pseudo-Muslim groups led by Amin, and they were responsible for safeguarding my personal movements within Kampala whenever I came from Tanzania. As Muslims, these comrades were valuable on both counts. In fact, in order to blend better in the environment, I also pretended to be a Muslim by using Muslim names and wearing Muslim caps. Among some of my names and disguises were 'Kassim' in Nairobi, and 'Abdalla' and 'Musa' in Dar es Salaam. I also posed as a PhD student going by the name of 'Mugarura', using an East African inter-state pass.

On one occasion I was in the Polana Hotel in Maputo, Mozambique, using my PhD student cover when I found myself in the company of three officials of the Economic Commission for Africa, including Professor Adebayo Adedeji, then executive secretary of the ECA. They asked me what my job was and I told them a tall story about my 'research' on 'the role of ideology in liberation movements'. Of course, there was no such research, but I had made sure to select a topic with which I was very conversant so that I would sound authoritative if I had to discuss it with anyone.

At different times, other people were involved in our work in Uganda, especially in the Kampala cell: Eriya Kategaya and Ruhakana Rugunda at the beginning, and later, Akena p'Ojok, who became our contact for the Gulu area. However, we fell out with Akena p'Ojok in 1972 over the handling of secrets and collective responsibility. He appeared to have secret contacts with Obote which we thought were most dangerous.

We also had bases at Makerere University and Kyambogo Teacher Training College, while in the east of Uganda our main area of contact was Mbale where we were supported, for example by Maumbe Mukhwana. In Busoga, Samuel Kagulire Kasadha, who had been the estate engineer at Makerere, was one of our people – he was later killed by Amin. These contacts in the east enabled us to set up a camp in the forest of Bunya in south Iganga. Bases were also established in Acholi, at Awere, 60 miles (97 km) east of Gulu, and at Atyak, 45 miles (72 km) north-west of Gulu.

The purpose of all these preparations was to have a springboard ready for the time when we started fighting. By the second half of 1972, we had about 50 trained cadres established in Uganda, and the work was going well. At this point, however, Obote ruined all our plans with his ill-conceived invasion of September 1972.

Chapter 6

FIGHTING AMIN (2)
[SEPTEMBER 1972]

THE DECISION TO INVADE

The work was progressing well but, because of Obote's intrigues, the Tanzanians were persuaded to allow the invasion of Uganda in 1972. This was a huge mistake. Not only did it fail, but it also disrupted our work. Obote favoured an invasion because he feared a popular people's struggle. He did not want ordinary Ugandans to take part in the struggle to liberate themselves. He told me on one occasion that he was worried that once people had been given guns, it would be difficult to take them away again. I asked him why he should want to remove the guns if people were using them to defend their rights.

Since he had presided over a sectarian government, based on the support of tribes from the north, Obote feared the democratisation of the instruments of state power. He wanted guns and power to remain in the hands of the few people he could easily manipulate. For our part, we argued that it was not only better to have as many people as possible participating in the struggle, but that this was also desirable in order to secure peace and guarantee the rights of the population against future dictatorships. The invasion of 1972 was, therefore, very disruptive. It resulted in many deaths, especially in western Uganda, in the Mbarara area, and in Acholi, where many prominent people were murdered.

The first I knew of the invasion plan was on 14 September when the late Prime Minister of Tanzania, Edward Sokoine, who at that time was Minister of Defence, came to see me in Bukoba to tell me that the invasion would take place that very evening. I asked him who was taking part and he told me that the main force was composed of about 1300 of Obote's people who had been training in the Sudan and that we were expected to go along too.

Obote's advisers seem to have thought that using 1300 people in a surprise attack from the south, while at the same time landing a planeload of troops at Entebbe Airport, would create panic and make the whole government system collapse. This idea arose because they were with colonially trained soldiers. In the colonial armies, Africans were cannon fodder; they were never promoted beyond the rank of NCO; nor were they trained to think and plan strategy – that was left to the European officers. Therefore, colonially trained soldiers have distorted beliefs about warfare. They believe in drama and psychological shocks, not in substance and strength. They believe in commando-style operations, surprise attacks, assassinations and so on. They want fighting to be easy and they are really very subjective in their thinking. That is why they admire Israel; but Israel's glamorous operations come from a strong base and their commando raids are peripheral to their basic strength. We revolutionaries, on the other hand, must always move on the basis of strength and organisation.

It is difficult to understand why the Tanzanians took the risk of allowing such a dangerous scheme to be launched from their territory, especially when it was not even properly planned. My understanding was that Obote fed them with wrong information which gave the impression that there was a large fifth column of his supporters within the Ugandan population at large, as well as within the army. According to this interpretation, a limited attack from outside would precipitate an internal uprising which would overthrow Amin. I told Sokoine that this was absolute nonsense.

The reality was that an open invasion of any sort was the last thing our movement needed at that time. I had recently returned from Uganda where I had met Edward Rugumayo, then Amin's Minister of Education. I had had a long discussion with him and he had told me that, within the government, there were four other people whom he could trust to go along with our plan to launch a protracted guerrilla struggle. These were William Naburri, Obitre Gama, William Ndahendekire and Lt Col. Sarapio Kakuhikire. I had briefed Dr Nyerere about my contacts and it seems that he had in turn told Obote. I can only think that this scanty information may have excited Obote and prompted him to try and pre-empt this promising development because he knew that he would not benefit if our plans succeeded.

Obote later claimed that I had led him to believe that there would be enough forces coming over to our side if we invaded, but this was merely an attempt to shift the blame after the invasion had proved a complete fiasco. If Obote believed that I had identified an internal force, why did he not include me in the planning of the action? If he really wanted to utilise an 'internal force', he should have discussed his plans with me, since I was the person who had the contacts. How could he count on my contacts without informing either me or them? The real explanation is that Obote, always a schemer, was trying to use some of the information we were giving him for his own purposes. Whenever I told him that there was a great deal of disillusionment in Uganda, he would say: 'Who did you talk to?', and I would tell him. His strategy was not so much to hammer all this discontent into a concerted force, but rather to take advantage of it, using his own small force. Obote was only really interested in using his opponents' existing weaknesses to seize an opportunity to get back into power. If an opposition leader does not alert people inside the country about his or her intentions, and yet goes ahead and attacks their barracks, they will fight the attackers, as they did us, even if they are discontented with the existing regime.

Apart from lack of adequate preparation, Obote's planned invasion was also inappropriate because by then Amin had started making plenty of mistakes. Even some of the people who had initially welcomed him were coming to realise that the man was a disaster. Such people began to get in touch with those of us who were working from outside the country. They had originally thought that perhaps they could work with Amin. 'After all,' they had argued, 'Obote was the one who created all this confusion by promoting Amin; so let's try Amin and see.' Now, however, people like Rugumayo were beginning to realise that supporting Amin was an unproductive exercise.

Had this line of argument been cultivated more seriously, it might have helped in removing Amin earlier, although without fundamentally destroying the existing power structure – which, in turn, would have caused more problems in the future. It was especially important that the army, which was really a colonial relic, should be disbanded completely and a new people's army created on the basis of a new ideology of nationalism rather than tribalism. My contacts with Rugumayo were, however, thoroughly disrupted by Obote's intrigues because after the failure of the invasion, Rugumayo had to flee the country. He and some of his colleagues were angry with me, thinking that I had known of the invasion plan and had not warned them. But as I have said already, I had no prior knowledge of the plan.

The deterioration of my relationship with the Rugumayo group was not the only fallout from the failed invasion. Even other members of Fronasa blamed me for not having disassociated myself from the invasion. Despite my own grave reservations about the whole invasion plan, I had reluctantly agreed to go along with it. My decision was based upon two carefully calculated points. Firstly, I thought that although Obote's group could not capture power as they hoped, they could at least capture Masaka and Mbarara. That would have given us an opportunity to intensify our efforts of organising an armed insurrection in the semi-liberated zones. As it turned out, they were not even able to take the two towns. My second point was that, whatever happened, we should not alienate the Tanzanians because theirs was the only government in the whole of Africa which was ready to support us. They had taken considerable risks in doing this, especially *vis-à-vis* the British, the Israelis and the South Africans. The divisions between African nationalists, the former colonial powers, and the South African racists were very acute in those days of the Cold War. It would have been disastrous to lose Tanzania's support by merely focusing on our own Fronasa interests.

With hindsight, we could logically only have avoided being involved in the invasion if it had taken place on 14 September, as originally planned. When preparations dragged on, however, and the invasion did not take place until the 17th, it became clear to me that we could not keep out without alienating the Tanzanians, especially if the venture failed. Because of our differences with the

Obote group, they had always made allegations against us that we were Amin's agents! Had we failed to take part in the invasion, having had knowledge of it since the 14th, we would have been accused of having leaked information to Amin. Indeed, in spite of our participation, Obote's group did accuse us of having stolen the ammunition truck and argued that this was the reason for the defeat of Obote's supporters in Mbarara. This was in spite of the fact that his people abandoned six trucks full of ammunition which were later captured by Amin's soldiers.

Such was the low level of politics, the intrigues and the lies that were always spun by Obote and his group. Even today, some pro-Obote people are still using such contemptible methods in order to promote their interests. Obote used to say that politics is 'dirty', and there is no doubt that he was a good practitioner of that kind of politics. Unfortunately, he ruined Uganda in the process of pursuing his 'dirty politics'. His group used to believe that the end justified the means – any means, no matter how despicable. Most of the time, unfortunately, with the UPC the ends were even more despicable than the means.

THE INVASION PLAN

Obote's plan was for a three-pronged attack. One small group was supposed to land at Entebbe Airport from Kilimanjaro Airport, near Arusha in Tanzania, using a hijacked East African Airways DC-9 aircraft under the charge of an untrained pilot named James Lalobo. This man had failed a pilot conversion test from a Fokker 27 aircraft to a DC-9. Yet, in spite of that, Obote had chosen to entrust him with such a vital mission. The plane was supposed to carry 100 people to capture Entebbe Airport; but on takeoff from Dar es Salaam, the pilot forgot to retract the undercarriage and it was left hanging down all the way to Kilimanjaro Airport. He also forgot to unlock the tyre mechanism, with the result that the tyres burst on landing and the pilot was almost killed. The plane was grounded at Kilimanjaro and the 100 men took no further part in the operation.

Meanwhile, the main force of 1300 men, plus our Fronasa platoon, was divided into two groups. One group of about 1000 was supposed to go through Mutukula and capture Masaka barracks. The second group, which included our platoon, plus Obote's people who had been training in Tanzania at a place called Kigwa, were to capture Mbarara barracks.

Our platoon of about 40 men did not include the people whom we had been training in Mozambique, but consisted mainly of recruits from Uganda. At that time, the Tanzanians were giving us some training facilities in Bukoba. I was using this group mostly to infiltrate arms into Uganda. For some distance, the Kagera River forms the border between Uganda and Tanzania, and then at mile 35 from Mbarara, the river crosses into Tanzania and then back into Uganda again before finally flowing into Lake Victoria. The part of Tanzania on the north side of the river is known as the Kagera Salient and that was where we were operating from. In order to transport arms across the border, we would wade through the river carrying guns on our heads. On our return we would walk back into Tanzania through the Salient and then, because we were carrying no arms, we could openly cross the Kagera by the large bridge at Kyaka.

I went with the Mbarara invasion group thinking that, since we had already organised a base in the Kabale area, we might capture Mbarara using our contacts there and quickly build up a force strong enough to fight the counter-attack which I was sure Amin's men would launch. This part of the plan should have been achievable because of the disorganisation in Amin's army. I did not believe that these two groups alone could have captured power in Uganda itself, but I did think that they were capable at least of taking the towns of Masaka and Mbarara, from where, subsequently, we could have launched a protracted people's war, using the hinterland for guerrilla operations.

When the Tanzanian Minister of Defence, Sokoine, first told me on 14 September that the invasion was planned for later that day, I warned him that our supporters inside Uganda had not been alerted about the impending action. As far as we were concerned, we could not be expected to be ready at such short notice. Then we learned that the invasion had been postponed for a few days and I held a discussion with Mwesigwa Black and a few senior comrades who were in Bukoba at the time. Although most were not happy with these developments, we concluded, for the reasons outlined above, that we had to co-operate with the plan now that it had been postponed. With this in mind I sent James Birihanze ahead to warn our comrades of the impending action. Birihanze, however, failed to reach Uganda, though we did not know this until after the invasion. He had not been able to cross through Mutukula because, apparently, Amin's people had become suspicious. Consequently, our people inside Uganda were never informed of the invasion and were, therefore, not able to make any contribution. In the event, the fighters that we did have were so ill-trained and ill-equipped that the whole operation was a total disaster. We had no support arms: no mortars, no RPGs, no machine-guns – just simple rifles, many of them semi-automatic, SAR 56s.

16 AND 17 SEPTEMBER 1972

The so-called 'invasion' of September 1972 was in reality an encounter between two groups of fools: Amin's group on the one hand, and ours on the other. Obote's 1300 fighters had been assembled at Kaboya near Bukoba. On the morning of the 15th, we learned that the airborne group had failed, having crash-landed at Kilimanjaro Airport. Nevertheless, Sokoine decided that the two land prongs should go ahead, otherwise news of the plan would leak. I warned him that while Amin's army was not a fighting force, it would be a big error to rely on Obote's group or on stories told by him. I even suggested, in spite of my longstanding aversion to the idea, that Tanzania would be better advised to use its own troops rather than rely on Obote's stories. In spite of all this, the decision was taken to go ahead. On the evening of 16 September, I went with our one platoon and joined the Obote forces at Kaboya.

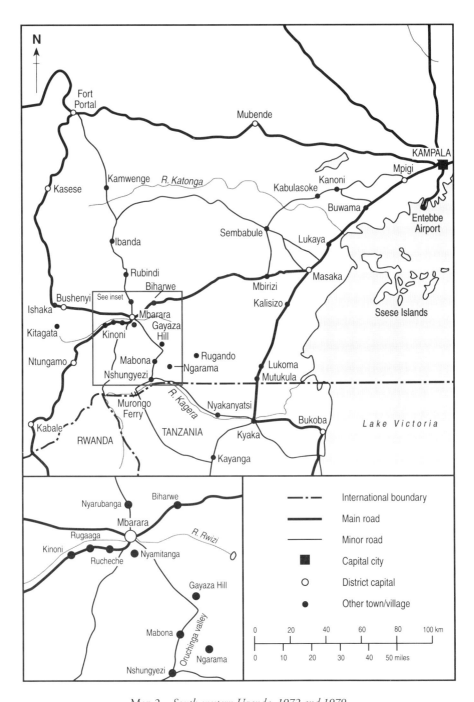

Map 2   *South-western Uganda, 1972 and 1979*

I was allocated one Bedford lorry to carry my platoon. Alongside eight other lorries, carrying 300 of Obote's men, led by Captain Oyile, Lt Okot and Lt Okumu, we were to form the group that would attack Mbarara through Kyaka, Nyakanyatsi and Nshungyezi. We went with the Masaka group and separated after Kyaka Bridge. We drove with dimmed lights through the Kagera Salient, up to a point near Kakunyu where we found the last Tanzanian army unit. This was around 3.00 a.m. Then the quarrels among the Obote group started. 'We are too few,' they complained. My answer was: 'What did you expect?' They had been told that they would find 'friendly forces' inside Uganda waiting to come over to their side and they were given the impression that there would be no serious fighting because there was so much division within Amin's army. I told them that since the Masaka group had already moved forward, we had no alternative but to go on, and if the idea was to surprise the enemy, the sooner we started moving the better. There was no clear chain of command, but since Captain Oyile was leading the larger group, consisting of Obote's people, he was assumed to be the overall leader.

After much wrangling among Obote's people, we drove up to the border. Amin's border guard was a small force of only one section, some distance inside Uganda at the PWD camp at Ryabatuura. Three of our sections, including one from my platoon, were sent to attack the border guard, who were totally taken by surprise and fled. By this time it was around 7.00 a.m. We drove up to Nshungyezi with my vehicle taking the lead at Ryabatuura because I noticed that the others were reluctant to move.

We occupied Nshungyezi junction and Obote's men began gaining courage. One of their drivers, a man called Odur, took over the lead from my truck. Odur had been a member of Obote's intelligence service. He was later killed in the attack on Mbarara. From Nshungyezi, we turned right towards Mbarara and almost immediately we encountered the commanding officer of Amin's Simba Battalion, based at Mbarara, driving towards us in a white Peugeot 504. Because of the confusion inherent in the whole operation, there were no procedures in place regarding how we should react to any vehicles we might encounter on the way. There was, therefore, total chaos when someone noticed that the Peugeot was carrying people in uniform. Amin's commanding officer, known as Ali Fadhul, was about to stop in despair, but when he noticed the confusion in our convoy, he decided to drive on at full speed, passing us and heading for Kikagati. It was a lucky escape for him; he is now in prison, having been tried and convicted for crimes he committed when he rejoined his unit after the invasion had failed. We drove on as fast as we could towards Mbarara.

All of a sudden, just before Kaberebere Trading Centre, I saw a lorry full of Amin's soldiers travelling towards us. Wondering why the leading lorry had not challenged them, I ordered our platoon to open fire. We poured sustained fire on them but they did not reply. Their lorry stopped and the soldiers jumped off. I assumed that they had taken up firing positions in the surrounding bushes and banana plantations. When there was no answering fire for some minutes, I ordered the men to hold their fire. Meanwhile, the rest of our convoy at the rear were shooting aimlessly, almost endangering our own side.

Together with two other comrades, I crawled up to the enemy lorry, only to find that it had been totally abandoned and left with all its weapons on board. The poor chaps had been so terrified, they fled without their arms or ammunition and without firing a single shot. About five of them were captured, however, and killed by Obote's thugs. This sparked off a serious quarrel between Obote's commanders and myself.

Although nobody had fired at us during this encounter, I lost not only my driver but also a few others of our comrades, including Raiti Omongin, who simply fled into the valley and across the opposite hill. We shouted after them, but they did not return. I kept hoping they would find their way back to us, but we did not see them again. Although this was my first armed encounter with the enemy, I had no feeling of fear at the time. During the whole invasion episode, my main emotion was one of anger, at this squandering of human life. I knew that this was not a properly managed conflict. It did not reflect the relative strengths of the protagonists. The other side was neither very strong nor better organised; it was simply that our own side was completely disorganised. Once I realised that, I was not afraid, for I knew that this failure to manage could be corrected. Until we achieved that, however, it was clear that we were our own worst enemies.

Realising that we were wasting valuable time, I assumed command and ordered our advance, taking the wheel of the Bedford lorry myself. Apart from three brief driving lessons in Dar es Salaam, I had never driven a vehicle before – which was hardly surprising, given my peasant background where machines are generally a mystery and a rarity. Somehow, I managed to drive the lorry and take command at the same time, which was quite a reckless venture!

We encountered several roadblocks mounted by a few soldiers, but they were no impediment to our reckless, unplanned advance. We stopped briefly at Nyamitanga, after which we drove through Mbarara town, my vehicle still in second place in the convoy. We avoided the main street, diverting as if we were going to Kakoba, and then taking the road near the bus park.

At Agip Motel we encountered one of Amin's jeeps. I stopped our lorry and opened fire on them, the whole of my group joining in. All the occupants were killed and the jeep overturned, and we drove on towards Mbarara barracks. At Nyamityobora forest, however, things changed dramatically for our adventurous convoy. Two more of Amin's jeeps, one armed with a 106mm recoilless gun and the other with a general purpose machine gun (GPMG), attacked us. The 106mm opened fire and hit the leading lorry of our convoy.

That one shell changed the course of the whole adventure: our untrained group broke up and fled. A few of us answered the fire from the jeeps, drove off the 106mm gun and captured the jeep with the GPMG, but our group as a whole had disintegrated. After some confusion, I managed to gather together some 70 fighters. All the others had fled, including all the leading Obote commanders: Captain

Oyile and Lieutenants Okot and Okumu. All of them were subsequently killed, not in the fighting, but in the days following the invasion. They were hounded out of their hideouts and handed over to Amin's thugs.

The remnant of the invasion force broke into two. My group took the left side of the Mbarara-Masaka road, moving towards the quarter-guard of Mbarara barracks. Near the location of the present shops opposite the quarter-guard, we encountered a group of Amin's NCOs, led by a very large man. I told my people to take cover and allow the enemy to come nearer to us. When they were a few metres away, we opened fire. Some of the enemy took cover behind strategically placed anthills and returned fire. An Obote soldier named Oketa, who was a very good shot but totally undisciplined, threw grenades at them. He was the only person with any grenades on him, a fact which in itself makes abundantly clear the extent of disorganisation and unpreparedness of our group.

One or two of Amin's soldiers continued firing at us. In order to avoid casualties on our side, I advised – I would not say 'commanded' since there was no command structure – our group to avoid the rest of Amin's soldiers, cross the Masaka road and move against the barracks from the direction of Kakoba. When we got to the barracks fence, we found the group which had taken the right side of the road trying to climb over it, with a company of Amin's soldiers firing at them. This area is very open and was thus a very good killing ground for the enemy. Seven of our boys were killed trying to climb the fence. After assessing the situation, I advised the two groups to withdraw to Nyamityobora forest.

We stayed in the forest until 2.00 p.m., resting and reflecting on our losses, while Amin's soldiers randomly lobbed shells at us with light mortars. Many of my comrades, not to mention Obote's supporters, had either been killed or lost in the stampede created by the 106mm gun in the morning. These included close comrades such as Mwesigwa Black, Raiti Omongin, Kahunga Bagira, and others who were all subsequently captured and killed by Amin's troops in the days that followed. Obote also lost some potentially useful people, for example Peter Natooli, who had been a student at Makerere.

After we had rested a while, I advised that we should cut our losses and go back to Tanzania. It took some time to convince the remnants of our force to withdraw in an orderly fashion. They were still drunk on the lies of their leaders who had been telling them that there was a substantial fifth column waiting inside Uganda to assist them take over power as soon as a few shots were fired at the border. They had been led to believe that this would be an easy war. It is characteristic of all opportunists and reactionaries to shrink from telling the truth because their intentions are always to exploit the people. If people are struggling and fighting for their own rights, why should they be shielded from the arduous and bloody struggles they must endure in order to achieve freedom? It is only those who wish to use and deceive the people who tell them lies about easy victories.

After several hours of argument, I managed to persuade 46 fighters to withdraw, but we could only muster drivers for three lorries, and those included myself. Although I had miraculously learnt to drive that day, I could not yet turn a lorry round. One Mugisu comrade called George, who is still alive, managed to turn the lorry round for me. With our three lorries and the 46 remaining people, we started our retreat to the border. I had told the drivers of the other two lorries to stop at the petrol station below the former Ankole Hotel and fill up with diesel so that we would not run out of fuel on the way, but only my lorry stopped. The other two simply drove on. Because of my inexperience in driving, I had difficulty in turning the lorry into the petrol station, but I managed to get close enough to fill it, after knocking down part of the low wall near the pump.

This fuel-stop, though necessary, nearly spelt disaster for my group. Unknown to us, Amin's soldiers, who had fled from the barracks, were now advancing to try to cut off our retreat. They were under the command of an officer named Colonel Gowan. The point they had chosen at which to cut us off was the very spot where I was standing filling up my lorry. Because of the general laxity typical of inexperienced fighters, I had allowed one of our boys called Nyakaana to walk from the petrol station up to a housing estate nearby to go and see his brother. These are the kind of mistakes young revolutionaries can make. What could possibly have been so important about Nyakaana seeing his brother at that particular moment?

After filling my lorry with diesel, I waited 20 minutes for Nyakaana to return but he did not. I learned later that, slightly beyond the petrol station, Nyakaana had met Amin's soldiers advancing to cut off our retreat. Instead of coming back to warn us, Nyakaana ran away and hid. Here we were waiting for him to return, wasting valuable minutes of our margin of safety, and all the while Amin's soldiers were advancing on us. Of the 46 people I had managed to get out of Mbarara, I only had about six in the back of my lorry. Had we not fortuitously driven off just before the arrival of Amin's soldiers, our very survival would have been put in jeopardy.

Soon after we had left, Amin's soldiers arrived and killed the pump attendant for no other reason than that he had given us diesel. What could the poor man have done? How could he have denied us fuel when we were armed and he was not? However, that was typical of Amin's army. After that we drove to the border without incident. Of the 330 fighters and nine lorries which had started off for Mbarara that morning, only 46 people and three lorries returned. All the others were either killed in action or captured and then murdered.

Afterwards, Amin displayed a huge stack of the bodies of people who had been killed by his army. In reality, these people were not killed in the fighting. After the dispersal which had followed the encounter with the 106mm jeep at Nyamityobora, many of the untrained fighters had either gone into hiding in peasants' homes or tried to make their own way back to Tanzania. Since many of the fighters were Acholis, they did not know the Mbarara area at all. Moreover, because of the hurried preparations, many had only been issued with SAR-56 rifles, which are semi-automatic and only carry ten bullets. Without reserve ammunition clips, these poor chaps could not have defended themselves against enemy agents or excited mobs. Many were picked up by civilians and handed over to Amin's executioners. There had been no real fighting in Mbarara: it had simply been a tragic farce.

Meanwhile, those on the Masaka front had not fared any better. Tito Okello and Oyite Ojok had managed to surprise Amin's men at Mutukula. They destroyed a few jeeps carrying GPMGs which had been recklessly racing towards the battle area as if trying to catch up with a wedding party, an action characteristic of Amin's so-called generals. Although Ojok had more than 1000 fighters, however, he did not get beyond Kalisizo, 12 miles (19 km) from Masaka, where they ran out of ammunition. In the advance on Kalisizo, they had captured a jeep with a radio communication set and, apparently, Okello himself started using it to call for reinforcements, without changing the frequency. Even if he had changed the frequency, it would still have been dangerous to use it without a code. When Amin's people realised who it was, they spoke to him on the radio and advised him to withdraw up to eight miles (12 km) from Mutukula where he would find ammunition ready for him.

In the meantime, Amin had flown troops behind Okello's lines, landing them at Lukoma airstrip, five miles from the Tanzania border. When Okello's convoy arrived at the agreed point sometime during the night, they fell into the ambush and disintegrated. Many soldiers were killed and others were scattered. Many civilian UPC leaders were also either killed or captured there. They included people like Joshua Wakholi, Alex Ojera and Picho Ali. The incompetence of the leaders was incredible. How a convoy could travel without an advance group and without prior reconnaissance information, especially as it had already lost the element of surprise, was simply incomprehensible.

COUNTING THE COST

Our lorry reached the Tanzanian border without further incident and there we merged with the rest of our Mbarara group, a total of 46 survivors. One Sgt Ageta declared himself leader and I was made a corporal. I did not resist these arrangements because I hoped to persuade the group to go back inside Uganda and establish a guerrilla base there. Using the fighters and arms we had left, we could have established a guerrilla base which we could have used to overthrow Amin within a year or two. The problem, however, was the conception and the objectives of the UPC leadership. The UPC feared a guerrilla war because their leadership was built on a sectarian, tribal base. They did not even believe in the UPC itself as such. Obote's habit of dividing people along ethnic lines had made him afraid to mobilise and arm people outside his Acholi-Langi group. This is not to say, however, that there was no friction between the Langis and Acholis themselves. Such are the fruits of the endless factionalism inherent in the politics of opportunism.

That same night, 17 September, the remnants of our group were told to proceed to Kyaka, which is 40 miles (70 km) from Nshungyezi. I was very tired but I still had to drive my lorry. We slept in the lorries and the following morning, 18 September, I was taken to see Lt Col. Marrealle, who was the chief of operations of the Tanzanian People's Defence Force (TPDF). He gave me an unforgettable breakfast consisting of a mug of tea, bread and corned beef fried with onions. Sometime later, Sokoine arrived from Bukoba and told me that I must go back to Mbarara. The company of troops which Ojok had hoped to use in the DC-9 plane at Kilimanjaro Airport had now arrived at Kyaka. It included Odongo Oduka, who had been one of Obote's bodyguards and also people like Francis Agwa and Amani Obote. Sokoine appointed me the leader of this group which was to be added to the remnants of the Mbarara group.

The Okello-Ojok group had not yet returned from the disaster at Lukoma airstrip and we prepared to leave that evening. My plan was to go back to the hills in Nshungyezi and mount a roadblock there. We could, indeed, have opened a guerrilla front in the hills of Kikagati and Mwizi. Basing ourselves there, we could have reactivated our contacts in the south-west of the country, gathered together the Fronasa cadres from inside and outside the country, recruited more people, and started a protracted people's war in Uganda. We did not manage to set off until late in the evening because the group was reluctant and scared to move forward, now that they realised the kind of lies they had been told of an easy victory. We did, however, have some useful weapons, including a 75mm recoilless gun.

We went up to the border at Kakunyu, but my group, of which 95 per cent were Obote's people, refused to move any further. They rightly said that they had been trained as a regular force and could not convert easily to carrying out guerrilla operations. I had no alternative but to order them back to Kyaka, an order they accepted with uncharacteristic enthusiasm. When we got to Kyaka Bridge, we were told to divert to Mutukula, where we met the defeated Okello group. Ojok had not yet arrived. I tried to persuade them of the advantages of guerrilla warfare but with very little success.

After some time, I was summoned back to Kyaka by Edward Sokoine. When I arrived, he tried to explain to me some new ways of using the Obote group but I refused point blank to have anything to do with them. We exchanged a few hot words and he concluded that I was not a good man to have around. He drove me to Bukoba and I went back to my camp at Kaboya to await further orders. I had requested that our small Fronasa group of 14 people be brought from the Frelimo zone of Mozambique so that we could start a guerrilla campaign using this as a nucleus.

Some days later, I was taken to Nyakanyatsi along the Kyaka-Mbarara road to meet the reassembled, but defeated, Ojok group. Out of the 1300 fighters on the Mbarara and Masaka sectors, only 847 could be traced. Thus, over a mere three days, 453 fighters had been captured or killed, and that was the end of the invasion. Soon afterwards, Amin's planes bombed Bukoba and Mwanza, killing nine Tanzanian civilians and wounding eleven. Thereafter, the political situation in Tanzania turned very sour for us, and even for President Nyerere. The right wing in Tanzania, which was very rabid in those days, seized on the disaster with such comments as: 'Nyerere is inviting war on us. People in Bukoba and Mwanza are dying because of the personal friendship between him and Obote.' The Tanzanian president was criticised by his own people, not only for having allowed the invasion to take place from Tanzanian soil, but also for having done so without the knowledge of the Tanzanian army. At the same time he faced international condemnation from the Organisation of African Unity (OAU), while Libya flew in arms and Palestinian commandos to help Amin defend Ugandan soil.

With the two countries apparently on the brink of war, President Siad Barre of Somalia brokered a peace agreement. On 7 October 1972 the foreign ministers of Uganda and Tanzania signed the 'Mogadishu Accord', by which Tanzania effectively recognised Amin's regime as the legitimate government of Uganda. This was a heavy blow for all opponents of Amin.

The whole invasion experience had been very traumatic for our movement and there were many recriminations. Since I was the person principally concerned, I carried much of the blame. I was accused of militarism, dictatorial tendencies, and so on. Of course, I felt a sense of personal responsibility since about half the people in my platoon were killed, including my good friend Mwesigwa Black. At first I thought that perhaps I should not have associated myself with the plan; but as soon as I reflected on that, I realised that such a course of action would have been totally unhelpful to us. Given the international political situation at the time, and the fact that Tanzania was the only country which had any sympathy for our cause, I reiterated my assessment that my decision to stick with the Tanzanians through thick and thin had been the correct one. Therefore, although I still blamed myself to a certain extent, I also maintain that, on balance, it was the best we could have done in the circumstances. There had really been no alternative. The correctness of my assessment was borne out by later events such as the 1978/79 war, the role Fronasa was able to play through taking advantage of the goodwill of the Tanzanians, and even the eventual victory of the National Resistance Movement. This victory was, I believe, in itself a vindication of my 1972 assessment. It would, of course, have been better if the whole debacle had never happened; but since we could not prevent it from occurring, we had to stick with our friends. After all, any setback was a tactical, rather than a strategic one.

Chapter 7

FIGHTING AMIN (3)
[1972–6]

AFTER MOGADISHU

Following the signing of the Mogadishu Accord in October 1972, the atmosphere in Tanzania became hostile. By the terms of the agreement, the Tanzanian government was obliged to halt all propaganda against Amin and to cease all support for 'subversive forces'. This severely hampered our activities. Indeed, because of the pressure of Nyerere's critics within Tanzania, we were supposed to have been rounded up and put in refugee camps, but our Fronasa group refused to co-operate.

On one trip I made to Murongo shortly afterwards in an attempt to discover what was happening inside Uganda, I was arrested by the TPDF. I spent the night having water poured on me, after which I was badly beaten by a whole platoon commanded by someone called Kiswaga. The Tanzanian army also had its origins in a colonial set-up, and that is how they punish people. They strip the victim to the waist and throw cold water on him. (This is a kind of torture, for being half-naked the person becomes very cold.) When he is nearly dry, they pour more water on him. All this happened in spite of the fact that I was travelling in a vehicle provided by the Bukoba Regional Security Officer, Mr Karumanga. All the colonial armies in Africa were brutalised, although only a few went to the extremes of Amin's soldiers. Instead of interrogating somebody to detect inconsistencies in his statements, or locking him up in jail, they beat him up and tortured him, and learnt no information of any value.

Thereafter, I was a frequent guest of the Tanzanian prison warders in Bukoba, Tabora, Dar es Salaam and elsewhere. Some people within Tanzania even suggested that we Fronasa activists should be handed over to Amin. They said they were sure no harm would come to us since we were his agents. Amin would have been very happy if we had been handed over to him, but it was especially bad luck for Obote that this plan did not materialise. One is amazed as to why these Tanzanian reactionaries were thinking of handing us over to Amin, of all people.

Why not deport us to some other country? Fortunately, however, it seems that President Nyerere and some other Tanzanians resisted these pressures and thus saved our lives.

After the Fronasa group had been at Kaboya for some time, some of us were arrested and jailed at Bukoba and then later transferred to Tabora where we stayed for some days. In Tabora, we were not put in prison proper but in a police back-yard. We were later taken under escort to Dar es Salaam, with instructions to report to Mr Sokoine. At that time we had no money so we had nothing to eat all the way to Dar es Salaam, which is 500 miles from Tabora. When we reached Dar es Salaam Police Station, we were told that since it was a weekend, we would have to stay in prison until Monday morning. When I refused to give in to this treat-ment, the prison warders got hold of my head, the Fronasa cadres got hold of my legs and I became the subject of a tug-of-war between the two warring groups.

When a high-ranking police officer called Pundungu was informed about the fracas, he came to the prison and put us in guest houses in Dar es Salaam. The Tanzanians later declared us *personae non gratae* because we had refused to register as refugees.

Around late November and early December 1972, while our papers were being processed, I sneaked away to Nachingwea in southern Tanzania to see Samora Machel and brief him about what had happened. I told him that we would now start infiltrating cadres and fighters back into Uganda to resume our plan which had been interrupted by the ill-planned invasion.

I had known Samora from way back in 1968 when I had led a student delega-tion to the liberated areas of Mozambique. Then he had been Frelimo's Secretary for Defence, while Dr Eduardo Mondlane was President. When Mondlane was killed by a Portuguese bomb in 1969, Samora was elected a member of the tri-umvirate and later emerged as President of Frelimo. When we went into exile in 1971, Samora offered us help immediately. The offer was mainly directed at our group because of our old contacts with Frelimo and, at the end of 1971, this had enabled us to send a few people for training to northern Mozambique. In 1972, the Tanzanians formally asked Samora to help us by providing us with training facilities and arms. Samora continued to help us, off and on, until 1978 when a batch of 28 cadres finished their two-year training course in Montepuez, in Mozambique's Cabo Delgado Province. By that time, Mozambique was indepen-dent. Unfortunately, by the time Samora was killed on 19 October 1986, he had not yet had a chance to visit Uganda. I have, however, maintained close contacts with his successor, Joachim Chissano, and his widow, Graca Machel.

On this occasion, Samora gave me US\$15 000, which helped us infiltrate our trained Fronasa cadres back into Uganda. The money was in cash, which we han-dled and distributed among the cells ourselves. We kept no specific record of this distribution because there was personal trust amongst us. In the early stages of our movement, the leaders were also fighters and so we did not have a bureaucracy with offices and files. The only papers I have on that period are the memoranda I used to write to Nyerere, and even these are only in my possession because I have retrieved them from him since 1986. I never kept any documents on me at the time, not even copies of the memoranda. This was very important because it made infiltration by the enemy very difficult. In fact, we were one of the few organisations that had almost zero infiltration. We viewed our job then as one of maintaining the safety and growth of the movement, rather than keeping records for posterity. Even when we became strong, in the second phase of the struggle, we never kept records, except for sending coded messages in military message books. A message might read: 'Do as we previously discussed,' which would be impossible for anyone intercepting the book to decipher. Otherwise, we used couriers to carry verbal messages. This kind of primitive organisation was very effective indeed. Even when we captured Kampala in 1986, many Western agencies had not thought that we had the capacity to do so. We had made a conscious decision not even to keep minutes of meetings.

THE STRUGGLE INSIDE UGANDA

Following the failure of the invasion, Amin's soldiers had run amok and murdered very many people including Francis Walugembe, Shaban Nkutu, Ben Kiwanuka, Nekemiya Bananuka, Alex Ojera, Joshua Wakholi and Picho Ali. The last three were captured alive during the disorganised invasion and murdered. The illiterate, uncultured and cowardly ex-colonial soldiers thought that they could intimidate the people by committing such atrocities. Instead, the conditions they created generated more resolve among the people and hatred for this gang of ignoramuses who acted extra-judicially even when they were in power. The whole ethos of Amin's army threatened the unarmed people of Uganda. Life was at its cheapest: an unfavourable opinion from one of the illiterate NCOs was enough to take away a human life. This was the tyranny which we proposed to fight by protracted armed struggle.

The plan for our struggle inside Uganda was to start with the 100 guns we had infiltrated into the country before the September 1972 invasion. I had with me 14 Fronasa cadres who had been trained by Frelimo, but who had not had a chance to participate in the September fighting. These included Maumbe Mukhwana and Augustine Ruzindana. There were other cadres who had been trained earlier and who were already inside Uganda. These included Valeriano Rwaheru, Abwooli Malibo and Martin Mwesiga. Altogether, we had about 30 cadres trained by Frelimo at various periods during 1971 and 1972. This number did not include the 30 or so boys I myself had trained at Kaboya and who had participated in the Mbarara fighting. Many of them had been killed following the disaster of September 1972.

After meeting Samora in Nachingwea, I had an opportunity to meet President Nyerere and explain to him what had happened in Mbarara. Obote was, as always, safe in Dar es Salaam and, as usual, telling lies, such as the idiotic declaration that the idea of attacking Uganda had not been to capture power. Apparently, the purpose had simply been for us to go there and test the water, as it were. If the situation became difficult, according to this lie, we were then supposed to have gone back to Tanzania. He even said that 'his' invasion had failed because Museveni had stolen the ammunition truck and driven it away. That was when I decided never to deal with Obote again. In that debacle we had lost many good colleagues.

Following a meeting between Nyerere and myself, some of our group proceeded to Kenya and re-entered Uganda from there. Over the whole period of the anti-Amin struggle up to 1978, we used to enter and leave Uganda through Kenya. We did this without the knowledge or connivance of the government of Kenya and it was only on a few occasions that the Kenyans noticed our presence in their country. We could no longer use the Bukoba route because of the tension there. It was not difficult at that time for people who were not publicly known to get into Uganda. The problem was for someone like myself who had assumed some prominence in the politics of the early 1970s.

We re-entered Uganda in December 1972 and started preparing again to begin guerrilla warfare, now relying on our inside forces, as we had advocated from the very beginning. Although people were demoralised after the failure of the invasion, our work initially progressed well. By the end of the year, we had established several cells all over the country. Maumbe Mukhwana led a group in Mbale, Kawuliza Kasadha a group in Busoga, Akena p'Ojok one in Acholi. Zubairi Bakari led the Kampala cell and Joseph Bitwaari the one in Kabale. There was a group in Toro led by Abwooli Malibo and there was another group at Kyambogo Teacher Training College led by James 'Muharabu' Karuhanga. The Mbarara group of the Bananukas had been decimated after September 1972. The Tororo group which had been led by Raiti Omongin had also disintegrated following his presumed capture and death during the Mbarara fighting of September 1972. Only one comrade remained from that group, a primary school teacher called Ochwo who is still alive today.

When I re-entered Uganda, I stayed with James Kasozi at Ndeeba, together with Martin Mwesiga. Eriya Kategaya was then still working with some private lawyers. The plan was to establish three or four bases in various forests in Uganda. Wukwu 'Kazimoto' Mpima was detailed to establish a base in the forest in Bunya, using the contact of Kawuliza Kasadha, estates manager at Makerere University. The others were in Kigezi, Bugisu and Acholi – in Pabo. We would start with attacks against small enemy groups, ambushes against their convoys and other limited operations of that nature. Given Amin's unpopularity, we hoped these methods would spread and become effective quite quickly. At the same time we would start recruiting more fighters and intensify training.

In those days, Amin had quite a formidable force. He had more than doubled the size of the army to 20 000 from the 8000 at the time of his *coup* in January 1971. He had a reasonable array of APCs, tanks and MiG-21 jet fighters. However, his illiterate commanders were quite incompetent. Amin's soldiers were cowardly and inexperienced because they had not been battle-tested, and, of course, they had no theoretical understanding of warfare. They had joined the army not to make sacrifices for the country, but in order to make money. They had a very low level of political consciousness and very poor leadership. In spite of their fierce appearance and brutality against defenceless civilians, they were little more than bullies. They would, therefore, have been relatively easy to defeat, especially bearing in mind that they had completely alienated the people. The main task for the liberation movement, therefore, was to consolidate itself.

SETBACKS ON THE EASTERN FRONT

Our problems started soon after the camp in Bunya forest had been established. Among the Bunya group were two boys who had been recruited by Joseph Bitwaari and James Karambuzi. Apparently they found life in the bush too arduous and they decided to desert and go back home. As they did not know the area well, and had neither money nor documents, they were arrested by villagers in the area. When they were interrogated, they revealed all they knew and Amin's soldiers were despatched immediately to attack the forest camp. Although the few fighters remaining in the camp managed to repulse the attack, some of our local contacts were arrested, including William Nkoko, who was later publicly executed in Jinja. Other contacts such as James Mbigiti and Kasadha were also arrested and killed. A few survived in the Jinja area, however, including a photographer called Rubanga.

Having repulsed Amin's soldiers, the Kazimoto group decided to make for Mbale to contact Maumbe Makhwana, who was the only contact they knew. They travelled through Busoga with the assistance of some villagers and when they reached the main road somewhere in Iganga District, they sent one member of the group on to Mbale to contact Maumbe. Meanwhile, without knowing that the Kazimoto group had been discovered, I left Kampala with Mwesiga and Rwaheru in our Volkswagen 1600. We went through Jinja and Magamaga and then turned off on the Kaluba road. It was around 8.00 p.m. and already dark. After driving for about five miles (eight kilometres) on the Kaluba road, we met two trucks. One was parked on our side of the road and there was another coming from the opposite direction. This was an army lorry and it stopped alongside our Volkswagen. I was driving and was, therefore, the person nearest the army vehicle.

The driver leaned out of the window and asked us where we were going. I did not reply immediately and, after a thoughtful moment, he got down from his lorry and ordered us out of the car. While I was still trying to engage the hand-brake, so that I could get out, Rwaheru, who was in the front passenger seat to my left, got out of the car and shot the soldier who was standing near the front door of our car. The man did not die immediately, but he lost his balance and started shouting: 'Maama! Maama!' I had by now got out of the car and I, too, shot him. His partner in the passenger seat slid out and hid underneath the truck, too frightened to move.

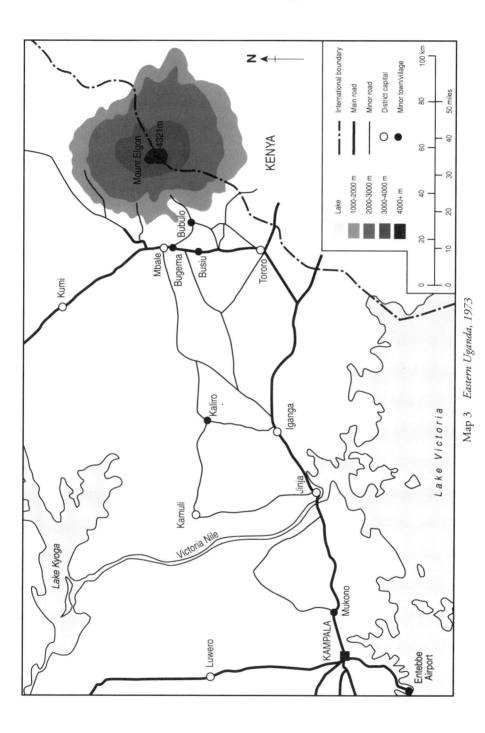

Map 3   *Eastern Uganda, 1973*

We did not know whether he was armed, or who was in the other truck, and we hurriedly got back into the car and turned it round. As I turned the car, the wheels were impeded by the dead body. I had to depress the accelerator several times before the car would mount over the body. We headed for the road junction five miles away, and on to Mbale. We rightly concluded that our Kazimoto group had been encountered and that they were being hunted down as they made their way towards Mbale. Maumbe was our main contact in the area and he was well known so it was essential that we reach him quickly and warn him of events.

We drove without incident through Tororo but, just before the Manafa river, we saw some lights ahead of us and suspected that it might be a roadblock. We got out of the car, abandoned it and walked through the bush all the way to Mbale like harmless civilians. We must have covered 20 miles (32 km) on foot that night, considering the meandering route we had to take. We crossed the Manafa river to the west of the Tororo-Mbale road and arrived in Mbale town at seven o'clock the following morning. We briefed Maumbe about what had happened and told him to expect the Kazimotos. Later, we left for Kampala to wait for the Kazimoto group to resurface. Eventually, an emissary from that group appeared in Mbale, and Maumbe evacuated them to Busiu, between Mbale and Tororo. I went there to see them and informed them that the new plan was to position them on Mt Elgon.

TRAGEDY IN MBALE

This was our second attempt at establishing a base on Mt Elgon. The first had been the ill-prepared attempt of August 1971. On this occasion we were determined to be better organised. With Kazimoto's group in Busiu, we worked feverishly, especially to acquire warm clothing for the very cold mountain weather we had experienced the previous year. While we were still working on the logistics of setting up our camp, another disaster struck. One of Maumbe's cousins wanted to spite Maumbe for refusing to give him some cigarettes and, knowing something of Maumbe's work, he reported to the authorities that there were some guerrillas in the area. Fortunately Maumbe learned of the betrayal and managed to evacuate the group to the mountain before Amin's soldiers arrived.

Meanwhile, Martin Mwesiga, Kazimoto and I travelled to Mbale to join the group, without knowing that its presence had been detected. We drove up to the house in Busiu and found it deserted. As we were driving away, we saw a suspicious-looking Peugeot 404 coming out of a nearby road, but we continued on our way to Mbale. When we got near Mbale town, the same Peugeot pulled up alongside our car for a few seconds and then drove on. We got to house number 49, Maluku Housing Estate. The time was 3.00 p.m. Maumbe was not at home but his wife was. She said he would arrive soon and that we should wait for him. We weighed up whether we should go straight back to Kampala and decided we should wait a while for Maumbe. Time, however, was not on our side.

At around 5.00 p.m., we saw a contingent of about 15 military policemen coming through the estate. We sent someone outside to find out what they were after. Our messenger came back saying that they were looking for a thief. I wanted to open fire on them because I was not convinced that they would use 15 military policemen just to look for a thief. Martin Mwesiga, however, dissuaded me, arguing that, firstly, we had student identity cards, secondly, we had been told that they were looking for a thief, and thirdly, we were in a house with women and children whom we should not endanger. We had left all our SMGs locked up in the car outside. If the assumption that they were not looking for us was incorrect, then we were in a very vulnerable position indeed. Our consultation lasted barely two minutes before Amin's people were upon us.

They surrounded the house in a very unprofessional manner, without cocking their guns. They only asked one question, regarding our identity. We said we were students and, straightaway, they told us to get into our vehicle and drive with them to the barracks. That convinced me, beyond any shadow of a doubt, that the time to act was then. I had the car keys and one of the soldiers, poking a rifle into my side, told me to open and enter the car. Taking them by surprise, I jumped over the hedge, hoping that my colleagues would follow my example and scatter in different directions. At that time I did not realise that they had not done so.

I ran towards a eucalyptus forest below the housing estate. The people in the housing estate, seeing me running pursued by soldiers, thought I was a thief and tried to intercept me, but I brandished my pistol and scared them away as I ran. Meanwhile, the soldier following me started firing, but it is not easy to hit a moving target, especially for the incapable, badly trained African soldier of Amin's army. He kept on firing at me and missing. I reached a big tree, took cover and fired on my pursuers with my pistol. When the soldiers realised that I was armed, they broke off the chase. These were soldiers accustomed to shooting at unarmed members of the public. They were not used to answering fire with fire.

I went into a thicket of tall grass, which turned out to be a worse enemy than Amin's incompetent soldiers. Struggling with the tall grass was so difficult that if Amin's cowardly, bullying soldiers had had the courage to pursue me, I would have been an easy target, but they had apparently given up the chase. I shall never forget those 300 metres or so of tall grass through which I crashed my way. The odds were squarely stacked against me. I was moving very slowly through the tall, thick grass, leaving a clear track which any pursuer could have followed. I was also growing very tired. Of course, I could have waited at the edge of the bush so that I could shoot my pursuers from behind the cover of the grass, but I was afraid to do this as I was so close to the army barracks, from where reinforcements could be quickly mustered. While it would have been impossible for my pursuers to see me through the thick grass, a large volley of bullets fired into the grass would have been most problematic for me, to say the least. For that reason I opted for speed in order to get out of the area and, later on, for concealment, taking advantage of the fact that few people in Mbale would recognise me.

Soon I was able to get out of the grass and run along a water drainage channel with the feeling of lightness one has when running downhill after climbing a mountain. I branched off the drainage channel and entered the eucalyptus forest, which was easy walking. After about 20 minutes, I entered a banana plantation in a village. Then I heard a large number of soldiers trying to comb through the high grass from which I had just emerged and I made for the main road at Bugema.

As I did not know what had happened to my colleagues, I decided to walk back to Mbale, coming from the Tororo road side, to find out what had happened. It was about 7.00 p.m. when I came near the military police barracks. There I met a young man walking in the opposite direction who asked where I was going. I told him that I was going to town to catch a bus to Kampala. Who was I, he wanted to know? I told him that I was a student, and he advised me very strongly not to proceed any further in that direction. I should, instead, go back where I had come from. When I asked him why, he told me that some guerrillas had fought a battle with some soldiers in the town. Two of the soldiers and two of the guerrillas had been killed but one of the guerrillas had escaped. It was then that I realised that my two colleagues, Martin Mwesiga and Wukwu 'Kazimoto' Mpima had been killed. They had not managed to get away.

The deaths of Martin Mwesiga and Wukwu Mpima were a great loss for the movement, and for me personally. Martin in particular had been a close friend of mine since the age of nine.

Martin had been convinced that we could pass ourselves off as students and I blamed myself for not having insisted that we could not. I had thought that since we were armed with pistols, one of us could have kept firing at the soldiers while the others got the guns from the boot of the car. These soldiers were very unprofessional: you only had to fire at them and they stopped chasing you.

I went back with the boy to Bugema, booked into a lodge and slept. From that day on, I learnt to become more assertive in my decision-making. Originally, the group had been consultative – every decision was arrived at by consensus. But this practice was dangerous when it applied to military situations. This is the problem in young revolutionary groups – the belief in collective decision-making. Yet, I think the revolution must have sacrifices, otherwise you will not learn anything.

Very early the following morning, I started walking along the main road at the edge of Bugema barracks. I saw Amin's soldiers inside the barracks fence in an all-round defensive formation, evidently expecting a guerrilla attack on the barracks. I was not concerned about the soldiers inside the barracks, but I was worried about those at the roadblock opposite the barracks' main gate. They had stopped a long line of vehicles and were beating people up. I decided to leave the road and divert to the right.

I walked through nearby villages under the cover of banana plantations and re-entered the road, past the point of the roadblock at the junction of Bubulo-Mbale-Tororo roads. There were a lot of army vehicles moving towards Mbale and I saw a jeep mounted with GPMGs coming from the direction of Bubulo. I knew that they were following up our colleagues who had gone up to the mountain – the ones with whom we were supposed to have linked up the previous day.

I was now in a dilemma as to what to do with the TT pistol which had saved me the day before. I had possessed two magazines, a total of 16 rounds, when we had been attacked by Amin's people. Unfortunately the magazine had fallen out of the pistol when I was firing at the soldiers. This left just one bullet in the chamber, but I had kept the second magazine in the side pocket of my trousers, so I had a total of nine bullets altogether. I had not changed the clothes I was wearing and so there was a possibility that some of the soldiers might recognise me and convey my identity to all the other roadblocks. If that was the case, it was crucial that I keep my pistol so that I could fight my way out if necessary. I did not want to be captured and I was resolved to shoot whichever soldier tried to search me closely, grab his bigger gun (they had SLRs and G-3s) and use it against the others.

On the other hand, if the soldiers I had fought the previous day did not recognise me, then keeping my pistol and taking it through roadblocks might draw attention to me. With clandestine operations, all things being equal, it is better to be absolutely legal: do not carry anything incriminating, have all your documents in order, and depend on credible disguised identity as your main defence. Moving through roadblocks with a pistol was inviting trouble. On balance, however, since I would not give Amin the pleasure of capturing me alive, I decided to keep my pistol, whatever the circumstances. A bus heading for Kampala came and I climbed into it to go to Tororo. It had already passed through the Bugema roadblock which I had avoided. At Tororo I took a taxi and went up to Jinja without incident.

Another risk I was taking was to remain inside Uganda at all, given all the heightened alert caused by our fight with Amin's men. It would have been better to leave the country immediately through Kenya, but I felt I had to go to Kampala to warn the people there so that they would not come to Mbale without knowing what had happened. Furthermore, our people in Kampala were not on the telephone, or if they were, I did not know their numbers. At Jinja I boarded a taxi heading for Kampala and we went without incident up to Namanve forest, about ten miles from Kampala, where our taxi was stopped at a roadblock manned by a whole company of soldiers.

All the passengers were ordered out. One soldier looked at me closely and I, too, looked straight at him. He did not even ask me for my identity card: he simply asked me what I did and I told him that I was a student. He then told me to re-enter the car without any more questions. Had he attempted to search me, I would have shot him and grabbed his gun. It would not have been easy to fight a whole company, but I thought I could have escaped, grabbed a vehicle from someone and driven off. Fortunately, that did not happen. We all re-entered the taxi and drove off through the line of soldiers on either side of the road. From that day, I lost faith in the use of roadblocks as effective security measures. Soldiers manning roadblocks get tired because of the endless stream of travellers, and the moment they are tired may be the very one when fugitives pass through the road-block. Alternatively, the fugitive may simply bypass the roadblock, as I did on many occasions. It is better to mount roadblocks only for very limited periods seeking specific information.

As we neared Kampala, I alighted from the taxi at Banda and went to James Karuhanga's house at Kyambogo where he was teaching. I found Valeriano Rwaheru there and we called Kategaya. I briefed them about what had happened to our good friends Martin Mwesiga and Kazimoto. Then I left the pistol with Rwaheru and in the evening I went to Kampala and caught a bus headed for Kenya. I had changed my clothes and I no longer had the pistol so, with all the legal identity documents, I had no difficulty in going through to Kenya and on to Tanzania to mobilise new support.

FURTHER SETBACKS AND BETRAYALS

Meanwhile, Rwaheru remained behind. I instructed him firstly to transfer two comrades, David Kangire and Victor Amanya to Atiak, Gulu District, so that they could start training the groups there. We had the potential for two groups in Acholi: one in Pabo hills near Atiak, and another around Awere, comprised mainly of ex-soldiers under Sgt Lino Owili, formerly of the Uganda Army. My second instruction to Rwaheru was to wait until the group which had been trying to establish itself on Mt Elgon and in the Bunya forest reassembled so that we could resume operations with at least two groups. There was also a third group around Kampala, comprising Hajjis Bakari and Kibuye. This group had the urban respon-sibilities of co-ordination, transporting people and materials, and carrying out operations if and when the need arose.

Had we succeeded in establishing these three groups, the struggle against Amin would have come to a head long before 1978. However, that was not to be. Our biggest mistake was to have leaders also acting as co-ordinators, dashing around in vehicles from one end of the country to the other. Had the leaders stayed put, each in his own zone, and in the bush, not in houses, we would not have missed the moment. While it is true that we did not have enough guns, the 100 or so guns that we had infiltrated into the country would have been enough for a modest beginning. During the second phase of our revolution, from 1981 to 1986, we adopted this more stable mode of operation and were able to achieve victory.

In 1973, although we were courageous and aware of the need to establish a rural political/military base (indeed, we were attempting to do this), we did not appreciate the gravity of mixing the two roles of rural commander and urban co-ordinator. In revolutionary warfare, a commander should always remain with his main forces and not engage in the subsidiary tasks of a co-ordinator. The role of co-ordination should be left to others, or couriers should be used. Rushing around may be romantic – you try to do everything yourself: you do not want to put somebody in danger where you cannot go yourself – but, comparatively, it is more serious and devastating for the organisation to lose a leader than to lose a courier. During the 1981–6 period, we observed this principle closely. In fact, in the five years of the war in the Luwero Triangle, I only left the bush twice: from June to December 1981, and from March to September 1985, and on these occasions only when it was crucial to do so. We were conscious of this problem in 1972–3, but because we had a very limited number of capable co-ordinators, it was tempting to 'try and accomplish something before going permanently to the bush.' In subsequent years, we either left most of the unfinished business in town to be managed by others, capable or otherwise, or we let that business take care of itself for a while.

As instructed, Rwaheru tried to carry out the deployments we had agreed upon. He sent Victor Amanya and David Kangire to Gulu, only for them to be betrayed by one of our 'contacts' there, one Latigo, a former General Service functionary who had shared a room with me at Rex Hotel in Dar es Salaam in 1971 before he had mysteriously gone back to live in Uganda. Kategaya and I had, a little earlier, narrowly survived the treachery of this same Latigo. In our co-ordinating efforts, accompanied by one Jacob Okello of the Uganda Development Corporation, we had driven to Awere, Acholi, in Kategaya's car, a brand new Renault, to meet the group of ex-soldiers led by Sgt Lino Owili. We already had contacts in the Gulu area through Akena p'Ojok, who had joined our committee in 1972 and had already helped us take arms to Atiak. We drove through Gulu town up to Awere without incident and found Lino in a village overlooking Awere Bridge, across the River Aswa. We agreed that Lino should organise the ex-soldiers and policemen in Acholi who had fled Amin's massacres and create a unit that would start operations against Amin's rule. We would share with them the few arms we had.

As we were about to leave, Lino told me that there was a man called Latigo who knew me and would like to see me as we had been together in Dar es Salaam. I told Lino that I did not want to see the man as I did not trust him. Soon after we left Awere, Latigo came and Lino told him that we had just left. I think he also described the car in which we were travelling. Having left Awere, we again drove through Gulu town and headed south for Kampala, with Kategaya driving. As we got to Bobi, we hit a sheep which was crossing the road. The accident damaged our radiator which soon overheated and brought the vehicle to a halt. We pushed the car off the road and found our way back to Gulu on foot.

We booked a room in a roadside lodge on the southern edge of the town. We stayed inside the room and, soon afterwards, Latigo arrived asking the lodge owner if he had seen Jacob Okello with two other people. The lodge owner said that he had not and Latigo went away. We were in a very dangerous area because, in those days, Gulu was a major air base for Amin's MiGs and there were a lot of Air Force personnel in the area. Had Latigo seen us, he would have been able, within minutes, to mobilise security personnel to surround us. We managed to get a minibus taxi around 10.00 p.m. arriving in Kampala at 2.00 a.m.

The taxi driver dropped us near Mulago where I had rented a house. Kategaya and Okello also went to their houses. When Kategaya got to his home, in some flats near Makerere facing Bakuli, the gateman told him that two people had climbed over the fence and gone round to the basement of the block using a torch to look at the vehicles parked there. It was obvious that they were looking for Kategaya's car. Latigo must have given the car registration number to someone who had telegraphed it to Amin's agents in Kampala. When the two men had not found the car in the car park, they had not bothered to enter Kategaya's flat.

This same Latigo later betrayed Kangire, Labeja and Obwona when they were trying to move some guns from Atiak to Awere. It seems Lino had not heeded my caution about Latigo because he was a relative of his. When Kangire arrived in Gulu to begin his work, Lino briefed Latigo about our group's movements. Since Latigo had a car, he was even asked to transport Kangire and his colleagues, but instead he handed them over to Amin's agents. Once Kangire was arrested, he was asked about his contacts and it was he who mentioned Karuhanga's house at Kyambogo which we were using.

A few days after Kangire's arrest, at around 11.00 a.m., while Rwaheru was at Kyambogo with Karuhanga, a platoon of Amin's soldiers surrounded the house. Karuhanga, who was in the sitting-room, was arrested and told to show the security men around. Meanwhile, Rwaheru had locked himself in the bedroom and when the soldiers failed to open the door, they demanded that Karuhanga tell them who was inside. Karuhanga told then that it was his wife who had been frightened by their coming to the house. Meanwhile, Rwaheru climbed on to a bed, cut the ventilator netting over the door and lobbed a stick-grenade into the midst of the soldiers who were crowded into the corridor of the house. The fools had never seen a stick-grenade before – they probably thought it was a hammer. Seeing the grenade, Karuhanga fled into the toilet and locked the door.

The grenade exploded, killing all the men in the corridor. Rwaheru then opened the bedroom door and lobbed another grenade into the sitting-room, killing more of the enemy. In all he killed eleven of them. Unfortunately, while he was preparing to throw a third grenade, it exploded in his hands and killed him. He had not thrown it quickly enough. James Birihanze, a graduate of literature from Dar es Salaam University, had also been in the house that day, but we have never been able to find out what happened to him as his body was not recovered from there. He may have run out of the house wounded and died in another place. After bringing reinforcements, and realising Rwaheru was dead, Amin's thugs entered the house and got Karuhanga out of the toilet where he had hidden himself.

In March 1973, James Karuhanga was publicly executed in front of his parents in Mbarara, although he had been captured in Kyambogo, near Kampala. On that notorious day in March, public executions were carried out in several towns around Uganda. People who had been captured in Kampala or Gulu were taken to their home areas to be executed before their families – such was the mentality of the regime. Joseph Bitwaari and James Karambuzi were arrested and publicly executed in their home town of Kabale. In Gulu, Obowan from Atiak and Laboja from Awere were executed as a result of Latigo's betrayal.

Not all those executed that day had necessarily been involved in guerrilla activity. Abwooli Malibo, arrested in one of the tea rooms in Kampala, was executed in Fort Portal. He had maintained some contacts with us although, after training in Frelimo camps, he had drifted away from clandestine work. Masaba and Namirundu were killed in Mbale. Masaba had nothing to do with us, but Namirundu, a schoolboy aged 17, and a relative of Maumbe Makhwana's, had helped cook for our people at Maumbe's house. Rashid Ntale and William Nkoko, who had been our village contacts in Butembe-Bunya, just next to the *gombolola* headquarters at Kityerera, were executed in Jinja. In Kampala, two thieves who had nothing whatever to do with us were executed at Clock Tower.

Because of all these tragedies and mishaps, most of which were a direct consequence of the mode of operations we were using – a mode exacerbated by the unfortunate international situation – we had to make a tactical retreat. We had already been declared *personae non gratae* in Tanzania since the Mogadishu Accord of October 1972, and no other neighbouring country was willing to accommodate us. The essentials of the Mogadishu agreement were that we should not operate from Tanzania, and that Nyerere should agree, effectively, to recognise Amin's regime.

In spite of our setbacks and mistakes, however, President Nyerere was encouraged by the efforts we had made. Our clandestine operations after 1972 showed that we had the capacity to do some work because we had some useful contacts inside Uganda. Although Nyerere did not give us any new guns, ammunition or money – and to that extent he had accepted the Mogadishu Agreement – he offered us new training facilities, using a Frelimo base in Nachingwea.

We recruited 54 boys, mostly from Bugisu, and started training them at Nachingwea. Unfortunately, once again, these boys had not been well selected. They had mostly been working in towns like Nairobi and had a *kiyaaye* (*lumpen proletariat*) culture. They began misbehaving in the Frelimo camp and soon after their training, the Tanzanian government dispersed them. For example they would start drinking and moving out of the camps, thus exposing their cover – their Ugandan background was not supposed to be known. This was another setback because they were the group we had hoped to start using against Amin, beginning in September 1973.

Nevertheless, the various incidents that we managed to spark off in Uganda, though minor in themselves, had a significant psychological effect on Amin's regime because they were happening deep inside Uganda in places as far apart as Gulu, Mbale, Kampala and Kabale. They had no international implications since they were not happening at Uganda's borders. Amin was thus deprived of any external excuse. Originally Tanzania had been projected as the problem, with the regime declaring: 'Uganda is peaceful and Ugandans have accepted Amin: it is Nyerere who is bringing us problems because he wants to force his friend, Obote, back into power.' But now there was a group which, first of all, was not under Obote's leadership: we had made a press statement to that effect. Secondly, we were not operating at the border; and thirdly, the incidents were scattered all over the country. They seemed to be emanating from within the population itself. Nyerere was especially happy with that state of affairs because it took the pressure off.

LIFE IN EXILE

After this series of setbacks, some of the comrades left Tanzania to look for work elsewhere. Kategaya got a job in Zambia, but others, including myself, found jobs in Tanzania. Before that, however, in 1973, I had married Janet Kataaha whom I had known since our childhood in 1958. Our families lived in the same sub-county of Ntungamo in Mbarara District, but I had not seen her for some years until December 1972, when we met in Nairobi as I was on my way through from Tanzania to Uganda. She was living there as part of the family of a Ugandan lawyer named John Kazzora.

Kazzora was one of those British-trained lawyers who had imbibed British ways: he dressed like the British, drank wine with meals, listened to classical music, and so on. He had been a Democratic Party supporter from our area, Mbarara. As such, he was one of those people who had initially welcomed Amin because they were so fed up with Obote. In fact, he was a sort of adviser to Amin – one of those who thought that as long as Amin was willing to take advice, they could use him to do some good.

By the second half of 1972, people such as Kazzora and Edward Rugumayo, Amin's first Minister of Education, whom I had met in Kampala, were becoming disillusioned with Amin. Thus a broad spectrum of disillusionment was emerging and, I believe, had Obote not pre-empted it, we could have got rid of Amin in 1973 or 1974. However, that was not to be. Rugumayo found himself compromised by his association with me and had to flee the country after the abortive invasion of September 1972, while Kazzora fled with his family from Uganda to Nairobi in late 1972 following the murder of the Chief Justice, Benedicto Kiwanuka. Amin's thugs had attacked Kazzora's office and killed a lawyer and his clerk.

Because of the political categorisations of those days, Kazzora thought of himself as a 'rightist', while people like myself and Edward Rugumayo were thought of as 'leftists'. For my part, I never really accepted these false categorisations. I considered that in a backward situation like the one obtaining in Uganda, the talk of right and left was phoney. The real divide was between the developed parts of the world and the backward ones. The conflict between the Western powers and the Soviet Union was reflected in African politics because of the ignorance and opportunism of the post-independence leaders. Very soon, some groups were describing themselves as 'pro-West' and others as 'pro-East'! Those who were pro-East did not talk to those who were pro-West, and vice-versa. Whoever dared to cross that divide was regarded as a traitor. The consolidation of African unity was not regarded as paramount by most African politicians in those Cold War decades. Instead, the ideal was to be a loyal member of one or other of the ideological blocs, in spite of the fact that our own social evolution did not reflect such contradictions or sharp class antagonisms.

Although my own views had not yet properly coalesced, I did not think that these divisions were correct. Because of our opposition to Western imperialism, we were automatically labelled pro-East. Intuitively, I did not like this categorisation, so I had no qualms about establishing contact with John Kazzora, who was supposed to be rabidly pro-West. Such contacts highlighted the artificial perceptions of African politics in those days and in practical terms it was also useful in case we wanted to talk to the British. The British did not know our group, and if they had, they would have disapproved, because they would have thought of us as 'communists'. People like Kazzora had a useful role in explaining that, although we were radicals, we did not have a 'communist' programme for the country. All we were seeking was decent governance for our people.

It was at the Hilton Hotel in Nairobi that I accidentally met the Kazzora family in December 1972, soon after their arrival from Uganda. I had not met John Kazzora himself before, in spite of the fact that he came from my home area, but I knew other members of his family well, including Janet Kataaha and Jennifer Nakunda, now Kutesa. The two had been with me in primary school at Kyamate, though Janet was a few years behind me: she was about the same age as my sister. Janet's parents had died when she was still young and she had grown up with Kazzora, who is her cousin. Kazzora had paid for her to go to an 'A' level college in Aberystwyth in Wales and she was supposed to go on to do her university education there, still on the private sponsorship of John Kazzora. When he was forced to flee into exile, however, he could no longer afford to pay the fees and she had returned from Britain to live with him in Nairobi.

Soon after this first meeting with Kazzora, and his agreement to work with us, Amin put pressure on the Kenyan government which obliged him to leave for England. Kazzora had thus already left by the time I returned to Nairobi in January 1973, but he had nominated Janet to work as a liaison and courier between himself and me. After a little while, I decided that the liaison should also handle other matters.

Janet and I were married in August 1973 and our first child, Muhoozi, was born on 24 April 1974, one day before the Portuguese Revolution which overthrew fascism in Portugal and paved the way for the decolonisation of the Portuguese colonies. At the time we were living at Kurasini, a suburb of Dar es Salaam, and we were so short of funds that our electricity had been cut off because of non-payment of the bill. In fact, we were not able to have it restored until Muhoozi was three months old. You should have seen his jumps and laughs when the lights first came on! He had never seen a lit bulb before! It was clear to me that

I needed to get immediate employment to stop my new young family from starving.

From 1974 to 1977, I concentrated on two things: personal survival and keeping Fronasa alive and active. Partly as a means of combining the two aims, I took the job of post-secondary teacher at Moshi Co-operative College, starting in August 1974. I taught Economics and what we used to call Development Studies for a diploma mostly to co-operative officials. It was like the course we had introduced at Dar es Salaam University although this one concentrated mostly on project analysis. I had a small house there with my family. One reason for choosing to work in Moshi was because the town was near Kenya, so that I could keep in touch with Uganda through Kenya. Fronasa did not have any money of its own and it was very difficult trying to keep the organisation alive using my salary alone.

During this period, I refrained from entering Uganda as we had decided that it was better to use people who were not well known. While working in Moshi, I maintained contacts with Haruna Kibuye and Zubairi Bakari, the latter now assistant district administrator in Mukono. Later on, through one Kajungu, then living in Nairobi, I contacted Amama Mbabazi and Kahinda Otafiire and recruited another colleague called Dennis Echowu. Using part of my salary, I would go regularly to Nairobi or Kisumu to meet these contacts.

In those days, there were only a few towns in Tanzania where you could telephone direct to Kenya or Uganda without going through the operator in the Post Office. These included Dar es Salaam, Arusha and Mwanza. It was important for confidentiality not to go through the Post Office and since I could not dial direct from Moshi, I travelled frequently to Arusha, 65 miles (105 km) away, to telephone Kampala and Nairobi. I would arrange for meetings in Nairobi, which was our physical contact place, while Arusha was the telephone contact town. The regime in Uganda did not think of tapping telephones to find out what was going on. Amin's people were just killers – they could not follow up anything in a systematic manner. Of course, one cannot say much on the telephone but we used codes. We had arranged, for instance, that Arusha should be called Jinja, and Nairobi should be called Mbarara. So all I had to do was tell my contacts: 'Your friend will meet his friend in Jinja on Saturday.'

Apart from the obvious need for heightened security, it was important that we learnt some broader lessons from the tragedies and mistakes of 1972 and 1973. In 1974–5, as we went through the lowest point in our political activities, I made three resolutions. Firstly, I would never again listen to external advice or yield to external pressure, as far as the strategy of liberating Uganda was concerned. Secondly, I would not entrust the future training of major groups of cadres to anyone else until the movement had developed a credible military force and political network. I would in future train the groups myself, or at least directly supervise their training; and finally, I would never again do the urban co-ordinating job, even for short periods. My base would henceforth be in the bush with the main forces.

Chapter 8

FIGHTING AMIN (4)
[1976–9]

In late 1975 I accidentally met Edward Sokoine at Monduli Trading Centre. It had been three years since our last meeting at Bukoba. We talked and he invited me to Dar es Salaam, where he introduced me to Lt Col. Sama, an officer in military intelligence. Later on, for further co-ordination, he introduced me to Lt Issonda, also from military intelligence. These contacts proved useful as, in 1976, they allowed us to recruit some more boys and they contacted Frelimo on our behalf. Through our contact Dennis Echowu, we recruited 28 boys from Uganda and sent them to Montepuez, in Mozambique's Cabo Delgado Province. Mozambique had, at this stage, been independent for a year.

Our second child, Natasha, was born on 12 March 1976 and in September 1976 I resigned from my teaching post at Moshi and moved back to Dar es Salaam with my family to work full-time for the struggle. At about this time, my younger brother came to visit us in Tanzania. He was born in 1960 and so was much younger than me. My mother had named him Caleb Akwandwanaho ('Akwandwanaho' means 'God has been my defender'). At the time of his visit he was still in secondary school. I was very worried about the safety of my family in Uganda and so I decided not to send him back, especially as he was the only brother I had. I thought that one day Amin would kill my family simply because they were my relatives – that is how Amin's regime behaved.

With that sort of insecurity in Uganda, I argued that now was not the time for him to concentrate on studies. It was better to keep alive and to make a contribution to the liberation of the country. Therefore, I encouraged him to join the group I had sent to train in Mozambique. As a 16-year-old, he was of course delighted at the prospect. Young people are easily excited by guns, although they may not always know the political implications. My brother took the *nom de guerre* of Salim Saleh, which was the name by which we knew him from then on.

I left Janet in Dar es Salaam with the children and went to Mozambique to train with Salim Saleh and the new recruits. Among this group of boys were Fred Rwigyema, Chefe Ali, Ivan Koreta and others still active in the NRA who are not so well known. The Montepuez group of 28, whose training I supervised person-ally between 1976 and 1978, were among the most useful military cadres in our whole struggle. They helped me start the western axis in 1978 in the battle against Amin, and they provided the core of the 9000 fighting men whom we had recruited in Uganda by April 1979. Because he was still very young, I kept my brother Saleh out of the direct fighting in 1979: I kept him in Dar es Salaam as a military liaison officer between us and the Tanzanians. In due course, however, he was to prove a brave and brilliant leader in the military struggle of the 1980s.

FIGHTING SECTARIANISM AND TRIBALISM

I took personal charge of the Montepuez group and stayed with the boys during the training months in Mozambique because I feared that some of the recruits might be undisciplined *bayaaye*, like those of 1973, and they might have caused us problems. With my presence in the camp, however, we were able to suppress most of their negative tendencies and attitudes. I did some political work with them, explaining to them our vision for the liberation of Uganda, but we combined this kind of political education with strong discipline. We even arrested a few of them and put them in jail. Some people make the mistake of thinking that liberation movements should only be run by 'politicisation' (*siasa*). This is not correct. Sometimes it is necessary to take strong action against indiscipline. It is better to combine politicisation with administrative action. Otherwise, excessive liberalism can lead to wrong results in the same way that lack of internal democracy can also create problems. Apart from the problems of drinking alcohol, escaping from the camp to chase after women, stealing rations, and so on, we also had to combat tribal sentiments based on ignorance.

Samora Machel described tribalism in Africa as 'the commander-in-chief' of enemy forces, meaning that it is the greatest single tool by which ignorant oppor-tunists destroy the unity and strength of unpoliticised African groups. We had proof of this ourselves. As soon as one gathers a group of no more than ten from different tribes, the opportunists will seek to discover who are the 'majority' among the group. Then someone will claim that, as he is from the largest tribe, he should be the section leader. The group of 53 that we took to train in Nachingwea in 1972–3 was made up mostly of Bagisu and this problem of the 'majority' tribe came up.

During the anti-Amin war of 1978–9, I gathered a group of 200 at Nyamyaga in Karagwe, Tanzania. The majority of them were Banyankore-Bakiga. However, the leadership of the group was mainly from the 28 Montepuez group who had mostly been Kumam. Somebody called Bagarukayo, also known as Bushaijabwengwe, an ignorant peasant from Mbarara, organised a protest demanding that I should 'liberate' the Banyankore from the *Badugudugu* (people who speak a language you do not understand). What was the fault of the *Badugudugu*? 'They are training us too hard', was the reply – and this from a man whose nickname, *Bushaijabwengwe*, means 'brave as a leopard'!

The way we treated Bushaijabwengwe may be instructive. I arrested him immediately and put him in *endaki*, an underground tunnel, half-naked. It can be very cold at night. He decided to go on hunger strike. We told him that we did not mind him dying because, after all, he had been trying to murder our organisation by fragmenting it into tribal factions. After a little while, I decided to intimidate him. I told him that since he had decided to go on hunger strike, we were going to shoot him in order to expedite his death. He immediately fell on his knees, quaking and begging for mercy as he had many young children to look after, and so on. Of course, we did not intend to shoot him but the firm way I dealt with that kind of opportunism contained tribalism in Fronasa and the young recruits started looking at each other as members of Fronasa rather than as individuals. Many of the leaders, mainly from Kaberamaido, were accepted although the majority of the fighters were Banyankore-Bakiga.

During a liberation struggle, sectarianism must be opposed at all costs. Tribalistic opportunism has caused trouble for liberation movements in Mozambique, Guinea-Bissau, Angola and Zimbabwe, and we had many trials and tribulations over these issues in our own movement in Uganda. It was only by successfully combating this evil, however, that we were able to defeat the reactionary regimes that were crippling our country.

TACTICS AND INFILTRATION

Once I had finished training the group of 28, I had to decide what to do with them. There was pressure from some circles to use them for the assassination of Idi Amin, but I rejected this tactic because I did not see that any durable advantage could be gained from such an action unless we had a follow-up capacity. Killing Amin on its own could actually have been counter-productive. Amin was in many respects a good enemy to have because he was stupid. To remove him by assassination, without removing his whole regime, might have resulted in the coming to power of somebody more intelligent but from the same reactionary clique. It was, therefore, in our own interests to preserve Amin until we could get rid of his entire regime. Amin's frequent mistakes were our allies.

These are the kind of debates that used to cripple action in those days because people did not yet have a thorough view of the problem. Assassinations would not only *not* have solved the problem, they would have misused our human and material resources, as had happened in 1972 when we had been forced into association with Obote's plans, against our better judgement. I therefore resisted the use of these young men in anything other than the creation of bases. I insisted on this because I knew that it was the only way to create a durable capacity for our group.

By the end of 1977, we were successfully infiltrating the boys back into Uganda and we continued with this work through 1978. These boys were sent into Uganda without any arms. This was another lesson we had learnt from the past.

Carrying arms exposes the cadre to risks, and this is undesirable until the group has sufficient capacity to protect itself. A small mistake at a roadblock may result in being discovered with a gun, and immediately the authorities will know that the cadre is politically motivated.

In August 1978, as part of the infiltration project, I visited Uganda again for the first time since 1973. I went with a man called Sabiiti to the border area of Kigaragara. We walked across the border at night, made some contacts and went back to Kakunyu village in Tanzania. Since the best security for clandestine workers lay in outward legality rather than in carrying guns, what we needed were identity documents and a constant presence in an area. With this in mind, we planned to organise some trading activity between Uganda and Kenya as a form of cover. The idea was that we should buy some coffee. Since many of Amin's people were also engaged in smuggling, we decided to join them, with the double purpose of making contacts and earning some money along the way. Even if we were caught smuggling coffee, it would not have been as serious as getting caught in clandestine political activities. In any case, the so-called authorities were also smugglers, so we could probably have argued our way out if caught. The smuggling plan did not materialise, however, because time ran out as Amin himself brought this phase of our struggle to an end.

AMIN'S ATTACK ON TANZANIA

On 30 October 1978, Amin's troops invaded the Kagera Salient. I think the main factor behind this invasion was the incapacity of Amin and his group. They must have merely been posturing: it could not have been that they underestimated the capacity of the Tanzanian army because even in the brief skirmishes of 1971 and 1972, the Tanzanian army had not fought badly. Therefore, the explanation for this blunder on Amin's part must have been his ignorance. Hopelessly out of his depth, Amin was always fond of doing and saying outrageous things. He wanted to behave like the Israelis who in 1967 had captured the Sinai Peninsula from Egypt in just six days. His limited knowledge could not fathom the consequences of such an act. He appears to have thought that by invading Tanzania, he was 'teaching President Nyerere a lesson'!

President Nyerere's reaction, however, was music to our ears. While addressing officials of the recently formed Chama cha Mapinduzi (CCM – 'Revolutionary Party' – created in 1977 from a union of TANU and the Afro-Shirazi Party of Zanzibar), Nyerere said that Amin's attack had given Tanzanians the cause (*sabaabu*), and they already had the will (*nia*) and the means (*uwezo*) to fight him. The Tanzanians had in fact had the will to fight Amin since the brief encounters of 1972, and especially since the bombing of Mwanza and Bukoba. The Tanzanian People's Defence Force (TPDF) had also developed the means to fight, having bought a great deal of Soviet equipment, including SAMs, MiG fighters and medium-range artillery. Amin had, therefore, played right into our hands.

Never since Amin's *coup* in 1971 had I felt so buoyant as I did on the day following the invasion. I knew that Amin was finished. President Nyerere had always wanted to give us full support, although some elements in Tanzania did not approve of this. These Tanzanian opponents of ours fell into two groups. One consisted of those who had secretly welcomed Amin's coup in 1971 and who wished for a similar one in Tanzania. These were generally the same people who were opposed to the Tanzanian government's socialist policies, and favoured the adoption of free-market economic policies. Others, influenced by some Western countries, did not welcome the support that Tanzania was giving to liberation movements in southern Africa.

It should be made clear that Nyerere's and Kaunda's governments were to a large extent responsible for the collapse of Portuguese colonialism in Africa and, hence, for the fall of fascism in Portugal itself. Indeed, the initiatives and sacrifices of the governments and peoples of Tanzania and Zambia played a major role in the extension of the frontiers of African freedom, and, in due course, helped bring about the fall of Ian Smith's regime in Rhodesia. However, some elements in Tanzania did not support this process and, when we came on the scene, they saw us as an additional problem. There was a third group of people opposed to Tanzania helping us, because they genuinely believed that Tanzanian security was being compromised by all the refugees who were arriving from neighbouring countries: the fear of sacrifice always works in favour of dictatorships in Africa.

When Amin attacked Tanzania on 30 October 1978, however, Nyerere's hand was strengthened and those who opposed us were weakened. I remember walking along State House Drive in Dar es Salaam, on my way to consult with Edward Sokoine, with a feeling of complete satisfaction about the future course of events. I knew that this time Amin could not recover his position, given his weaknesses within Uganda itself, and his lack of internal strength to withstand the pressures.

My wife, however, did not share my feeling of satisfaction. She knew I planned to go to the front and she was very concerned. She was also sceptical about the possibility of success. I think she saw our chances as rather remote. She felt that perhaps we should spend a little more time looking after ourselves, although she was not against the idea of liberation in itself. By this time, our family had increased with the birth of our second daughter, Patience, in May 1978. I pointed out that if we all concentrated on doing things for ourselves as a family, there would be nobody to do the work that was necessary to liberate the country. So there was a kind of tug-of-war in our family over this issue. Of course, there was the very real fear on my wife's part that I might go and not come back.

PREPARATIONS FOR WAR

As usual, there was much confusion, as the Tanzanians were being manipulated by Ugandan opportunists. All sorts of Ugandan groups sprang up claiming they could overthrow Amin with dramatic actions. Landings at Entebbe Airport, attacks on

Tororo from across Lake Victoria, and so on, were some of the schemes that were floated around. Indeed, some of these schemes were actually attempted, with fatal consequences for the participants. One of the groups drowned in Lake Victoria. For our part, we refused to be associated with such hare-brained schemes. We told everybody concerned that in order to defeat Amin, we had to develop an alternative people's force. Merely pinning our hopes on a military *coup* from within Amin's army, or depending on any other quackery by small groups would simply not do and we would not be a party to it. The wheeling, dealing and lying went on through November.

During that time, I went to Nairobi to meet my contacts from Uganda. I went armed with Nyerere's speech to the CCM officials and started distributing copies of it to Ugandans. The Kenyan Special Branch learnt of my activities and decided to trap me. The man they sent to do it was a Kenyan European by the name of Patrick Shaw. This man had featured in the kidnapping and murder of J.M. Kariuki way back in 1976. I hear he suffered from insomnia and let out his frustrations on any unfortunate victim who crossed his path. He obviously savoured the idea of my becoming his next victim.

While sitting in the Nairobi Hilton Hotel with a friend, I saw a fat white man looking over a newspaper that he was pretending to read. I inquired from my friend who the man was and he told me that it was the infamous Shaw. I told my friend to stay where he was and I asked a waiter to re-charge my cup with more coffee. I spread out my newspaper as if I were reading it and then got up as if going for a short call, but in reality I was leaving the hotel. Shaw had found somebody capable of outwitting him. I turned the corner of the Hilton, and took a taxi to Serena Hotel where I changed taxis and asked the driver to deliver me to the bus park. From there I took a *matatu* to Namanga, on the Tanzanian border, about 100 miles (160 km) south of Nairobi.

Since I was using an alibi, Shaw could not have got me even if he had alerted the Kenya border police. In any case, I was a most respected gentleman at Namanga, both on the Kenyan and Tanzanian sides of the border. I had earned that respect through regularly surrendering to the customs and immigration any Kenyan shillings I was carrying. Thus, on both sides, I was known as 'Mzee Kassim', a long-distance trader of no mean proportions. Shaw, therefore, was hopelessly out of his depth in trying to confront me. Having waited in vain for over an hour for me to return to my coffee and newspaper, Shaw arrested my friend and took him to the police station to question him about the man with whom he had been sitting. After four days of frustration, Shaw released my friend, as he had not been the target in the first place. Back in Dar es Salaam, I waited in my Upanga flat while the poor Tanzanians waded through the confusion created by the Ugandan charlatans.

All this time, Amin's troops were massed on the north bank of the Kagera (see Map 2, page 64), looting and attacking villagers. Amin declared the Kagera Salient annexed and his troops looted the Kagera Sugar Mill and Mishenyi Ranch. The pastoralists of western Uganda believe that it was the cattle of Mishenyi Ranch (known as *empunyu* because of their whitish colour) which put a curse on Amin because of the way they were treated. The cattle were driven on foot all the way to Mbarara, 90 miles (145 km) away, and distributed to Amin's clowns. On 3 November, Amin's men eventually succeeded in blowing up the Kagera River Bridge at Kyaka, having lost several MiGs to Tanzanian anti-aircraft fire in the process. Over the next week the Tanzanians assembled their forces on the south side of the river and on 14 November 1978 they launched a huge barrage of artillery across the Kagera, using BM21s, 122mm howitzers and other smaller guns. Amin's ill-prepared troops, who had not even dug trenches, were either killed or fled back to Mutukula. Within a week the Tanzanians had put a pontoon bridge across the river, re-occupied the Kagera Salient and restored the integrity of their country's borders. As the Tanzanian troops moved through the salient, they found grim evidence of its brief occupation by Amin's thugs in the shape of the decapitated and mutilated bodies of Tanzanian civilians.

Sometime in December, while in my flat waiting for the word that the TPDF was ready to pursue the war onto Ugandan soil, I received a call from Major Butiku, President Nyerere's private secretary. He was telephoning from Bukoba where Nyerere had gone to thank the troops for regaining their country's territory. He told me that President Nyerere had secured a slot for me at the front line, and said he would give me the details when he got back to Dar es Salaam.

When Joseph Butiku came to Dar es Salaam, he briefed me as promised. I was to be attached to Brigadier Silas Mayunga, who was on the left of the front line, that is, in Karagwe, Tanzania, opposite Kikagati in Uganda. Since 1976, I had been working with Captain Issonda from Tanzania's military intelligence. At that time, some our boys were still in Mozambique, so I reassembled them, added some others and moved the group to Morogoro for a brush-up exercise and target prac-tice. This group formed the nucleus of the western front as our contribution in the war against Amin. They became very important because this nucleus remained intact and was expanded. This was in contrast to earlier groups which had always been interfered with by factors beyond our control. Because of our previous expe-riences, I became very protective towards this group and used it according to our wishes. I had trained them myself and was, therefore, in a position to shape their development.

When we left for the front line, we travelled through Arusha, Babati, Singida, Kahama, Biharamulo and eventually on to Bukoba and Karagwe. It was raining and our vehicle kept getting stuck on the way. When we arrived at Karagwe, we met Brigadier (later Major-General) Silas Mayunga at Kayanga, the administrative headquarters of Karagwe. Brigadier Mayunga commanded Brigade 206 of the TPDF and he apportioned us our sector on the front line. We were to be based at Nyamiyaga Primary School, four miles from where the Kagera River forms the boundary between Uganda and Tanzania. After spending two nights in a school near Kayanga, we left for Nyamiyaga through Rwambaizi and Kibaale where there was a Tanzanian company. We passed their position and went on to ours. We reached our position on the front line on 23 December 1978 and set up camp at Nyamiyaga Primary School. Across the border from our position was Kyezimbire Primary School in Isingiro county, Mbarara District. We stayed there training new recruits through January and into February 1979.

On one occasion, I led a fighting patrol across the border into the Rugaaga area. The fact that I led the fighters myself did not escape the notice of the Tanzanian officers, many of whom I had not worked with previously. There were a few who had been captains in 1972 and who were now colonels, and these officers knew something about our background. Sometime after I had returned from our foray into Uganda, I was summoned to Brigadier Mayunga's headquarters at Nyakanyatsi. I must say that I found Mayunga easy to work with and he did not try to obstruct my work, such as the recruitment exercises I was carrying out. He even gave me a Land Rover to help me. He seemed to appreciate Fronasa's potential more than other people did.

Apparently, however, a high-ranking Tanzanian official had visited the front line and issued what would have been a disastrous directive. The directive said that all support should thenceforth go to Obote alone because none of the other Ugandan groups were serious. This shift in policy appears to have been occasioned by the sinking of a boat in Lake Victoria carrying some people led by Major Patrick Kimumwe. They had set off to go and attack Entebbe Airport. This was one of the hare-brained schemes authored by the many opportunists who abounded in Dar es Salaam. The Kimumwe group was anti-Obote and the Tanzanians had reacted to this latest disaster by saying that all support should now go to Obote alone. The purpose of my summons to Nyakanyatsi was for the Tanzanians to ask me what I thought about that decision.

It seems that Mayunga had inquired during that high-level meeting what would happen to Fronasa if all support was now to go to Obote alone. Following Mayunga's intervention, the meeting decided that I should be called and asked my opinion. To hear my reply, apart from Mayunga, were Col. Moses Nnange, Deputy Minister of Defence, and Lt Nyaborogo, political commissar for Brigade 206. I was really surprised that the Tanzanian leadership could have contemplated such a mistake at such a late hour. This shows how difficult it is to solve internal problems by relying on external support – even if that support is coming from brothers.

I shocked the meeting when I replied as follows: 'If you talk of supporting Obote to the exclusion of all other groups, I shall be put in a dilemma as to whom to fight – Amin or the Tanzanians!' I went through the history of Uganda, outlining Obote's historical blunders and treachery between 1962 and 1971. I concluded by saying that only two options could be contemplated: either the Tanzanians should support Obote, while at the same time also supporting other groups, or they should establish a broad-based, united front which would be able to welcome everybody, including Obote. I pointed out that ever since 1971, I had been advocating a broad-based united front and Obote had rejected it all along. If the second option was chosen, then a meeting of Ugandan exiles should be called to decide what form the united front should take.

My strong reaction was obviously registered by the members of the meeting. Colonel Nnange said that he would come to visit our camp at Nyamiyaga. He did indeed come and inspect the Fronasa troops. I had written a paper about my views on the situation and it seems that the Tanzanian government then decided to continue with the policy of supporting all groups. Later they opted for a united front.

THE BEGINNING OF THE END FOR AMIN

From the day we arrived on the front line, we had started recruiting Ugandans who were working as labourers in Tanzania. Because of the bad economic situation in Uganda, many people had migrated from parts of Kigezi and Ankole to seek jobs in Tanzania. So when this opportunity presented itself, we recruited them into our force while we were still in Karagwe. We trained them on crash programmes and by the second week of February we had a force of about 300.

On the eastern front, meanwhile, the Tanzanian army had crossed the Ugandan border from the Kagera Salient on 21 January and captured the border town of Mutukula. Amin's soldiers had fled in disarray. The invasion proper began some three weeks later.

On 11 February, the force under my command crossed into Uganda at Murongo Ferry together with the Tanzanian force which was stationed there. Crossing the Kagera was not easy as there was no bridge and the ferry had been destroyed by Amin's soldiers. There were only two motor boats available. The current of the Kagera river is very strong and trying to cross it in a straight line would have landed us 200 metres downstream where the banks were very steep. We tried to tie a rope to the boat so that we could hold it manually in case it was swept downstream. However, the heavy rope kept on getting stuck in the mud. We decided to launch the boat upstream so that it would come at an oblique angle to the intended landing site on the opposite bank. This technique eventually worked. It is very difficult to understand why Amin's troops did not confront us during our crossing. It would not have been at all easy for us to cross that particular point under hostile fire. As it was, we finished crossing at around 2.00 a.m.

Having crossed with one Tanzanian battalion and one Fronasa company, we lost touch for some time with the Tanzanian company which was supposed to attack Ntundu Hill near Kikagati. A section of my company was detailed to attack the abandoned power station which it was suspected was harbouring the enemy. The power station was duly attacked and there was a great stampede inside. The greater the stampede, the more our people fired into the old power station using RPGs and machine-guns. In the end, the stampeding enemy turned out to be a herd of goats! The area had been deserted for some weeks because of the border tension and the goats had been left abandoned. The following day, we advanced along Kyaka road for some miles and then diverted to the left to Ngarama sub-county. We joined some other forces and all of us advanced towards Mabona in the Oruchinga valley, at mile 20 on the Mbarara-Kabale road, where we planned to form a defensive line.

At that time, Brigade 206 was comprised of about seven battalions – 2KJ (*Kikosi kya Jeshi*), 14KJ, 20KJ, Task Force, Special Force, 79KJ and 25KJ, plus our own Fronasa force. Meanwhile, on the Mutukula side, the 20th Division of the TPDF was advancing from Kabwoba and they established their defensive line at Kabwoko towards Masaka.

Our advance on the Oruchinga valley faced little opposition except for two encounters. Lt Col. Mayunga's 2KJ fought against Amin's battalion from Fort Portal at Ishozi, which is situated on the other side of Ngarama in the direction of the Oruchinga valley. Amin's battalion was nicknamed 'Mountains of the Moon'. Many of the vehicles in the battalion were destroyed although 2KJ, which was mainly a militia battalion, was also partially dispersed. 20KJ under Lt Col. Shimanya, given the task of capturing the crossing point facing mile 20 near Mabona, fell into an ambush and 24 soldiers were killed. Eventually the ambush was overrun and by the end of 11 February the front line was established along the general line of Kitindo, Mabona and Oruchinga.

I set up my headquarters in Ngarama sub-county and intensified recruitment. I led forward patrols several times and on a number of occasions I passed the front line at Mabona and climbed the high Kagarama Hill in order to conduct recon- naissance and carry out some mobilisation. Amin's soldiers were at Gayaza Hill, firing 106mm shells at us. I held public rallies several times at Kagarama, attracting people from the valleys beyond places like Nyakigyera.

For the next two weeks, the situation was uncertain and full of suspense because of our fear that the TPDF might withdraw on account of pressure from within the OAU. The OAU was trying to mediate in the war and Tanzania was demanding that the OAU condemn the invasion of its territory and also support Tanzania's demand for compensation. The OAU, as usual, was vacillating, and for a while we were worried that it might give in to Tanzanian demands and rob us of this chance to get rid of Amin. I was also apprehensive that the Tanzanians might allow Obote's group to come to my sector and cause confusion there. Indeed, at one stage, Edward Rurangaranga was sent by Obote to our sector, precisely for that purpose.

Obote was very worried about the emergence of a non-Nilotic armed group which he knew was my principal aim, in other words to destroy the sectarian monopoly of arms. Obote's scheme, therefore, was to delay the emergence of our non-sectarian force by sending Rurangaranga, Rwakasiisi, Nduhuura and Kabogorwa and others of their ilk, to foment divisions between the Bairu and Bahima people of Ankole by bringing back the old UPC/DP politics. I met Rurangaranga at Ngarama and asked him what his mission was. He said: *Kuhumuriza abantu baitu*, 'To allay the fears of our people'. I told him that I had already been doing that for one month and that, therefore, his belated contribution was unnecessary. I asked him whether he would like to come with me to carry out some reconnaissance as I had been doing for about a month. He said: *Kanoreeba okuguru kwangye okukwabaire,* 'Can't you see that I am crippled?' I told him that in that case we did not need his services. He left, only to return later with his friends Rwakasiisi and others. He went to Nairobi and I heard later that he claimed to have 'left Museveni killing Bairu' in the Mbarara area.

Meanwhile, we intensified our recruitment so that in case the Tanzanians did withdraw, we would be able to stand on our own against Amin's forces. As matters turned out, however, nothing came of the OAU mediation efforts and on 26 February we received orders to advance on Mbarara. On the morning of the 27th, we captured Gayaza Hill and went beyond it up to Masha, 11 miles (18 km) from Mbarara. Again there was little fighting because Amin's soldiers ran away. Our medium artillery, based at a road camp at mile 14, shelled Mbarara the whole of that afternoon. We slept until midnight and then started marching. Altogether, on the march against Mbarara, there were seven Tanzanian battalions (later increased to nine) and our one company. By then, however, we had a further 1000 men training at Ngarama. By the time Amin's regime collapsed, on 11 April, the Fronasa force had grown to 9000.

As our numbers grew, we did not organise our force into the regular battalion sizes used by other armies. Instead, we organised it into columns, each comprising approximately 400 men. Such a column would be armed with very light weapons – AK-47s, machine-guns, RPGs and landmines, and our main mode of transport was walking. Altogether we had 22 columns (guerrilla battalions), named after our fallen fighters: Mwesiga, Rwaheru and so on. Such a force would have been enough to defeat Amin's army by itself. It was just a matter of time.

At midnight on 27 February, we advanced on Mbarara and by morning we had entered the town. We captured it easily because there was no resistance. Amin's soldiers had been intimidated by our weight of fire and the noise of our guns which they thought were very powerful. Again this showed the ignorance of in-capable commanders who were not able to appreciate the strength of our forces and weaponry. There was no military reason why they should have fled so precipi-tately.

The Tanzanian forces were supported by three tanks, some APCs and batteries of BM-21, 122 howitzers, 130mm field guns and 85mm guns. My company was attached to the lead battalion, 25KJ, under Lt Col. Kamanda. We arrived at Nyamitanga around 6.00 a.m. and crouched, in single file, along the road. When it was light, about 35 minutes later, the two tanks fired some shells to see whether there was any enemy willing to fight. There was no answer. We proceeded down-hill and Kamanda and myself were the first to step onto Ngaromwenda Bridge across the River Rwizi. The TPDF battalions fanned across Mbarara, checking the town up to and including the barracks, which they found abandoned.

Once in Mbarara, we established a defensive position around the town with the TPDF's 14KJ Battalion facing Biharwe, 2KJ facing Nyarubanga on the

Kyamugorani side, 25KJ and 79KJ facing Ruharo, and the Special Force facing Rugando. The artillery was positioned at Nyamitanga while our own Ugandan forces remained in reserve. At the same time as we entered Mbarara, the Mutukula forces also entered Masaka. We stayed in Mbarara recruiting and expanding our Fronasa companies. On one occasion, Amin's forces launched a counter-attack against our positions on the Ruharo side. They came in the evening from Itendero, trying to recapture the town, but they were repulsed with quite a number of casualties on their side. There was also a minor counter-attack by some of Amin's forces from the Rubindi area through Rubaya, but it was easily repulsed by 2KJ Battalion facing Nyarubanga.

A more serious attack, however, took place on 21 March. It had been a fine morning and I had planned a rally at Kinoni, Rwampara, in the afternoon of that day. At around 10.00 a.m., a friend of mine named Kahuurwa rode in breathlessly on a bicycle to tell me that he did not think the rally could take place because Amin's people were advancing on the very spot where we had been planning to hold it. I was at Kamukuzi, the old king's palace, when I got this information, while Brigadier Mayunga had moved his headquarters back to Nyamitanga. I drove with Kahuurwa to Nyamitanga to confer with Mayunga about the situation. When I arrived, I found Mayunga a very worried man. I had not realised that the situation was so serious, but Mayunga told me that Amin's people had indeed attacked and, as he was speaking, he had lost contact with his commander in the sector. 'Losing contact' with one's commander is part of the jargon of regular armies with which I was becoming familiar by then. Although I had fought in 1972 and had been with Frelimo previous to that, I did not accumulate much knowledge of the internal culture and parlance of regular armies. I had learnt by now, however, that 'losing contact' simply means a unit has become so disorganised that they can no longer contact the section commander by radio. This is quite an ominous sign during a war and, not surprisingly, I came to loathe those words in subsequent battles. I suggested to Mayunga that, since I knew the area well, I should go and check what was going on. He readily agreed and I alerted three or so Fronasa companies that I was leaving for the battle area.

At Rucheche, on mile 8, I found the whole of 80KJ Battalion, with its commanding officer, Major Mosha, and one tank, in full retreat. I asked them what had happened. Their first words were: *Waharabu wa mezidi* ('The Arabs have become too strong'). Of course, there were no Arabs involved in this particular attack, but, since the Libyans and the Palestinians were known to have supported Amin, especially on the central Mutukula–Kampala axis, to an ordinary soldier everybody opposing us was an Arab. I stopped the soldiers and asked them whether they were going to walk all the way to Dar es Salaam. They answered in the negative. I told them that standing and fighting was better than giving the enemy a chance to disorganise our defence. I pointed out that when you are fighting a war, security lies in actual fighting, not in fleeing. The soldiers rallied and we re-formed them and began returning to mile 12 from where they had withdrawn.

Apparently, the panic had been created by a tank pulling out of the firing line to re-load. The other soldiers had thought it was a signal for withdrawal. It took an hour to reach mile 12, at Rugando *gombolola* headquarters, the original front line. By that time, more and more Fronasa troops were arriving by truck, but we found no enemy in sight. We only found eight bodies of our Tanzanian comrades.

Two battalions had been deployed in a forward position in this sector. On the right of the road, in an area well-covered by banana plantations was deployed Major Kessy's Special Battalion, which had accompanied us from Murongo, while on the left was Major Mosha's 80KJ Battalion. The left-hand side of the road was more open, with the buildings of the sub-county headquarters as the prominent feature. It appears that when Amin's soldiers had attacked 80KJ Battalion, they had not been aware of the Special Battalion in the banana plantations on the right of our sector. Kessy had acted very well. As Amin's group of about 1000-strong was attacking 80KJ, he had advanced and attacked them on their left flank. This threw them completely off balance and they retreated towards Ntungamo with a lot of casualties.

After we had defeated Amin's forces at Rugando, some retreated to Fort Portal and others had established a position at Rubindi, 25 miles (40 km) along the Ibanda road. In the days following the Moshi Conference of 24–6 March, some of our forces advanced through Kinoni, having been divided into two brigades. One retained the designation 206KJ and the other was named Minziro, after a forest on the Uganda-Tanzania border where some fighting had taken place. One of the brigades moved through Kinoni, Ntungamo, Kitagata, Ishaka and on to Fort Portal and Kasese. The other took the Ibanda-Kamwenge route, also heading towards Fort Portal. Meanwhile, the forces on the Masaka side had been advancing as well. Brigade 205 was deployed in Sembabule, moving through Mbirizi, Kabamba, Mubende, and on to Hoima. The aim was to link up with the Task Force Division in Hoima.

Although Amin had an army of 20 000, I never saw him launch a brigade-size attack. He would launch battalion-size attacks in a haphazard manner, simply hoping that somehow the enemy would just go away. The African armies created by the colonialists were adequate as long as they had European officers who did all the thinking and strategic planning. This was true not only in the case of Amin's army, but also other in countries such as Liberia and Rwanda. In this way, the colonialists really did Africa a disservice. I was surprised, for instance, when we were crossing the River Katonga, between Masaka and Kampala, that Amin's people did not find some means of stopping the crossing at that very difficult point. Such a move would not have needed many people. Just as they could not manage the economy, both civilian and military colonial-type agents could not put up an organised fight against us. The reason was their low calibre, poor education, weak character and lack of exposure to real experience.

Chapter 9

THE UGANDA NATIONAL LIBERATION FRONT

[1979–80]

THE SEARCH FOR A POLITICAL FRONT

When I arrived back in Mbarara from the Rugando front on the evening of 21 March, I found a message calling me to report to Dar es Salaam. I did not relish having to leave the war front as this would divert me from some very useful work, but this was an official summons, so I had no option but to go. That very night, I drove to Bukoba, arriving the following morning. I took a plane via Mwanza and reached Dar es Salaam at around seven o'clock the next evening, 22 March. My family were, needless to say, extremely relieved to see me still alive and well.

Soon after my arrival, I had a telephone call from Major Butiku telling me that I was to go and see Dr Nyerere that night. Nyerere told me that a conference had been called, bringing together all the Ugandan factions, but that Obote had become obstructive. The concept of a broad-based conference was not a new one. Since 1971, some of us had taken the line that Obote could not be a uniting factor. We had also pointed out to some of our friends outside Uganda, especially the Tanzanians, that the UPC was not an appropriate vehicle for liberation. We had persistently argued that we needed a more broad-based platform as a launch-pad for the liberation struggle.

Obote's line had always been that the UPC alone was enough to defeat Amin and emancipate the people of Uganda. The implication in that argument was, of course, that Obote himself would be the natural leader of the UPC liberation movement. Our Tanzanian friends vacillated on this point, although some of them seemed to accept our view that a more broad-based movement would more effectively spearhead the struggle for the liberation of Uganda. Others, however, insisted on using the UPC and Obote as the only platform for liberation.

When Amin attacked Tanzania in October 1978, the Tanzanians had risen to the occasion. They mobilised their forces, determined to confront Amin, throw him out of their country and, if possible, follow him into Uganda and punish him. They had, not unreasonably, expected that the Ugandans would wish to do the same. Because of the indecision over the question of the most appropriate vehicle for liberation, however, most of the Ugandans in exile were not of much assistance. Those of us who were capable of doing something useful for the struggle were not given as much help as Obote, in spite of the fact that he was so narrow-minded and so tribally inclined that he could not conceive of a national, de-tribalised, liberation movement.

Obote was unable to come to terms with the idea of a non-northern army because his tenure of power had been based on manipulating that factor. He had based his rule on an Acholi-Langi army with a scattering of other northern peoples. They had monopolised all access to the instruments of force and thus ensured his undemocratic hold on power. There was, therefore, no way he could countenance the idea of a national liberation movement with a national liberation army. Yet the creation of such a movement would be necessary and inevitable if the whole population had to be mobilised. We had been trying to point this out to our Tanzanian friends, but some of them had not believed us. They thought that we were simply prejudiced against Obote.

Nyerere had begun to grow disillusioned with Obote following the performance of one of his groups led by Robert Serumaga. This group made an ill-planned attempt to launch a pre-emptive strike across Lake Victoria in January 1979, reminiscent of the farcical 'airborne attack' on Entebbe in 1972, which never even got off the ground at Kilimanjaro Airport. One of the overloaded boats capsized, drowning all its 82 occupants, while the rest turned back to Tanzania rather than attempt a landing in Ugandan waters. Even then, however, Nyerere had still taken the position that Obote should receive all the support that was to be provided by Tanzania in the fight against Amin. Although our group had all along been offering an alternative to Obote and his intrigues, the Tanzanians had not accepted it easily. It would be unfair to expect them to understand the situation inside Uganda. They had tended to overestimate Obote, whom they regarded as a socialist, a nationalist and a patriot and, therefore, as a positive force in the politics not only of Uganda, but of Africa as a whole. The reality, however, was the opposite. The fact of the matter was that not only was Obote useless as far as the pan-African struggle for liberation was concerned, he was actually a very negative force whose sectarianism further aggravated Uganda's problems.

This debate, however, had been brought to an end in February 1979, as soon as the Tanzanians started making shallow penetrations inside Ugandan territory at the start of the war. Obote's group was put in charge of the Ugandan contingent of the Mutuluka prong of attack and occupied areas such as Kyotera, Kabwoko and Kalisizo. The contingent was led by Tito Okello and Oyite Ojok. In my sector, I immediately started a massive recruitment exercise, taking in every available youth who cared to volunteer. On the Masaka side, however, there was no recruitment because Obote's group did not want to recruit from the 'wrong' tribes who lived in that part of the country. They had an eye to a repeat of the northern tribal domination of the army in the post-liberation period. Even Paulo Muwanga, who at that time was the administrator for Masaka, in spite of being a UPC supporter, was frustrated by the Obote group's obstructiveness and their impeding of recruitment. This behaviour, more than anything else, opened President Nyerere's eyes to Obote's ways and methods and, I think, influenced him in choosing a non-Obote option in his attempts to solve Uganda's problems.

I had been hammering this line of argument for many years, but the Tanzanians had not understood it until they were convinced by their own experience with Obote's group in Masaka. After Masaka, one could see that Nyerere was thoroughly disgusted with Obote and this led him to accept the idea of a broad-based conference. Other people, for example Dan Nabudere, with his group at the University of Dar es Salaam, Bishop Festo Kivengere, who had known Nyerere for a long time, and Idi Simba, who had been director of the East African Development Bank, played a role in crystallising the situation for the Tanzanian president and influencing him towards our position.

Dr Nyerere told me that Obote would not be allowed to attend the conference because his obstructiveness would wreck it. The purpose of calling me from Mbarara, therefore, was to enable me to attend the conference. I had no hesitation in attending, but I had grave misgivings about the methods that had been used to convene it. The following morning I left for Moshi, where the conference was to be held. We were being accommodated at the YMCA hostel where I had stayed in 1974 with my wife and son.

THE MOSHI CONFERENCE 1979

Obote had at first refused to attend the conference and tried to prevent his people from attending it too. When, however, he found that the conference was going to take place anyway, he decided to come after all. But President Nyerere, knowing that Obote would be a divisive factor, stopped him from attending. Instead, he persuaded him to write a letter wishing the conference success:

> I send greetings to all the participants at this momentous conference. I am willing but unable to come and join you. I shall, however, be with you in spirit and have every hope that decisions of the conference will be the beginning of a new Uganda.
>
> The eyes of the world are on the conference. Those eyes are important but the most important eyes are those of Ugandans. Many of the participants have come a long way and even those from nearby, were all propelled by one desire: to find a way for a common effort against terror at home. There is, therefore, a most positive basis for the conference. I trust that the conference will build on that fact to the exclusion of all extraneous consideration.
>
> I wish you success and want to assure you that though absent from the conference, I shall play my part in the implementation of positive conference decisions.

The conference failed to start on 23 March as scheduled. It was delayed by a day because of problems arising from the many Obote delegations attempting to swamp the conference with his supporters. There was 'Lusaka Discussion Group', 'Lusaka' this and 'Lusaka' that, all of them representing Obote. In addition Otema Allimadi and Luwuliza Kirunda were present, comprising the 'official' Obote delegation. Paulo Muwanga, in uniform, accompanied by other 'fighters' in the persons of Rurangaranga, Mugwisa, Rwakasiisi, Nduhuura and Kabogorwa had 'just arrived from the front line'. The quackery in the conference room was verging on the absurd and, as a result, the whole conference was a fraud.

Nevertheless, the Tanzanians needed it, since their army had done most of the fighting. Although the OAU had abandoned its mediation efforts, there were still some diplomatic murmurings about the 'dangerous precedent' that had been set by Tanzania in 'invading' Uganda. Nobody in Africa was making it his business to remember that the people of Uganda had had more than their share of problems inflicted on them by Amin, nor did anybody remember that a regime that cannot defend the sovereignty of its country is not worthy of staying in power.

Immediately we entered the conference hall, I raised the following questions: How had attendance at the conference been decided? Who was supposed to attend and why? How would delegates reach decisions – by vote or by consensus? If there was to be voting, what weight would be given to each vote? Was contribution to the struggle to be used as a yardstick or not? Was previous political significance in the party political days to count as a factor or not?

Unfortunately, these issues were not seriously discussed. The main concern of the delegates was to form a group and present it as the vanguard of the anti-Amin struggle. On the one hand, the Tanzanians were anxious to put together a Ugandan front, other than Obote, whom they now knew was a liability both inside and outside Uganda – a front which would help the Tanzanians show that the fight against Amin was a popular national one, not a foreign-imposed one. On the other hand, our own Ugandan opportunists were already jumping on the bandwagon of the Tanzanian army in order to grab the top jobs for themselves after liberation. There could, therefore, be no serious discussion of the real issues involved. My objections were brushed aside and, in fact, because of the positions I took up, I managed to make myself quite unpopular at Moshi.

Irrespective of their contribution to the struggle or political importance prior to the Amin regime, all groups were given equal weight. Apart from the numerous Obote groups, Fronasa, which by that time had 9000 fighters, was given two delegates. The different Obote 'discussion' groups, in addition to the main Obote delegation led by Otema Allimadi, received two delegates each. The 'Muthaiga Discussion Group', created a few days before the conference, was similarly given two delegates. This group represented people who had been merely living in exile in Nairobi's Muthaiga suburb. I tried to point out the flaws of this arrangement, but the Tanzanian officials on the scene brushed me aside.

By the end of the conference, we had elected Professor Yusufu Lule as chairman of a new, broad-based movement, the Uganda National Liberation Front (UNLF). The concept was good but the mechanisms of bringing it into reality were not. In a liberation struggle there are only two bases for legitimacy: contribution to the liberation struggle – military, political, diplomatic – or evidence of previous or current political support. Our view had been that the principal anti-Amin armed groups, Obote's faction and Fronasa, as well as the old political parties which had taken part in the 1962 elections (their sectarianism notwithstanding) should be the participants in the meeting. If we had used these two criteria, life might then have been easier for the UNLF.

Many people thought that Fronasa simply wanted to use its military capability to monopolise power. Therefore, in their utterances, they demeaned the role played by the Ugandan armed groups in order to diminish their legitimacy. At the same time they extolled the role of the Tanzanians as the only people who were about to liberate Uganda. These were the same people who in a few months' time would be cursing Tanzania for having installed Binaisa and, later, Obote. We opposed all this and, in fact, my position was that I did not see why the Tanzanians should continue to fight all the way up to Kampala. They had formed a spearhead and they had taken revenge for Amin's invasion of their territory – the rest of the work should have been left to Ugandans. This was a point I raised in several fora: it made me very unpopular with the Tanzanians and led to our isolation at the conference. Thus we had a situation whereby the Tanzanians were very friendly with the armchair revolutionaries who were pampering the egos of the TPDF commanders. I thought all of this was very dangerous for our country.

I asked the participants questions such as: 'Who are you? Whom do you represent? What is your legitimacy?' Many of the delegates were very angry with me for asking such questions, so much so that when it came to forming the Military Commission, Paulo Muwanga was elected chairman instead of myself. Even for me to be elected vice-chairman was at the intervention of President Nyerere after the conference. I am very pleased, however, that I was isolated in that group at Moshi, because everything I prophesied turned out to be correct: the demise of UNLF, the fraudulent elections of 1980, the bush war of 1981–6, and the defeat of the UPC by the NRM.

The idea of the UNLF was not a bad one. It was the idea of a broad-based united front that I had worked for since 1971 and which later crystallised into the NRM. But the UNLF was fraudulently constituted and that was its Achilles' heel.

The outcome of the conference was that precisely the elements who had done nothing, or very little, in the struggle against Amin, were favoured. A typical attitude at Moshi was an implied hostility to the freedom-fighters. This hostility emanated chiefly from people who suffered inferiority complexes because of their own lack of contribution to the cause of fighting Amin's criminal regime. Therefore, to some of us, it was not surprising that soon after its formation, the UNLF experienced upheavals in its ranks. The situation that was created was bound to cause problems in the future. At Moshi were sown the seeds for its eventual disintegration.

Nevertheless, Moshi did facilitate the formation of the UNLF, with Professor Yusufu Lule as its head. Lule had been promoted by groups who reasoned that he was an old man who was not politically ambitious. However, that was really quite naive, because as soon as Lule was announced as the head of the UNLF, various forces started vying to use him as a vehicle for gaining access to power and positions of influence. There is, of course, no such thing as a neutral political actor. Very soon, traditionalist and conservative elements in Uganda started claiming him as their man. Therefore, when Kampala fell on 11 April 1979, we did not have a cohesive group at all. Moreover, the people who were advising Lule were not experienced enough to be able to identify areas that could or should have been emphasised for the safety and growth of the movement.

THE UGANDA NATIONAL LIBERATION FRONT

Three organs to run the movement were created at Moshi. They were the National Consultative Council (NCC), which was supposed to be the interim legislature, the National Executive Council (NEC), which was the cabinet, and the Military Commission. Elections or nominations to these bodies were haphazard: there was no formula at all. The basis for nomination to the NCC, which was chaired by Edward Rugumayo, were the *ad hoc* groups which had been formed purely for the purpose of attending the conference. The Military Commission was composed of people who said they possessed fighting capability – which meant Fronasa, Kikoosi Maalum, Save Uganda Movement, and others who had been in the old Uganda Army. Paulo Muwanga was made chairman of the Military Commission and there were four other members: Tito Okello, Zed Maruru, William Omaria and myself.

The functions of these organs were not well thought out; for example, the Military Commission's relationship with a future Ministry of Defence. That need not have been a major problem because the Military Commission could have operated as a defence sub-committee of the NCC, if the people who were making these decisions had been clear-headed. It could, for instance, have dealt with policy and not with administration, but the people who were on the commission were not the kind who could conceive defence policies within a broad national perspective. So the Moshi conference was, if anything, a missed opportunity, and the confused, chaotic situation which resulted from it laid the ground for future problems. There were two very serious flaws in the scenario which were potentially dangerous: firstly, the over-involvement of the Tanzanian troops in actually overthrowing Amin and, secondly, the lack of legitimacy of the groups that gathered at Moshi.

From the start, in 1971, I had been opposed to using non-Ugandan troops to overthrow Amin for the simple reason that the people of Uganda would be deprived of a chance to take their destiny into their own hands and it would leave the political problems of Uganda unresolved. Amin might go, but if the people of Uganda did not take their destiny into their own hands, or did not definitively lay a foundation for resolving their problems, what would be the gain? In 1971,

Somalia and Sudan, under pseudo-leftists Mohammed Siad Barre and Jafaar Nimeiri, had offered troops to overthrow Amin. I had welcomed the idea at the time in the hope of removing that obviously pro-imperialist buffoon in the full employ of the Israelis, the South Africans and the British who were dead set against African liberation movements. However, I was mindful of the opportunity cost, the loss of the chance for the people of Uganda to shape their own future. When, however, the intended ousting of Idi Amin by the Sudanese, Somali and Tanzanian force did not materialise, I moved more and more towards the idea of self-reliance, with material help being the only contribution acceptable from outside.

This notion, of course, had been blown off course by the events of 1972. Now there was a new opportunity which I felt should not be missed. In my view, the Tanzanian army should have had two clear aims in 1978–9: to expel Amin from the Kagera Salient, and to make a shallow penetration into Uganda – perhaps only up to Mbarara and Masaka – in order to erase the indignity of Amin having occupied a part of their territory. That would have enabled the TPDF to vindicate itself in the eyes of the people of Tanzania without embroiling itself in the complicated internal affairs of Uganda. It would also have obviated the diplomatic problems Tanzania faced, and avoided the crippling expense the country underwent. The war for liberation would have taken slightly longer, but it would have yielded better results in the end. It is even possible that the war of 1981–6 would not have been necessary if this path had been taken. Furthermore, an anti-Amin war waged only by Ugandans would have laid a firmer basis for resolving Uganda's political problems. As matters stood, however, the whole process was artificial, dishonest and completely fraudulent.

BACK TO THE FRONT LINE AFTER MOSHI

Eventually, I returned to Mbarara. Our force had been advancing together with the Tanzanians and by the time I arrived, they had moved up to Fort Portal. I was in Mbarara most of the time, organising meetings with civilians. Meanwhile, the main Tanzanian force was converging on Kampala.

Brigade 208 took the left flank from Masaka, moving through Kanoni and Kabulasoke and on to Mpigi. Brigade 201 moved up the centre towards Mpigi, along the Masaka-Kampala road through Lukaya and Buwama, while on the right flank Brigade 207 advanced along the Lake Victoria shoreline. Brigade 201 was temporarily halted at Lukaya by the Palestinian forces which Amin had brought in to support him, but a counter-attack from the left flank by Brigade 208 saved the situation. The plan had been to advance straight on to Kampala, bypassing the Entebbe peninsula, but from the high ground at Mpigi the TPDF commanders could see the coming and going of Libyan aircraft and it was felt that it would be too dangerous to leave the Libyan force, of unknown strength, at their backs while they moved on Kampala. Therefore, Brigade 208, under Brigadier Mwita Marwa, was dispatched to take Entebbe Airport.

After three days of bombardment, Brigade 208 moved in on 7 April and cap-tured Entebbe. Amin, who had been at Entebbe State House when the bombard-ment commenced, fled by helicopter to Jinja at the first signs of attack, swearing vengeance on any of his officers who followed his example. Once the Libyans based at Entebbe realised they could no longer escape by air, they tried to make it to Kampala by road, but they were caught in a TPDF ambush set up by Lt Col. Boma around the hills beyond Kisubi, five miles from Entebbe. In all some 300 Libyans were killed in or around Entebbe and 49 were captured by the TPDF.

Once the airport was captured, the Tanzanians moved in on a barely-defended Kampala, taking it on Wednesday 11 April. President Nyerere had ordered that the route to Jinja was to be left open, to allow any remaining Libyan forces and diplomats in Kampala to escape. He wanted to avoid any more diplomatic entan-glement, given the difficulties in which he was already embroiled. Unfortunately, this also left open an escape route for Amin and his top officials.

We had expected Amin to put up some resistance, because even though Kampala had fallen, it was not the end of the war. After the fall of Kampala I went to the capital, leaving the Fronasa forces on the western front in the charge of Chefe Ali.

THE LULE GOVERNMENT

Looting broke out the moment Kampala fell and had reached epidemic propor-tions by the afternoon of the following day. So it was in an atmosphere of mount-ing chaos that President Lule and the new UNLF government were sworn in in front of Parliament Building on Thursday 12 April.

There had been some jostling for position in the formation of the government, with the Tanzanians suggesting the name of Paulo Muwanga as Minister of Defence. Lule had refused and had taken the defence portfolio himself, but after some haggling with the Tanzanians, it was agreed that I should be the Minister of State for Defence, that is to say, an assistant to Professor Lule. So I was sworn into the UNLF government in this capacity. I had also been appointed vice-chairman of the Military Commission, with Muwanga as chairman. Because of my views on creating a national, non-sectarian army, there had been opposition to my appoint-ment as chairman of the Military Commission, which was supposed to control the new Uganda National Liberation Army (UNLA).

After we had been officially sworn in, we began the task of trying to run Uganda, but it was extremely difficult. Amin and his thugs had wrecked the coun-try, leaving it in a complete mess, economically, socially and politically. Our task was not helped, either, by the many competing forces in the coalition itself, owing allegiance to so many political interests, and nobody had enough authority to assert control over all of them.

The presence of the Tanzanian army also added to an already complicated situation, as each of the various Ugandan groups was trying to use them to enhance sectarian, rather than national, interests. Hence, the situation was chaotic and the country suffered greatly as a result of the ensuing indecision, bickering, rampant smuggling and deteriorating security. To complicate matters, Professor Lule became very apprehensive of the few Ugandans who had participated in the liberation war, in other words Fronasa and Obote's Kikoosi Maalum. I tried to advise him not to distrust these forces because they were, after all, still weak and could not be a decisive factor by themselves. In any case, they had made a contribution to the liberation of the country. Fronasa numbered about 9000 by this time, and Kikoosi Maalum about 1500.

Professor Lule went to the extent of writing an official letter to me, requiring me to disband the Fronasa forces we had just recruited. This was ridiculous because we were still fighting a war against Amin's soldiers in various parts of the country. It was inconceivable that anyone should seek to dissolve a freedom-fighting force even before the job they had set out to do was complete. How could we have justified disbanding this force at such a time, thus rendering it incapable of defending the cause it had fought for? This was, in effect, a way of sabotaging the whole idea of liberation, as if to say to future generations that he who was stupid enough to offer himself for the cause of freedom would only be fit for the dustbin as soon as his peers were in power.

Without a discussion in any forum, Professor Lule came to the conclusion that he needed 'a small, but professional army' of about 7000 officers and men. What professional opinion was he relying on? I, by then, had been promoted to full Minister of Defence, but Lule had not sought my opinion. If he had wanted an initial small force to guard Uganda at that time, it would have been easy enough to consolidate the 9000 Fronasa and 1500 Kikoosi Maalum into one force and then screen them on health grounds, citizenship, and so on, in order to come up with a figure of 7000. At a later date, there could have been another recruitment exercise to bring the numbers up to a full complement of 30 000 officers and men.

Another of Lule's problems was his morbid fear of and ignorance about Obote in particular, and northerners in general. This was reflected in his attitude to the pro-UPC factions in the NCC – Luwuliza Kirunda, Steven Ariko and so on. Much as we were critical of the UPC, one could not exclude them completely. They had to participate in the politics of the day, but according to the new rules of democracy. Professor Lule had an aide in the person of Semei Nyanzi, a highly polished, middle-class Acholi. However, elements around Lule were so myopic that Nyanzi was initially shut off from any information and finally removed from the job altogether. Yet, detribalised Ugandans such as Nyanzi, their other reactionary traits notwithstanding, were the very people who could help in creating the African middle class in Uganda that was and is so important both economically and politically.

Lule was also hampered by his aversion to democracy. The issue which eventually caused his removal was his refusal to submit his appointments to the NCC for vetting. He simply said that, as President, nobody could veto his appointments. In addition, he found it difficult to cultivate a national image, as for example when he failed to discourage Baganda chauvinists who had started calling him *Lule waffe* ('Our Lule'). Trying to help him once when he was speaking at Kayunga, in Mukono District, I told the gathering that they were in danger of 'spoiling our President' by referring to him as *Lule waffe*, whereas he had been elected by a cross-section of Ugandans. However, such friendly warnings simply fell on deaf ears. This fanatical Baganda support occurred in spite of the fact that those same forces had not been great friends of his in his younger days when he had refused to pay unqualified obeisance to the Kabaka. Such chauvinist Baganda attitudes made the UPC very uncomfortable. They thought that the KY and other non-UPC groups would use the interim period to consolidate their power. As we have seen, the constant danger of sectarianism is that different groups are always trying to undermine one another.

There were also struggles within the NCC, centred on the way that body had been created. Because there were so many factions, the NCC had no cohesion. One group in particular were known as the Nabudere-Rugumayo group. They were regarded as leftist and anti-Obote, but their anti-Obote stance had out-weighed their rationality. We had known them in the Uganda-Vietnam Solidarity Committee, and yet, contrary to our advice, they had joined Amin's adminstra-tion. When they eventually fled Uganda, they kept on condemning Tanzania's involvement in the anti-Amin struggle. However, when the Tanzanians put them in charge of organising the Moshi Conference, they tried to use that position to suppress the fighting groups – Fronasa and Kikoosi Maalum (KM). The Nabudere-Rugumayo group had supported socialism and national liberation movements in the past. I think, therefore, that their political problems emanated from the mistake they made in working with Amin, as other groups and individu-als did, without knowing that Amin would turn out to be a murderer. They had resented Obote so much that they believed anybody else would be better and should be supported, regardless of his record or what he stood for. Needless to say, we did not agree with this position.

Given Amin's ignorance and cultural backwardness, there were no grounds to assume that he could have been a positive influence on Uganda's politics. The Nabudere group had thought that they could work with Amin to push the pro-gressive cause forward and that Amin might, in future, bring about multi-party democracy. When, however, it became clear that Amin was a demented murderer and the Nabuderes and Rugumayos had to flee the country, they made the further mistake of trying to apologise for having supported Amin. From this they devel-oped an inferiority complex and perhaps even resentment against those who had opposed Amin from the beginning. This explains their unco-operative behaviour towards Fronasa during the UNLF days. Had their attitude been different, I think a great deal of damage could have been avoided.

Fronasa's relationship with Kikoosi Maalum was also quite problematic. Fronasa had been the principal opponents to KM in Tanzania and were the only armed alternative to them. Yet, since they were also opposed to Amin, we appeared to be on the same side. However, KM knew that with Amin out of the way, we were their real problem. They had a pathological fear of Fronasa, precisely because they recognised our capacity to organise, our clean record, and our superior ideology. Our opposition to sectarianism especially frightened them and it was also a mystery to their arch-reactionary mentality. On one occasion some of Obote's people asked me: 'Since you are not Acholi or Langi, who are the people being killed by Amin, why did you run away from Uganda?' In fact, on the basis of that logic, they went to the Tanzanians and told them that we were Idi Amin's agents because, first of all, we had no personal reasons to oppose Amin since he was not killing 'our people', and secondly, 'our friends', Dani Nabudere, Edward Rugumayo and Wanume Kibedi, were working with Amin. Had it not been for the personal knowledge Dr Nyerere had of some of us, plus his political sophistication, it would have been impossible for our group to continue using Tanzania as a base for our activities.

In spite of all this, our attitude to KM was readiness to co-operate with them – although preferably not to join them, because of their wrong-headed ideology and methods. This dual attitude to KM continued during the UNLF period. We sometimes acted together with them, yet always kept them at arm's length. They continued to exhibit hostility and fear towards us, which we ignored. Later on, during the anti-Obote struggle of 1981–6, we had the same problem with Amin groups such as the Uganda National Rescue Front (UNRF) led by Moses Ali, and other reactionary groups, for example Uganda Freedom Movement (UFM) and Federal Democratic Movement (Fedemo), which were trying to use the Baganda on a sectarian basis. In qualitative terms, there was not much difference between KM, UNRF, UFM or Fedemo. They were all ambitious groups trying to exploit sectarian platforms of one kind or another.

Our opposition to disbanding the fighting forces coincided with the NCC's struggle to assert itself *vis-à-vis* the President. These struggles culminated in the ousting of Lule on 19 June 1979, just 68 days after becoming President. This event was brought about in essence by the undemocratic culture which had developed among Ugandan leaders in that they failed to discuss issues openly. It was an unnecessary development since we could easily have debated whatever issue was at stake and come to some resolution. However, partly because the NCC failed to use democratic fora and partly because of the formation of cliques, what were essentially simple matters could not be resolved amicably. This, therefore, created more fissures in the UNLF.

When it became clear that Professor Lule would have to be removed, some quiet, informal discussions took place among us to try to find a successor. We decided that we should support Godfrey Binaisa, a Muganda, since we knew that the reactionaries on all sides would use tribal arguments to divide the people. Edward Rugumayo, the chairman of the NCC, spearheaded the opposition to Lule, sometimes unjustifiably, by raising in public issues which should have been raised in private. Rugumayo was a Mutooro, from the west of Uganda, and we knew that if Lule was removed and Rugumayo replaced him, the reactionaries on both sides would focus on the tribal issue in order to set the *wananchi* (local people) in the west against the *wananchi* in the central region of the country. In order to avoid this, I was among those who suggested that we choose Binaisa to replace Lule. As it turned out, it was a very unwise choice.

We had thought that we had reached agreement on the choice of Binaisa, but when this was raised at the meeting in the NCC, things did not turn out quite according to plan. One of the problems was that Fronasa only had two seats in the NCC. These were held by Father Christopher Okoth and Eriya Kategaya. I did not attend the meeting because at that time I was not a member of the Council, and Rugumayo, whom I had advised not to put his name forward, nevertheless did so. Thus it became a three-cornered fight between Rugumayo, Binaisa and Paulo Muwanga. On the first round of voting, Rugumayo won by a narrow margin from Binaisa, with Muwanga trailing in third place. The second round was between Rugumayo and Binaisa, and this time Binaisa won. Godfrey Binaisa, therefore, became President and I resumed my job as Minister of Defence.

THE BINAISA GOVERNMENT

At first we thought we could work with Binaisa, but very soon he started 'running off course'. He was more interested in business deals than in managing the affairs of state; and whilst he was a good speaker he was not serious enough about tackling the problems facing the country. State House was, as a result, always full of people looking for business favours. There was also a great deal of indecision over many issues. One example was the killing of some Muslims in Bushenyi District. They were killed by fellow villagers who had been incited by someone whose identity was known. We told Binaisa he should take action against this man but he refused to do anything. He was already calculating that some of the guilty people would be useful allies to him in his future struggles against some of us in the Bushenyi area.

Corruption, suspicion, intrigues and rumour-mongering were rampant and again no work was done in the country. There was no construction of roads, large amounts of coffee were being smuggled out of the country and security was deteriorating. It was during this time that many people were killed, including Dr Obache, Dr Jack Barlow and Kaija Katuramu who was a chartered surveyor. We investigated some of these cases and came near the solution, but each time someone would intervene to obstruct the investigation, and Binaisa refused to do anything about it. There was a suspicion that some of these killings were politically motivated, by people who wanted the UNLF to fail. However, neither Lule nor Binaisa gave us a free hand to deal with the insecurity, as they, too, were suspicious of our intentions and influence. They thought that if we solved these problems, we would gain more popularity and their own position would be undermined.

The law and order situation was getting out of control at this time. When some of us pointed out these problems, our opponents waged a campaign to the effect that Museveni wanted to build his own army. They were referring to the young boys we had recruited during the struggle against Amin. These boys had now become a problem for some people, instead of the asset they had been while there was fighting to be done.

A new army, integrating Fronasa and Kikoosi Maalum, was supposed to have been built, but the recruits for integration were not passed out after their training courses. The regular army was supposed to be re-formed as Amin's men retreated north, but there were logistical difficulties. Of the 9000 fighters we had recruited, only about 4000 were eventually integrated into the UNLA and trained at Kabamba, Mubende, Nakasongola and Masindi, because Oyite Ojok and his group were worried about an army which was not tribally biased in their favour. Ojok manipulated the Tanzanians, who still did not understand our situation very well, and they interfered with the smooth building of a new army on national lines. For instance, some of the young boys were disqualified on the grounds that they were Banyarwanda. They were put in camps and given no food so that they would desert the army. Later on, Ojok started recruiting illegal militias from the north of the country, as had been done in the 1960s.

In November 1979, Binaisa announced over the radio that he had removed me from the Ministry of Defence and transferred me to the Ministry of Regional Co-operation. This was an attempt to remove the freedom-fighters from the core of the government. We decided to challenge this decision in the NCC, which itself was full of people who had made no contribution to the liberation struggle. It was a tough fight for Binaisa and although he eventually managed to get a majority to support him, it was a warning to him that he would be inviting trouble if he did not respect people who had made sacrifices for freedom. I was, therefore, transferred to the Ministry of Regional Co-operation, although I remained vice-chairman of the Military Commission.

My removal from the Ministry of Defence was engineered by Obote's group using Binaisa, Paulo Muwanga and Oyite Ojok, although Obote himself did not return to Uganda until May 1980. This was part of their preparation to stage a *coup d'état.* They knew that as long as I was in charge of defence, it would be very difficult for them to stage such a *coup.* My removal would give them the freedom to use the army as a truly UPC tool. Their plan was to capture power eventually using the smoke-screen of rigged elections. They calculated (wrongly) that if I was out of the Ministry of Defence, I would not be able to organise anything.

There was very little for me to do in the Ministry of Regional Co-operation and the only significant thing I did while there – apart from starting to write this book – was to challenge the 'Umbridge formula'. Professor Umbridge was a Swiss who had been hired to devise a formula for dividing up the assets of the East African Community after the organisation had broken up in 1977. His formula was not a fair one because it laid down more or less that those who had more assets should

PLATE 1

1.1 The author as a student at Dar es Salaam University, Tanzania, in the late 1960s

1.2 Yoweri and Janet Museveni in Tanzania, 1973, soon after their marriage

1.4 Yoweri Kaguta Museveni with his parents, Amos Kaguta and Esteeri Kokundeka, in 1989

1.3 Yoweri and Janet Museveni with their first two children, Natasha and Muhoozi, in Tanzania, 1977

1.5 Major-General Salim Saleh (Caleb Akwandwanaho) in 1996

PLATE 2

2.1   The cast of Shakespeare's *Julius Caesar*, Ntare Senior Secondary School, 1964. The author is second from the right in the front row

2.2   The Museveni family at Kampala State House, April 1994

PLATE 3

3.1   Eriya Tukahirwa Kategaya in 1996

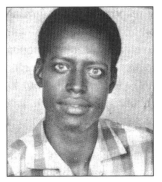

3.2   Mwesigwa Black
(Photo: courtesy J. Tumusiime)

3.3   Martin Mwesiga
(Photo: Dr Nassan Tandekwire)

3.4   The author in the early 1980s, as
chairman of the NRA High Command,
during the war in the Luwero Triangle

3.5   With Salim Saleh (to the right of the
picture) in 1984   (Photo: William Pike)

PLATE 4

With senior army officers at State House, Entebbe, 1987, including from left to right (front row) Tadeo Kanyankore, Elly Tumwine, Yoweri Museveni, Fred Rwigyema, David Tinyefuza; (second row) Proscovia Nalweyiso, Serwanga Lwanga, Pecos Kutesa, Joram Mugume, Stanley Muhangi, Chefe Ali, Patrick Lumumba, Julius Chihandae, Ivan Koreta; Anthony Kyakabale (wearing glasses, behind Proscovia Nalweyiso); John Mugume (wearing a beret, directly behind Elly Tumwine, three rows back); Fred Mugisha (between Chefe Ali and Patrick Lumumba); Sande Mukulu (wearing glasses, directly behind Fred Rwigyema); and Benon Tumukunde (end of fifth row on the right)

PLATE 5

5.1   Briefing diplomats and journalists outside Lubiri Barracks in Kampala, in 1986, after proclaiming a new government   (Photo: Popperfoto)

5.2   Addressing the Special Commemorative meeting of the General Assembly during the celebrations to mark the fiftieth anniversary of the United Nations in New York, 23 October 1995   (Photo: UN/DPI Photo/G. Kirch)

PLATE 6

6.1   From left: Yoweri Museveni, President Daniel arap Moi of Kenya and President Benjamin Mkapa of Tanzania, inaugurating the East African Co-operation Secretariat in Arusha, Tanzania, in March 1996

6.2   1996: the President looking after his cattle   (Photo: Peter Chappell)

PLATE 7

7.1 President Museveni travels extensively all over Uganda teaching people how to raise their household incomes (Photo: Elias Mwanje)

7.2 Casting his vote, Nshwere, on presidential election day, 9 May 1996
(Photo: Popperfoto)

PLATE 8

Being sworn in as the first directly elected President of Uganda, 12 May 1996

receive more. This meant that Uganda would end up getting much less than either Kenya or Tanzania, although in paying back loans, the three countries would divide the debt equally. I challenged this formula at a meeting in Arusha in January 1980, and I understand that it was made more equitable later, after I had left the Ministry.

The fact that Binaisa fell for the UPC's tricks must single him out for condemnation, because he, too, contributed to the Obote-engineered plots and intrigues. It had now become a matter of one intriguer using another: Obote's people believed they were using Binaisa to smooth their way to power, and he thought he was using them to consolidate his hold on it by eliminating people he saw as political or military heavyweights. Watching from the Ministry of Regional Co-operation, I knew that this could not last. Within a very short time there was conflict between Binaisa, Paulo Muwanga and Oyite Ojok. In February 1980, Binaisa tried to neutralise Paulo Muwanga by sending him to Geneva as Ambassador. Muwanga challenged this in the NCC, and after a debate, the President was forced to back down.

THE DEMISE OF THE UNLF

By March 1980, Obote was talking about returning to Uganda to contest elections under the banner of the UPC. Binaisa tried to counter this notion by announcing that elections would be held towards the end of the year, but only under the umbrella of the UNLF. No political parties would be allowed. This was ostensibly part of Binaisa's non-partisan image, but in practice he was trying to manoeuvre for himself. By May it was clear that Obote's planned return was imminent. Ever persistent in his intrigues, Binaisa tried to dismiss Oyite Ojok as Army Chief of Staff, which prompted the Obote clique, headed by Muwanga and Ojok, to decide that the time was ripe to get rid of Binaisa. Muwanga issued a proclamation declaring that the Military Commission, of which he was chairman, had taken over the government of the country with the backing of the army.

I was out of the country in Arusha at the time of the Muwanga/Ojok *coup*, but we had discussed the removal of Binaisa, even with the Ojoks. I, for one, had no objection, because he was a disturbing influence in whatever was planned. I supported his removal because then we would be able to confront Obote without a third force confusing matters. Binaisa had proved only a hindrance to our freedom of action. He was not a neutral force, yet he was perceived as such. He was effectively doing the work of the UPC by stopping us from organising in the country.

Two clear forces now emerged on the Military Commission. Numerically, we were in a minority on the Commission because I was the only active anti-Obote member. Paulo Muwanga, Oyite Ojok and William Omaria were pro-Obote. The other two, Tito Okello and Col. Zed Maruru, while not necessarily pro-Obote, were not actively against him either. So I was left alone to hold the line against Obote.

There were two possibilities. One was that the UPC would realise that they could not get away with their schemes, and would, therefore, settle down and negotiate. The other was that they would carry on with their manoeuvres and we would have to fight them. In either case, we needed a free hand and for the country to be aware that there were two, not three, forces competing for the control of the country. Therefore, when Muwanga and Ojok took power, the situation was very clear – more or less as it had been under Amin's regime.

The first casualty arising from the removal of Binaisa had been the UNLF itself. Although this umbrella group was full of intrigues and manipulations, engineered mainly by Rugumayo and Nabudere, the UNLF had, nevertheless, been a useful instrument. As a concept, it could have been improved upon and taken further. Therefore, its destruction in the process of removing Binaisa, and the consequent resurrection of the old political parties, was an enormous blunder. Obote returned to Uganda on 27 May 1980. He immediately started to reactivate the UPC and Muwanga announced that party political elections would be held that December. It was from that point that some of us knew that we would eventually have to resort to arms yet again to fight the system, and from then on, we decided to make our position very clear.

The country did not have the infrastructure to mount a viable election. There were no roads worth the name, and there were no vehicles to carry out a proper registration exercise. In view of this, some of us thought that any election should be postponed. When we put forward that suggestion, our opponents said: 'You see! These people are afraid of an election. They know that they have no support. That is why they don't want an election.' There was a lot of irresponsible jockeying for partisan advantage which was eventually responsible for the debacle of the 1980 election.

The demise of the UNLF had been caused by the greed and intrigues of UPC and DP leaders. Opportunistically and unrealistically, each of the two factions had thought that somehow they would gain the upper hand, although that would mean dividing the country again along sectarian lines. We who had belonged to Fronasa did not see how the political parties could have brought peace in Uganda. They had been sectarian right from their very foundation. The UPC had been used by the Protestant elite to consolidate the dominant position which they had attained by collaborating with the colonialists. Among their other machinations, the DP, on the other hand, represented the Catholic elite trying to gain advantage over the Protestants. Neither of these two groups thought of the welfare of the country as the motivating force behind politics: they were simply out to manipulate the population.

Having been in power for the period after independence, the UPC clique had had ample opportunity to alienate the masses. The DP, on the other hand, had not had that chance, so it was to them that the people turned in desperation after the dissolution of the UNLF. Even people who had not been DP supporters before, decided to join the party in order to present a front against the hated

Obote. We, on our part, knew that it was impossible for the DP, because of the ideological limitations of its leadership, to have won power and maintained it. So it was clear that two scenarios were emerging. One was that the UPC would rig the elections and claim victory. They would be in a position to sustain that claim with the support of the armed groups under their influence. The other possibility was that the DP, reinforced by the many people who had been disenchanted with the UPC over the years, could win the elections, but they would have to contend with the real possibility of a military *coup*.

THE UGANDA PATRIOTIC MOVEMENT

Any sane person who was neither greedy for power, nor politically and ideologically myopic, should have seen that the only viable option for Uganda at that time was a broad-based government in which all these factions could have attempted to work together. It would then have been easier to contain the adventurers in the various opportunistic groups. We, who were advocating unity, were placed in a dilemma because, given their past history, we could not possibly have joined either the UPC or the DP.

We had two alternatives. One was to stay out of the elections altogether and consolidate our presence in the armed forces. We could bide our time, knowing full well that the politicians would fail, and when our position was strong enough, we could use our military strength to get rid of the whole lot of them. The second option, as some of our people argued, was that we should present a third choice for the population. Personally, I was in favour of keeping out of the factional fights altogether because I did not want to identify myself in any way with any of the parties. My own support had been for the UNLF, and since it had now disintegrated, I wanted to keep out of politics and stay in the army, waiting for the politicians to fail, as they were bound to do.

Some of my colleagues, however, argued very strongly in favour of a third party. At one point I told them that they should go ahead without me, but they argued that the new party would not become viable if I was not involved, so I went along with my colleagues although I was not fully convinced. Following intense pressure from Bidandi-Ssali and Kategaya, I agreed to associate myself with the Uganda Patriotic Movement (UPM). My reluctance was prompted by my aversion to working for any divisive groups, even if it was not the expressed intention of any one of them. In spite of our refusal to join the DP, we tried very hard to unite all the other parties, apart from the UPC. We had hoped to unite, under one umbrella, the UPM with the DP and all those who had not declared any partisan loyalty, so that the UPC would be isolated. This plan did not work, however, because the DP leaders were unrealistically hoping that, by some miracle, they would be allowed to take power. They seemed to be living in a kind of dream-world.

Those involved in the formation of the UPM included Jaberi Bidandi-Ssali, Chango Machyo, Joshua Mugyenyi, Father Okoth, Jeremiah Opira, Erisa

Kironde, Rhoda Kalema and Sam and Gertrude Njuba. Others wanted to join but did not do so because they did not win high enough positions in the party or they realised that since the UPM was a new party, they would face an uphill struggle in getting elected. It was not easy for many of them to swim against the current and stick to principles. It was easier to swim with the current, regardless of the terminal point of the river.

So we formed the Uganda Patriotic Movement in spite of knowing that it would have a poor chance at the elections since issues were already polarised along sectarian lines. Moreover, as election day was set for 10 December 1980, we did not have much time to make adequate preparations. However, the argument in favour of our new party was that the third option we had presented to the country would be a useful one later on. We enjoyed quite a lot of support, but people said to us: 'Although we like your party, it is too new to defeat Obote on its own. We shall be splitting votes if we vote for you, so we shall concentrate our votes on the DP.' My argument remained that the political problems the country faced could not be answered merely by the exercise of holding an election. The general theme of the new party was to emphasise the need for the unity of the Ugandan people. We did not see why a DP Catholic should be against a UPC Protestant just because they happened to belong to different religions.

THE RIGGED ELECTIONS OF DECEMBER 1980

As we had predicted, the elections were rigged. During the campaigning I had taken the chance to warn the UPC that they should be prepared to face the consequences of a rigged poll.

The elections were contested by four parties: the DP, UPC, UPM and CP. The DP had the majority of popular support in the areas of west, central and eastern Uganda and Arua. The Ugandan people had hoped to defeat Obote through the ballot box and formed a great anti-Obote coalition involving the original members of the DP, mostly Catholics, those who had belonged to Kabaka Yekka, those who had deserted the UPC, and those who had no political affiliation. All these various factions chose the DP as the easiest political defence against the threat of Obote's return to power. Because the DP had never held power, however, it was an unknown quantity and could not act as a broad home for a more varied membership. Instead of acting as a resistance movement against Obote, factions soon surfaced within the DP. Frightened by the new members, the old Catholic originals started talking of themselves as the only legitimate members of the party, *banasangwaawo*, and referring to the newcomers as upstarts.

The party leadership, apart from relying too much on Catholic support, was also quite inept in its use of political tactics. Having belonged to the DP myself in the 1960s, I had quite a number of friends who wanted me to rejoin the DP. I did not agree to this, however, because I thought that uniting Ugandans was more important than electoral success. In this context, joining the old sectarian parties would have been the wrong move. Following the collapse of the UNLF under UPC and DP pressure, I believed that the correct thing to do in 1980 was to abstain from both those parties.

The UPC tried to pose as the major military force of the liberation struggle, having illegally recruited tribal militias from Acholi. They devoted much effort to confusing the Tanzanian officers who were based in Uganda, thinking that Tanzania's support for them would decide all. They even made it impossible for me to get an appointment to see Dr Nyerere, in spite of all the close contacts I had had before. Muwanga's people would bribe the Tanzanian officers in Uganda, who would pass on false information to Nyerere. The Tanzanian President would then act according to the information he was given.

Muwanga's government refused to amend the electoral law, hoping to use its loopholes to cheat through double voting, switching ballot boxes, false counting, gerrymandering constituencies, hooliganism and so on. My own constituency in Nyabushozi was gerrymandered. Taking advantage of the fact that voting was likely to be on a religious basis, the sub-counties of Nyakashashara, Sanga and Kashongi were removed from Nyabushozi and made part of another constituency. These sub-counties were mainly Protestant, cattle-keeping areas, and they were exchanged for Ibanda county, which is occupied by Catholics. Both the UPC and DP were involved in these practices in my area as both parties had an interest in making it difficult for me to win. By the time the elections were held, it was clear that whatever the outcome, there could be no satisfactory result which would benefit the country. All the UPC wanted was the facade of an election in order to legitimise the *coup* they were to carry out.

It was tragic to see incapable reactionaries taking our country towards civil conflict while thinking they were being very smart. The UPC declared that they would take power whether people voted for them or not. The moment we came to the conclusion that the old political groups had not learnt any lesson from our past history, we decided to give them enough time to make fools of themselves and then we would discipline them from our own base. In effect, we were saying: 'OK. Let this farce run its course. Then we shall play our own music, where there is no cheating, where there is only conviction. Manoeuvres are all very good for the air-conditioned room, but when it comes to mosquitoes, manoeuvres don't work very well.' If we had not allowed the farce to run its course, we would have been branded as troublemakers.

One complicating factor was the presence of Tanzanian forces. We did not want to fight the Tanzanians – unless of course we had to, as in the end we did. But the UPC were using our reluctance to fight the Tanzanians, to push through their schemes. Without the Tanzanian presence, the UPC would not have been able to carry on their games.

The UPC had always been composed of shallow politicians who thought that intrigue was the art of politics – the 'dirty game', of which Obote was supposed to be the 'master tactician', where tactics meant intrigue and double-talk. Obote, for instance, gave the equally shallow and opportunistic Kabaka Yekka grouping the promise that they would be allowed to keep Buganda as their own, with the freedom to exploit the peasants, denying them a voice. There would be no direct elections in Buganda, unlike in other parts of the country. Buganda would have its own High Court and its own police. There were to be Baganda 'ministers' at Mengo, and so on. These arrangements held echoes of the intrigues and double-talk of 1962–6.

Obote wanted power at any price. He thought it was a small matter to promise the reactionary forces in Buganda all they wanted and, when the Tanzanians had departed, turn against the agreement, relying on the army which, thanks to Ojok, was again dominated by people from his area. Yet again, the unprincipled alliance between the UPC and KY proved tragic for our country and was a testimony to the UPC's treachery, political incompetence and ideological bankruptcy.

This, then, was the configuration of the political forces in Uganda immediately following the overthrow of Amin. If the fight had been left to Ugandans alone, without the Tanzanian presence, it would not have been possible for the UPC to split the UNLF. But now, with the elections rigged, as we had predicted, we had to start preparing to fulfil our pledge to go to the bush and fight the injustices that had been inflicted upon our country.

Chapter 10

FIGHTING OBOTE (1)
[1981]

PLANNING FOR THE STRUGGLE

It seems that neither the UPC nor the Tanzanians believed that we would actually go to the bush and fight. They thought that the presence of Tanzanian forces, and the fact that they could easily be reinforced from Tanzania, would be sufficient to deter us. We would never dare challenge 11 000 Tanzanian soldiers stationed in Uganda. What a miscalculation they made! We knew that we were capable of challenging and defeating them as long as they took an unjust stance against the people of Uganda. As for the UPC leaders, they spent their time drinking in Nile Hotel. They did not have time to reflect on the consequences of their treacherous actions and they must have thought that our threat to go to the bush was an idle one. I must say that I was quite surprised at the foolhardiness of the UPC leaders, because we gave them clear warning. In spite of this, they went ahead with their treachery, and so we decided to implement our plan to take up arms again.

We did not go to the bush immediately because there was the possibility of getting a consignment of arms from outside the country to start us off. The arms did not, however, materialise. We had earlier reconnoitred some areas from which to launch the struggle, in particular the armouries in Uganda to find one which we could raid in order to capture enough arms to start the war. This was not easy because the tribal militia which the UPC had poured into the uniform of the UNLA kept their guns in their houses. There were, therefore, not many sizeable caches of arms around. Only the military training schools – Kabamba, Masindi, Nakasongola and Mubende – had significant quantities of rifles stored in armouries. We decided to select one of them, intensify our reconnaissance on it and then launch our attack.

Since we had 9000 men under arms by the middle of 1979, it may seem puzzling that we had no arms at all by the end of 1980. This was a direct result of a decision which I had taken in September 1979 to integrate all the armed groups and have their numbers documented – a decision taken on a point of principle.

121

The four training centres mentioned above were selected for retraining our fighters. At that stage, some of the Fronasa fighters such as Sam Katabarwa, Sam Magara and Kahinda Otafiire came to me and suggested that we should hide some guns so that if the UPC were to play tricks on us, we could fall back on those arms to continue the struggle. Much to their disappointment, I rejected this advice and told them to hand in every gun.

I had two reasons for this: a moral one and a tactical one. The moral reason was that as leaders in the UNLF, which was still alive at that stage, we could not cheat ourselves. A leader must do in private what he states in public. Two-faced leadership is abhorrent to me. The tactical reason was that if the cache of arms was discovered, Fronasa would be discredited in the eyes of Ugandans who would regard us as a group with a hidden agenda. Moreover, I knew that with a just cause and a determined and capable leadership, we could always acquire arms from somewhere if it became necessary to resort to them again. Some of my comrades were unhappy with this decision, but I was not prepared to compromise. I knew that to act otherwise would be a strategic mistake, because not to be trusted is the greatest strategic handicap for any political group. As a consequence of this decision, we did not have any arms apart from the 30 or so rifles which my bodyguards carried quite openly. The struggle was, therefore, held up by two factors: the anticipation of an arms consignment from outside the country and selecting a suitable target to attack within Uganda so as to get the arms that way.

We had quite some influence among the young army which had been formed after the collapse of Idi Amin. However, since we had no administrative control over it, whatever support we had was scattered all over the country. Our young men had been deliberately deployed in very remote areas – for example Karamoja and north-eastern Uganda – and it was very difficult to contact them. We therefore had to adopt a strategy that would allow us to marshal our forces slowly, using people from the old army (the UNLA), and the civilian population, at the same time as the enemy was being weakened. In other words, we had to opt for a protracted people's war. This type of strategy was not easily understood by some of our colleagues. Some wanted a quick solution and were not patient enough to understand the thinking behind a protracted people's struggle. They preferred to contemplate a *coup* or a number of assassinations.

A *coup* was not possible because, apart from the difficulties it entailed operationally, there was a force of Tanzanians 11 000 strong, of which a sizeable contingent was present in the areas of Kampala, Entebbe and Masaka. As for their second option, we regarded assassinations as cowardly and criminal acts which would have had no value in solving the fundamental problems the country faced. Such acts are indulged in by people who have no long-term view of their problems. These days people think it is fashionable to create armies and fight governments, but in order to create a liberation army, you must have a justified and popular cause, although that condition is not enough on its own. You must also be very skilled at organising and deploying the forces at your disposal. Above all, you must be able to suit necessary action to appropriate timing. A liberation movement, by its nature, is precarious because it does not have the logistical means of armies supported by the state. Any mistake along the line can cause a major defeat for the whole venture, or cause a setback which could take years to redress.

Having decided to launch a protracted people's struggle, I started organising it with the few young comrades whom I had recruited in the 1979 war. Prominent among them were Sam Magara, Ahmed Seguya, Fred Rubereza, Sam Katabarwa, Elly Tumwine, Salim Saleh and other young men who had become junior officers in the UNLA. We worked underground trying to get enough arms to start the war. After the elections I travelled frequently between Kampala and my home village in Nyabushozi county to ensure that the UPC did not discover my intentions. In order to put the UPC off my track, I even started building a house there and also began negotiations to buy land at Kanoni, in Ibanda county. As I had hoped, word went back to the UPC that I was busy looking for a way to support myself financially.

Earlier on, just before the elections, the UPC had gone to the extent of arresting me, my wife and son and detaining us for about five hours at a roadblock at Kireka, near Kampala. They kicked us and made us squat on the ground and I think they meant to kill us. This was when I was vice-chairman of the Military Commission, in effect the Vice-President of the country, which shows the primitive nature of the people who were running Uganda's state affairs at that time. If one does not agree with someone, how does it solve the problem to hold him at a roadblock? On that occasion, some of my comrades used force and rescued us.

After the elections, the situation became much worse. People who had voted for other parties were harassed and intimidated by the UPC, and some were even killed. Therefore, as we were making our preparations to go underground, the justification for our cause was becoming more and more evident. The main practical question at that time was: which military barracks should we attack in order to get enough arms to start us off? This was not at all an easy matter because the number of people we had quietly gathered together was still very small. Any large mobilisation exercise would have been easily detected. In fact, several leakages of our plans did occur and this greatly excited the UPC; but the government was also weak and they could not easily move against us without involving the Tanzanians.

The Tanzanians, for their part, were hesitant to fight us because they knew that we were a serious force of dedicated revolutionaries and this presented them with a dilemma. They would have preferred it if we had agreed to work with the UPC because that would have simplified their role in Uganda, but we could not, under any circumstances, work with the UPC. We knew that would have meant political death for our cause, the UPC having so discredited itself during the whole time it had been in power. There was thus mutual disappointment between us and the Tanzanians. For our part, we blamed them for having allowed unprincipled factions to divide the broad-based UNLF, and for theirs, they blamed us for refusing

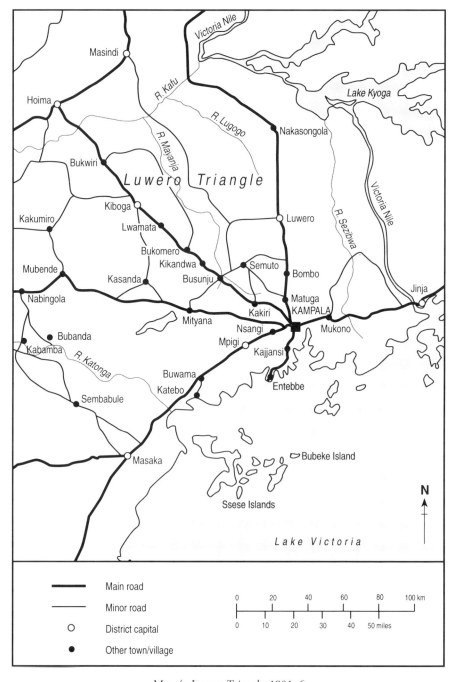

Map 4 *Luwero Triangle, 1981–6*

to work with the UPC. Nevertheless, there was some residual respect left between us and they were reluctant to be used by the UPC to fight us directly.

The problem of identifying a barracks which had enough arms in its store exercised our minds for a while, until we came up with two targets. One was Masindi Barracks, where there was a training wing, which meant that there would be some guns in the stores. Attacking it would not be easy, however, because the armoury was deep inside the barracks, about 1500 metres from the entry point. Since we only had a small group, a dash from the gate up to the armoury would not have been easy, especially as the barracks was very big. The other target was Kabamba, which had a store nearer the quarter-guard.

After much debate, we decided to attack Kabamba. The decision was based on two factors. Firstly, we had some people within Kabamba barracks who were collaborators of ours – the late Sergeant Patrick Kato and the present Brigadier Tadeo Kanyankore, and a number of other boys who had been recruited by Fronasa. Secondly, the armoury was near the quarter-guard and thus easily accessible. However, Kabamba was guarded by several companies of Tanzanian soldiers and it had about 1400 Ugandan trainees. Potentially, this was a sizeable force which could oppose us if we made a mistake. The secret of success lay in surprise. We aimed to gain access to the guns quickly and remove them, relying on the element of surprise to throw the entire garrison off balance. We had to bear in mind that other forces could be quickly summoned from the barracks at Mubende, which is quite near Kabamba.

THE WAR COMMENCES: KABAMBA I, 6 FEBRUARY 1981

The day chosen for the attack which would launch our campaign was Friday 6 February 1981. Our plan was to obtain a vehicle, drive quickly and secretly from Kampala, arrive near our target in the early hours of the morning, and take the barracks by surprise shortly after dawn. The day before our planned attack, about 30 volunteers assembled in Matthew Rukikaire's house in Makindye, a suburb of Kampala, and stayed in hiding there all day. Eventually the number grew to 34, but only 27 of us were armed. Meanwhile, Andrew Lutaya, now a lieutenant-colonel, obtained a lorry covered with a tarpaulin. He had managed to secure it from a *mwananchi* (local person) who did not suspect our purpose. At around 5.30 p.m., the main group left Kampala in the lorry. I stayed behind finalising other arrangements and left later the same evening, travelling by pick-up with Sam Magara.

There was no incident on our journey until we had just passed Katigondo, about 12 miles (19 km) from Masaka on the Nyendo-Sembabule Road, where we punctured a tyre. It was then that we discovered that the driver of our pick-up, Charles Tusiime, now a major in the army, had not brought a spare tyre. We got out and tried to get some villagers to help us but none would do so because there were a lot of car thefts in the area at the time. They thought we were car thieves.

I could not get a taxi where we had stopped, so I decided to walk the 12 miles (19 km) to Nyendo, near Masaka, leaving Magara and the driver trying to repair the tyre. The problem was how to link up with the main group, which had already gone far ahead. We had told them to stop after the junction of Rumegyere on the Masaka-Sembabule-Mubende road. I walked to Masaka through Katigondo and arrived at Nyendo around midnight.

I manufactured a story that I was going to Sembabule to attend a wedding. When the taxi drivers refused to help me, I asked one of them to drive me to the house of one of my acquaintants, Nathan Ruyondo, father of one of our commanders, Colonel Patrick Lumumba, who died in 1991. I arrived at his house and told him the Sembabule wedding story, adding that my car had broken down. I asked if I could borrow his Peugeot 304 car, which I told him I would bring back the following morning. I had hoped to use it to link up with the main group and return it with our driver the next morning. He believed my story and gave me the car.

It was about 2.00 a.m. when I got back to where Magara and the driver were still stuck with our pick-up. I decided we must leave the pick-up, so they joined me in the Peugeot and we headed for Kabamba. We managed to link up with the lorry after the junction of the Rwemiyaga-Sembabule and Sembabule-Kabamba roads, and found our comrades there wondering what to do. Since Magara and I were the ones in charge of the operation, they would have been in trouble if we had failed to turn up. The idea of sending back Mr Ruyondo's vehicle had to be abandoned because a second vehicle was an essential part of the operation. Now that the pick-up was not available, we had to use the Peugeot.

The plan was that the lorry would lead up to the barracks' quarter-guard, with the small car following behind. One of us would engage the quarter-guard staff in conversation, while the small vehicle would overshoot us and dash for the armoury. The few occupants of the car would seize the armoury and the rest would follow to reinforce them. When we arrived near Makolo, we stopped to wait for daybreak. We knew that the guards would be vigilant at night but that they would relax somewhat in the morning. The time when the trainees left the barracks and went for exercises would be the right moment for us to attack. Therefore, we decided to attack between 8.15 and 8.30 a.m.

We arrived at the quarter-guard, as planned, with the small car following the lorry. The front-seat passenger in the lorry, Elly Tumwine, started talking with the people at the quarter-guard, telling them that he had brought provisions from general headquarters. The small vehicle dashed past the lorry, as planned, but then the plan began to go wrong. When the soldier at the quarter-guard saw the Peugeot speeding past, he panicked and rushed to get his gun. Tumwine fired at him and the sound of the pistol alerted the one Tanzanian soldier who was inside the armoury. Tumwine should have struggled physically with the man instead of firing at him and that would have given us a few minutes to reach and get control of the armoury, which is about 100 metres from the quarter-guard.

The Tanzanian soldier got hold of some machine-guns and took position to fire at anyone trying to enter. Since the armoury was underground and made of concrete, by the time our people arrived, he was already entrenched in his position. We did not have enough weapons to dislodge him because we had no RPGs (rocket-propelled grenades) or bombs. We had only one anti-tank rifle grenade and when we had fired it, that was the end.

Although we could not get inside the armoury, we gained control of the communications rooms and the motor transport section. The trainees fled because they had no ammunition in their guns. Apart from the armoury, therefore, the barracks was effectively under our control. Since the armoury had been our objective, however, I decided that it was pointless to delay. So we collected the few guns that we could get hold of from the orderly room, the signals centre and the military transport section and prepared to depart. We captured eight vehicles, and with about six of our internal collaborators joining us, we drove off in the direction of Nabingola on the Mubende-Fort Portal Road.

This was quite a risky route to take because there were Tanzanian troops in Mubende town, which was only 23 miles (37 km) away, and there were also troops at Fort Portal. Therefore, we had to move speedily to Nabingola, 30 miles (48 km) from Mubende, and then follow the Fort Portal road as far as Kyenjonjo, only 33 miles (53 km) from Fort Portal, before the Tanzanian units could set up roadblocks at either place. Failure to move quickly could have been disastrous. At Kyenjojo we turned north on the Hoima road and travelled as far as Kagadi. We did not know whether there were troops in Hoima or not, and in any case, Hoima was too close to Masindi where there was a large number of troops. Given the many hours that had elapsed since the attack on Kabamba, roadblocks might have been established in force at Hoima. We were not yet in a position to risk any such confrontation. Hence, at Kagadi, we turned east towards Karuguuza and captured a few guns from Karuguuza Police Post. Then we turned north to avoid Kakumiro which was too closely situated to Mubende.

At Nsunga Police Post we captured a prize – a rocket-propelled grenade launcher. It was a Bulgarian RPG and an excellent piece of equipment. The only other RPG we had secured had been misplaced by Magara who had given it to somebody to keep and we had not been able to retrieve it before the attack on Kabamba, an omission which had contributed to our failure to gain entry to the armoury at Kabamba. This RPG had three rockets, though only two fuses, and had been left there by Amin's retreating soldiers. It was very useful later on.

A number of our comrades were somewhat demoralised by our failure to get guns from the Kabamba armoury. They did not see how the war could possibly be won if this was what happened on our first operation. For my part, however, I was sure that we would win in due course because in the first phases of such a war, survival itself is success. The Kabamba operation had met this criterion although we had failed to capture the big haul of guns we had expected. Our success lay in the fact that we had attacked a major military unit, captured a few guns, and got away without any loss. This act had thrown doubt on Obote's claim that he was in control of the situation and it provided a rallying point for the huge anti-Obote sentiment in the country. Therefore, the survival of our anti-Obote nucleus in the form of an armed challenge was, in itself, a success. During the whole operation, only one of our comrades, Julius Chihandae, had been wounded.

We eventually arrived in Kiboga, a distance of about 200 miles (320 km), at around 2.00 a.m. on 7 February. We drove through Kiboga town and turned northwards to Budimbo where we stayed at the farm of a supporter called Matovu. Some of our people had gone ahead earlier and reconnoitred this route. We got some food, cooked it and ate for the first time in over 48 hours. We stayed there, resting, until the following afternoon. Altogether, we now had 43 rifles although we had no support weapons, apart from the RPG we had got from Nsunga Police Post. The previous day, however, when we attacked Kabamba, we had had only 27 rifles. So we had made a net gain of 16 rifles and one RPG. This may not seem much, but we had not lost anybody, had only one comrade wounded, and so in our own terms it was quite a successful first operation.

EARLY STAGES OF THE WAR

Before leaving Matovu's farm, we organised ourselves into four sections each composed of between 10 and 12 people. Section one was led by Sam Magara, section two by Elly Tumwine, section three by Hannington Mugabi and section four by Jack Mucunguzi, while I was the overall commander.

In the afternoon of 8 February, we drove our convoy through Kiboga town, attacked the police post and took the guns we found there. We even held a rally in the town. The *wananchi* were not scared: rather they were enthusiastic and supportive. By the end of the day, the total number of our guns had risen to about 60. We camped near Kiboga town and sent out groups to attack police stations and capture more guns. One group went to Kasanda, and others to Busunju, Kakiri and Bukwiri. At that time most of our people wanted to keep the captured vehicles and this presented us with a problem. It was not easy to explain to them why it was a mistake to hang on to vehicles.

Vehicles are a danger to a guerrilla army in a number of ways. First of all, vehicles confine the force to roads, which makes it vulnerable to ambushes. Soldiers moving on foot can be more flexible. They can walk on roads, paths, through grassy savannah, forests or swamps, which makes it difficult for the enemy to predict their next move. Secondly, the most disastrous thing is to be ambushed inside a vehicle. A vehicle is a trap in which 30 or 40 people are an easy target for destruction with one RPG shell or machine-gun. If the same enemy were to confront the same 30 or 40 people dismounted, his work would be much more difficult and he would be at risk himself. The situation is even worse where the enemy is using landmines because a single landmine can blow up a lorry and destroy all its occupants.

On the morning of 9 February, I went to Bukomero to do some recruitment and when I came back I found that a number of Tanzanian soldiers, together with Ugandan recruits, had attacked our camp and the group I had left there had been dispersed. We had lost nobody, but Mugabi's group was now in Bukwiri, 20 miles (32 km) north of Kiboga, while Tumwine's section was stranded in Kasanda, 30 miles (48 km) south of Kiboga. The two were 50 miles (80 km) apart and although one group was with me, the fourth section was in Bukomero. This disorganisation had come about through our own mistake of insisting on using the vehicles which we should have abandoned after the attack on Kabamba. The problem now was to link up again.

I drove back to Bukomero, 35 miles (56 km) away, and collected the group which was there. We abandoned the vehicles and moved on foot into the valley of the River Mayanja, which flows north-west, roughly parallel with the Kiboga road, some 10 to 15 miles (i.e. about 20 km) distant from it. That night we covered around 20 miles (32 km) and arrived at a place called Kakinzi. We camped near a farm belonging to a man called Sebuliba. One of our people knew his son, Wasswa, who was very helpful. We stayed there for three or four days, trying to gather news of our other comrades in Bukwiri and Kasanda.

While we were still at Sebuliba's farm, some of our soldiers started questioning the wisdom of the whole enterprise. Although no one had yet died, they recalled our failure to capture guns at Kabamba, and the setback when the Tanzanians had attacked our camp at Kiboga. They wondered whether it was not too dangerous and whether we would not all end up getting killed. There was very evident pessimism, so we decided that those who wanted to leave should feel free to do so. Six or seven people left, but those who remained were more resolute.

This resolution was soon put to the test as the Tanzanians tracked us down to Sebuliba's farm and blew up his house. We responded by firing one of our precious RPG shells which drove them off. We decided it was time to go back to the main road and try to link up with our comrades. This time we established ourselves at Lwamata, half-way between Kiboga and Bukomero. The Tanzanians had established a camp in Kiboga and we stayed in the hills of Lwamata where we could keep in touch with the local people. In due course, both Tumwine's and Mugabi's sections rejoined us and our force was complete again, although some comrades had become lost in the confusion of the encounter with the Tanzanians on 9 February.

On 18 February, nine days after the Tanzanians had dispersed our forces, we launched an ambush against them near a place called Kyekumbya. The ambush was led by Elly Tumwine who left with his section at around 10.00 p.m. on the 17th and moved into position near Kyekumbya, on the Lwamata side, under the cover of darkness. They were in position by morning and spent the day waiting in total concealment, until an army vehicle appeared. We only had the one fused shell left for the Bulgarian RPG and Anthony Kyakabale, who is now a lieutenant-colonel, was selected to fire it. Assuming he scored a direct hit, the rest of the section were to fire their rifles for some minutes and then withdraw. I told them not to attempt to approach the vehicles to capture guns. My main interest at this stage was for our soldiers to overcome fear and see for themselves that it was feasible to destroy our opponents and preserve our still very small force.

They stayed in ambush until about 4.00 p.m. when an army vehicle came along. They waited until the vehicle had passed. At this point it was moving slowly because it was on a slope. Kyakabale stepped onto the road with his RPG at the ready. One of the Tanzanians at the back of the truck saw him and shouted out: *'Maama muzaazi!'* (Many African people call on their mothers, invoking their protection when they are in danger.) Kyakabale fired the rocket and hit the vehicle which overturned and caught fire, killing several soldiers. After firing their rifles for a while, Tumwine's section resisted the temptation to try and recover guns from the dead enemy, and instead made an orderly withdrawal, secure in the knowledge that they had made a successful strike against the enemy.

In guerrilla campaigns, especially when organising fighters from backward Third World countries, this type of demonstration is crucial. People from undeveloped societies have a fear of war machines which is born of ignorance. They believe that war machines are omnipotent and all-knowing. They are so mystified by weapons like machine-guns, tanks, APCs and cannons that they imagine that even when someone is under cover, these machines can somehow see that person. In the initial stages of a guerrilla campaign, therefore, it is imperative that the leaders demonstrate to the peasant soldiers that the machines and the enemy can actually be destroyed, while our fighters can preserve themselves. This will convince them that the war is winnable, provided one is fighting for the right cause. It must be emphasised to the peasant soldiers that while it is true that the machines are powerful and destructive, there are loopholes which we can use either to neutralise or to destroy them.

The effective use of ambush is one of the most important tactics in successful guerrilla warfare. Normally, and most importantly, the ambush site should be reconnoitred beforehand in order to ensure that it was the best site available. The best is one where there is good ground cover from which you can fire securely, where the possible target vehicle would be moving slowly, and from which you can see a reasonable distance in either direction; or a combination of any two of these conditions. Many liberation movements make the elementary mistake of using ambush sites that have not been properly selected. Even if it is a hastily laid ambush because the enemy has been sighted unexpectedly, the commander should quickly satisfy himself that at least some of the ideal conditions, such as good cover from enemy sight and fire, are fulfilled. If the conditions are not good, then the commander should withdraw.

During the war, we used two forms of ambush. Sometimes, as at Kyekumbya, we laid ambushes in populated areas, which was a complicated undertaking. We had to move to the ambush site between 10.00 p.m. and 5.00 a.m., a time when most people are asleep and nobody was moving about. We would stay there waiting for the enemy vehicles to come. If the population was still living in the area, we would have to be extra careful. There was always a look-out man who would alert the commander when the right target vehicle came, but it was important to ensure that no *mwananchi* saw us. If by bad luck a *mwananchi* saw the group, he had to be detained until the mission was accomplished and thereafter he would be released.

Alternatively, an ambush could be carried out in a depopulated area. Sometimes we advised the population to leave the war zones so that they would not get caught up in the fighting. It was mainly for the *wananchi*'s own safety that we did this; but it was also in our own interest because at that time we did not want to shoulder the heavy administrative burden of looking after the people. Nor did we want to divert our still tiny army to the task of guarding the population against Obote's attacks. Laying an ambush in a depopulated area was an easier task because all it required was for us move to the site when it was dark. There would be no danger of *wananchi* exposing the ambush, or the trouble of having to screen vehicles in order to distinguish army vehicles from civilian ones, because there would be no civilian vehicles in the area.

Shortly after our successful Kyekumbya ambush, the Tanzanians approached our camp at Lwamata, fired into the air and left. Our main problem, as we saw it at this stage, was a lack of adequate guns and ammunition. We would have been glad, for instance, of more shells for the RPG. There had been a few promises from various sources, but nothing had materialised. In retrospect, perhaps, it was good that we were not well armed right from the beginning. This concentrated our minds and we became better organised as a result. At the time, however, we felt the lack of arms quite acutely and we decided to contact our underground workers in Kampala who had been trying to secure some guns for us. Our Kampala comrades were led by Eriya Kategaya who had remained undercover in town. Other comrades such as Sam Katabarwa were in Nairobi, but we had lost touch with all these groups and did not have any news of them.

We set off from Lwamata aiming for Matuga, 16 miles (25 km) north of Kampala. Our guide and contact was a young man called Sam Wasswa, the son of Sebuliba at whose farm we had stayed until the Tanzanians had destroyed his house. (Wasswa is now a colonel in our army.) The first day we moved from Lwamata up to Kagoogo, to the farm of one of our supporters called Settuba who, unfortunately, was later killed. We travelled only at night.

From Kagoogo, we went up to Nakaziba, arriving in the early hours of the morning and hiding in the hills. After Nakaziba, Wasswa had no further contacts and thereafter we had to depend on the local people, which was more risky, though they generally supported us. Because they hated Obote so much, they gave us a guide called Bomboka, who was to die later during the war. It was he who introduced us to Edidian Luttamaguzi of Kikandwa near Semuto, who later became a hero of our movement. One of our battalions, Lutta, based in the Kufu-Kikandwa area, was named after him. He was part of the group of nine people who were murdered on 9 June 1981 on the orders of Bazilio Okello and Paulo Muwanga because they refused to reveal the whereabouts of our soldiers, in spite of the fact that they knew where they were. It is to commemorate that event that we have now declared 9 June Heroes' Day in Uganda.

It was night-time when we moved out of Nakaziba. We crossed the River Mayanja at Kakinga, passed through Sebuguzi and arrived in the Namirembe-Kirema area when it was almost morning. In those days, there were still public transport buses in these areas, and we were spotted by a priest at a junction in Kirema. The priest did not give us away, however, because the *wananchi* told him to keep quiet about us. So we managed to enter the forest below Kikandwa and thus reach Luttamaguzi's farm, where we stayed for about two days. Luttamaguzi then took us to Sentamu's farm on the other side of Kikandwa. Later on, we moved from there to Kalasa and hid in the *shamba* of an old woman who became a great supporter of ours and whom we nicknamed 'lieutenant-colonel'.

We stayed in Kalasa for two days and then moved on to Gombe where we stayed with a *mwananchi* called Kayima. We were there for another two days before moving on to near Matuga in a forest on the Matuga-Gombe road from where we tried again to make contact with Kampala. We waited there for several weeks for the promised guns, but nothing turned up. Meanwhile, we had delayed operations, hoping to replenish our supplies.

In those early days, we had to observe total concealment: we lit no fires during the day for fear that the smoke would betray us; and made no movement to or from the forest so that our presence would not be suspected. It is unbelievable how difficult it is for peasants to keep quiet. It was a constant struggle to get people to refrain from making noise. At night we would cook using very dry firewood which does not give off smoke, and we would sleep in the open air because we were not yet firmly enough based to start building huts. This involved simply covering one-self with a blanket, if such a comfort was available, or just lying by the fire trying to keep warm. While some slept, others would keep watch at the inlets to the forest, or at the fireside, just listening.

Food was bought through our local contacts among the population. Right from the beginning of our campaign, we operated a cash economy. We paid for everything because we did not want to use 'voluntary contributions' from the peasants for fear of the system being abused. In the areas near the leaders, you could get a genuine voluntary contribution of food, but we feared that in places further away, commanders might start extorting food from the peasants and this would damage our reputation. We would be given money by our supporters inside and outside the country, which we distributed among the units. In this way, the system we established benefited both ourselves and the peasants. In the Matuga area, apart from Mzee Kayima and his wife, we also had supporters like David Muwanga (who was later murdered by Bazilio Okello), Kyobe, Luyima, Semakula, Kazibwe Migadde and others.

BUILDING ADMINISTRATIVE AND
POLITICAL STRUCTURES

When we finally gave up expecting any guns to arrive, we decided to move further back, away from Matuga to Migadde hill, 17 miles (27 km) from Kampala. We hid in a forest behind the *shamba* of a man called Semakula and stayed there for a few days, still making contact with Kampala. It was at this time that the National Resistance Council (NRC) was formed.

We had already, at the beginning of the campaign, smuggled someone out of the bush to make a statement to the British Broadcasting Corporation (BBC) that we had launched an armed struggle against Obote's regime. Now various people, including Haji Moses Kigongo, came from Kampala to Migadde to ask how they could contribute to the struggle. I thought for a while and then said: 'OK. We have already formed the Popular Resistance Army with a committee to lead it, known as the High Command. Maybe what you should do is form a sister committee, which you could call the National Resistance Council, which could organise civilian committees to support the PRA.' Kigongo and another comrade went ahead and formed the NRC, and it became the basis of the council which existed until the parliamentary elections of June 1996, when a new house was elected by universal adult suffrage. It should be remembered, however, that when the NRC was formed, a war was going on and that originally its various committees were support committees for the PRA.

The Popular Resistance Army was headed by a High Command which dealt with both military and administrative matters. The High Command could be regarded as a sub-committee of a wider body known as the Army Council. Any commander of a unit, equivalent to a battalion, would be a member of the Army Council. The Army Council dealt with policy. In December 1981, we introduced into every unit an administrative committee consisting of all officers in the unit, plus the Regimental Sergeants-Major. The committee dealt with proposals to the High Command for promotions, appointments, and administrative matters in the units, such as buying food. There was also an operations committee in each unit comprised of the commanding officer, his second-in-command, the intelligence officer, and the officer for a specific operation who dealt with operational matters, such as actual battles.

Any local fighting operations such as ambushes, repulsing enemy attacks and mine-laying would be discussed collectively only by this smaller group. Other officers would not need to know about them. However, before the fighting, the officers and men who were supposed to take part in a battle would be isolated from the others to be briefed by the commander. After the briefing, he would ask whether there were any questions or doubts about the operation. If there were any doubts, the commander would explain further until everybody understood. The purpose of this was that there should be unity of opinion about the operation so that there would be no recriminations in case it failed. However, attacks against the enemy in entrenched positions, for example barracks, could only be carried out on my orders, in order for us to avoid making costly mistakes. I would authorise such an attack only after the commander had satisfied me that the plan was feasible; that the reconnaissance information was accurate; that the cost in lives to our men would be minimal; and that there were good chances of capturing weapons so that we would not expend our ammunition without gaining some return.

Once the National Resistance Council was set up, it was able to organise other committees to support the PRA with intelligence information, recruitment and food. This work could only be effectively done through a network of organised civilian committees. Thus the NRC operated at the national level with subsidiary committees at the local level. By August 1981, we had already created no-go areas for the government and our civilian committees, not the army, administered these areas and adjudicated cases. These civilian committees were named Resistance Councils and Resistance Committees (RCs). They were first constituted by our clandestine supporters, with nine councillors at every level from the village to the parish, sub-county and, later on, zonal (operational) level. The RCs dealt with administrative and judicial matters. Later on we made them elective, even when we were still in the bush. After we won the war, RCs were introduced throughout the country. There were also disciplinary committees, which were courts set up to deal with indiscipline and crime. In the case of capital crimes, the defendant would appeal to the High Command, whose decision was final. It was only for homicide that we imposed the death penalty.

During the whole of the bush war, there were only four or five capital offences. One case happened in 1985 when a man named Zabron, together with another soldier, while under the influence of alcohol, killed some villagers near Semuto. At the time, we already had our local courts so the two were tried according to its rules. During the trial, however, some people tried to take a quasi-Western legal position. They claimed that what had killed the villagers was not Zabron and his colleague, but the alcohol that had driven them to the act. We argued that such reasoning would not be understood by the villagers. It was also very dangerous because of tribalism. Zabron was from Ankole, as were some of the leaders of the army, including myself. Since the victims were Baganda, it would have seemed very bad if we had not followed the law of Moses – in other words an eye for an eye, a life for a life – and executed these two fellows. Because we were prepared to do this, the peasants were able to see that we were not like the old regimes which covered up crimes committed by their own supporters. Our courts used different concepts from Western ones (such as those of extenuating circumstances), which some of our people had tried to use in the Zabron case.

AN IMPORTANT VICTORY

When we failed to acquire any guns from our contacts in Kampala, we decided to launch our own operations to continue with the process of building up our army. On 18 March we ambushed and destroyed army vehicles at Kawanda where we captured ten rifles. After that ambush, we went back to Hoima road. That was our tactic – we never stayed in one place for long. We moved on to Nakaziba, planning to attack Kateera, 54 miles (87 km) from Kampala on the Hoima road.

We stayed there for several days, waiting for the reconnaissance information to materialise. I had sent Wasswa ahead to reconnoitre the Kateera area with strict instructions to establish clearly whether the soldiers there were Ugandan or Tanzanian. I had developed a policy that we should not attack the Tanzanians deliberately. Tanzanian soldiers were potential friends of ours who had unwittingly got involved in a situation created by the confusion in Uganda. If we were to fight them, it should only be in unplanned encounters or in self-defence. We hoped to persuade the Tanzanians to leave Uganda, rather than get involved in a war with us. Our quarrel was with Obote, not with them. Therefore, if possible, we should only attack Obote's soldiers.

So when Wasswa reported that the Kateera unit was composed of Tanzanian soldiers, I ordered our people back. We withdrew to Kikandwa and concentrated instead on reconnoitring Kakiri, where another army unit had been sent in response to our presence in the area. After much patient work, we obtained very good information on Kakiri, relying on one of our supporters named Mayanja, who still lives in Kikandwa. Later on, I sent two of our senior soldiers there: Patrick Lumumba and Sam Magara. I was very particular about reconnoitring and I would not authorise any operation without getting thorough information. Once I was satisfied, I led the group for the attack on Kakiri.

Kakiri was only 25 miles (40 km) from Kikandwa down the Hoima-Kampala road, but we had to take a roundabout route in order to avoid the main road. We left Kikandwa on the night of 4 April, passed by Bukatira Primary School, went through the villages of Kikubampanga and Luttabayima and arrived at Masuliita in the morning of the 5th. We hid in the farm of one of our supporters known as Nalongo, who still lives there today. We hid there the whole day, and when it was dark, we left Masuliita for the final part of the journey to Kakiri. We usually travelled between 10.00 p.m. and 5.00 a.m. to ensure that we did not meet anybody. As we were going towards Kakiri, however, we met a man on a bicycle. He passed us by but we did not know where he was going. This type of encounter with civilians was a potential source of trouble because they could leak information, even unintentionally.

When we neared our target, we turned right and entered a forest below Kakiri. The idea was that we should stay there for the whole day and carry out our attack in the evening when the soldiers would be assembled at evening parade. The idea of this was to ensure that all the soldiers were together so that we could kill or capture as many as possible and take away their guns. However, the place where we were hiding was near a well and the ground was very soft. The tracks we made in the wet soil were so deep that they would certainly have been noticed. I realised we would never be able to stay there the whole day without being discovered, so I called my commanders together and told them we must attack Kakiri immediately, which we did.

At about 8.00 a.m. on 6 April we launched our attack. Taking the enemy completely by surprise, we overran the station fairly easily, capturing 12 SMGs, one 60mm mortar, one GPMG and quite a few anti-tank guns. It was altogether a very successful operation. When we were preparing to withdraw, however, some Tanzanians arrived on the scene and in the ensuing fight, they lost one major and some other soldiers.

It was about 9.30 a.m. when we finally withdrew and headed back towards Masuliita. After a short distance we turned off the Kakiri-Masuliita road into a forest on the right. Soon afterwards, some Tanzanian forces arrived from Busunju and Kampala and tried to surround us in the forest. It had rained very heavily during the night and it was very heavy work for the 53 of us lugging our new weapons and ammunition along the forest tracks, since we had not brought any unarmed carriers along. Subsequently, owing to our experience at Kakiri, we developed a new policy of always going out on operations with unarmed groups to carry captured weapons. We nicknamed them 'commandos', to indicate to them that they were so experienced that they went into battle without the need for arms. Of course, the truth was that we had no arms to give them.

The Tanzanians surrounded the forest with their APCs, but we stayed hidden in the forest until evening when we emerged on the Bakka hill side. We could hear the Tanzanians just across the valley trying to pull their APCs out of the mud where they were stuck fast. We rejoined the Kakiri-Masuliita road at Ddambwe, crossed the River Mayanja and got back to our place at Nalongo's at four o'clock the next morning. We spent the whole of 7 April there resting and left the next night for Kikandwa, where we arrived triumphant at having scored what was an important victory for us.

CONSOLIDATING OUR FORCES

I preferred to lead the soldiers personally on these first operations in order to show them what to do. Thereafter, I did not have to accompany them because the commanders would have seen how to carry out an operation. The elements I wanted our commanders to take note of were: accurate reconnaissance, surprise, fighting battles of short duration, proper use of terrain to gain cover, and concealment in approach and withdrawal. If a guerrilla army masters these points, provided it is fighting for a just cause, it will eventually win the war. Of course, a lot also depends on the skills of the government forces. If they confine themselves to relying on heavy equipment and travelling on roads in their vehicles, they will lose the war. If they are flexible, and are prepared to walk on foot most of the time, provided their cause is a just one, they will cause problems for the insurgents. These are the methods the NRA used when fighting the insurgency in northern Uganda.

We stayed in Kikandwa for some time and decided to split our force into two because we now had a few more guns. We had built up the number of our guns again to 60, having lost some during the encounter with the Tanzanians at Kiboga on 9 February. The force led by Sam Magara was to operate along Bombo road, and the other, under Elly Tumwine, was to go through the Kakinga-Bukomero area and establish itself in Kasejere forest to the west of Hoima road, opening up the Singo front. I left with Sam Magara's group, headed for Matuga and went to Migadde to try to contact our Kampala people and establish how successful they had been in their search for guns. After some time, I returned to see what was happening on the Singo front. This was an important phase because we were about to try to operate on two fronts – on the Hoima road and on the Bombo road, a strategy which would enable us to split the enemy's forces.

Unfortunately, our people made some serious errors. They insisted on travelling on bicycles and motor-cycles, thus leaving very clear tracks in their wake. As a result, on 18 April, they were attacked by the Tanzanians at Kagogo. They do not seem to have been prepared and their response was correspondingly inadequate. We lost one comrade named Kazahuura, who was the first of our people to die in the liberation war. We also lost 13 guns that day, including the mortar and the GPMG. The whole group was dispersed and when I arrived at Kikandwa, I found them trickling in trying to join the force there. I decided to concentrate again on consolidating our forces.

I summoned Magara's force from Matuga and we waited until the rest of the Hoima road group had trickled back. After some time, we shifted to Kyererezi on the Mayanja river. The number of our personnel had now swollen to more than 200, as we had been recruiting from the surrounding villages. Our supporters in Kampala had also been ferreting out UNLA soldiers who wanted to come and join us. Indeed, the force had now become so large that it was difficult to conceal. We therefore decided to create six small zonal units out of it. These units formed the core of the battalions which lasted until the end of the war.

The six units were named in honour of African heroic figures. Two were named after noted Ugandan opponents of British imperialism in the late 19th century: Kabalega, the *Omukama* (king) of Bunyoro, and Mwanga, the *Kabaka* of Buganda. Kabalega, under Elly Tumwine, operated in Kapeeka, while Mwanga under Matayo Kyaligonza operated in Mukono. A third group, Lutta, was later named in memory of our own contemporary hero, Luttamaguzi. This group was commanded by Hannington Mugabi and operated in Kikandwa. The remaining three were named after international African heroes: Abdel Nasser, former President of Egypt, Nkrumah, first President of Ghana, and Mondlane, founding President of Frelimo. Abdel Nasser under Jack Mucunguzi operated along Gulu Road; Nkrumah, with Fred Mwesigye in command, was based in Singo; and Mondlane, led by Fred Rwigyema, operated in Kalasa, Makulubita area. Only Abdel Nasser had a reasonable number of guns – about 40; the other units had only 10 or 12 guns each. We also created another small unit of about six people to act as my bodyguard. Later, in January 1982, we created a Task Force, commanded by Kyaligonza and Lumumba, which operated in Gomba, Matuga, the Kampala area, Sanga and occasionally Mukono.

Chapter 11

FIGHTING OBOTE (2)
[1981–3]

MAKING CONTACTS ABROAD

About three months after our campaign against Obote had commenced, a Libyan diplomat called Mohammed Alfaghee initiated contacts with us. Alfaghee had been in the Libyan delegation in Kampala during the two years of the UNLF government (1979–80). We had, in fact, fought the Libyans when they had come to support Idi Amin and many had been captured and taken to Tanzania, although Dr Nyerere later released them. Libya had also returned the Ugandan planes which Amin had flown there when he made his escape. With these measures taken, the relationship between the UNLF and Libya had thawed. Now it appeared that Libya was promising to help us in our struggle.

I had encountered the diplomat on a number of occasions and we had cracked jokes together, but we had never had the chance to enjoy a proper conversation. When we went to the bush, he kept on inquiring about us. He spoke to one of our contacts, Sam Male, who happened to be working in the Libyan-Arab Bank in Kampala. Sam Male was in contact with Eriya Kategaya and when the Libyan met Kategaya, he insisted on talking to me. A meeting was duly set up and I met the man at Semakula's house in Migadde in May, where he conveyed Colonel Gaddafi's invitation to me to visit Libya.

I left for Libya on 6 June 1981. I was driven by Sikubwabo Kyeyune from Matuga, where I had been staying at Kyobe's house for about two weeks. We went through Wakiso, joined the Masaka road near Nsangi, turned off the main road at Buwama and headed for Katebo, near the present crocodile farm. There we boarded a small boat, powered by a 12hp outboard engine which Andrew Lutaya had 'liberated' from the stores of the Department of Fisheries at Entebbe. We set off from Katebo at 6.00 p.m. and headed for the Ssese Islands, landing at Bubeke Island where Lutaya knew a peasant who would help us. We arrived at Bubeke at 10.00 p.m. and Lutaya's friend gave us a meal of fish and *matooke*. I have never enjoyed eating fish. Being a cattleman from the savannah, I was

28 years old before I had my first taste of fish; even then this came about only under pressure from my late comrade, Samora Machel, who managed to persuade me by telling me that I should 'emancipate' myself from traditional prejudices.

At Bubeke, we transferred to a bigger boat, equipped with a 48hp engine, and set off at around 7.00 a.m. We bypassed the few small islands to the east of Bubeke and struck out for the open lake. Occasionally, the engine seized up and then we would drift on the lake while it was being repaired. Apart from Lutaya, the nucleus of my 'navy' consisted of Busagwa and Paddy. I had also taken Pecos Kutesa along as my aide. As usual, there was no sign of either the Tanzanian or the Ugandan governments on the lake, so the only danger to a law-breaker using the lake for his clandestine activities is the lake itself. It can get very rough, with waves that will easily swamp a boat.

Lutaya was obviously not given to heeding the Luganda saying: *Lubaale mbeera n'embiro nga kwotadde,* meaning: 'God helps those who help themselves.' As far as safety on the lake was concerned, Lutaya depended entirely on *Lubaale.* There were no lifejackets and no reserve engine: we were at the mercy of God and the elements. After some hours of travelling in the direction of Kenya, we lost sight of land for about two hours. More than 100 miles (160 km) of open water separates the easternmost Ssese island from the Kenyan island of Mfangano at the head of the Kavirondo Gulf where we were headed. Eventually we sighted Mfangano in the far distance. We passed south of Sigulu Island, one of the last islands on the Ugandan side of the lake and by 6.00 p.m., when we passed Mfangano Island and entered Kavirondo Gulf, we had been on the open lake for 11 hours. We were heading for Kisumu, at the eastern end of the Gulf, but we were not too sure of our direction. At around 10.00 p.m. we entered what looked like a reasonable-sized port, lit up with street lights. We did not know whether it was Kisumu, but we went ashore and made some enquiries, only to be told that we were in Homa Bay, on the south side of the Gulf, some 40 miles (64 km) west of our destination. Resignedly, we climbed back into the boat and chugged the length of Homa Bay, re-entered the Kavirondo Gulf and headed for Kisumu, which we finally reached at 6.00 a.m. on 8 June, a full 36 hours after we had left Katebo landing site.

Immediately we ran into problems with the 'authorities' because we had no smuggled merchandise. What sort of people were we, they wanted to know, coming across the water empty-handed? I wished that Lutaya had briefed me about this. It would have been easy enough to bring across some *bogoya* (yellow bananas) which are highly prized in Kenya. I do not remember how we managed to be allowed to enter the country but we were, leaving our precious boat in the custody of the smuggling 'authorities', with our machine-gun concealed somewhere inside it. Later on, we struck up a lasting relationship with some people in the Kenya Police who eased our subsequent comings and goings. Before the war was out, I crossed that dreadful lake two more times.

Being a fighter, I do not enjoy travelling by air or water because I do not like the thought of depending entirely on other people for my very existence. Even an infantryman on dry land, of course, has to depend on others to an extent, but in a crunch at least he can use his rifle and put up a fight. This is not so in the air or on water where one is competing with the elements. The fact that I had never learnt how to swim was also not calculated to enhance my relaxation during my three trips across Lake Victoria, especially if one remembers that the distance from Katebo to Kisumu is 220 miles (355 km).

Up the street in Kisumu we were met by Amama Mbabazi and Sam Katabarwa. As far as I remember, we got some money from them so that one of us could go back and quieten the smugglers and persuade them to look after our boat and our SMG. Later, I learned that the boat, built by Lutaya's Ssese Island people, and able to carry 12 tonnes, was 'borrowed' by our Kenyan smuggler friends to take some merchandise to Tanzania. The African smugglers are the only true believers in an African common market. It was very interesting for me, as the future leader of an African country, to experience from the other side the incapacity of African governments that impedes the activities of genuine common marketeers. These smugglers could do whatever they wanted and the authorities were conspicuous only by their absence.

By noon we were in Nairobi and I rejoined Janet and the children. Alice Kakwano had smuggled our older children out of Uganda by disguising them as her own. Janet had managed to slip out of the country with the baby, Diana, on 4 February, two days before we attacked Kabamba barracks. It had been a relief when they had left safely. Diana was now one year old and much changed. It was six months since I had last seen her. I, too, must have looked quite different: I was emaciated but very fit.

I met a few Kenyan officials, among them Kierini and G.G. Kariuki, but the annual OAU summit was approaching and the Kenyan authorities thought that my presence would 'embarrass' Obote! How gifted African leaders are in inventing and propagating such empty clichés! How does the presence of one human being in a city of one million people 'embarrass' another human being, however exalted his status? This is how the generation of African leaders who took over after independence fettered Africa and completely failed to address the real African crisis or find solutions to the continent's problems. They spent most of their time posturing, pampering their egos, indulging in meaningless ceremonies and displaying their fundamental ignorance about the dynamics of society. In any case, I had more useful things to do than remain in the same city with Obote.

THE PRA BECOMES THE NRA

I had my appointment to keep with Gaddafi on 19 June, but prior to that I had another task to fulfil: I wanted to forge a union between the PRA and Professor Yusufu Lule's Uganda Freedom Fighters (UFF).

After he had been removed from office in June 1979, Professor Lule had kept in touch with me, even though we had had our differences in policy and attitude. On one occasion, during the period of Binaisa's government, when I was attending a meeting in the Kenyan port city of Mombasa, Lule had contacted me and requested a meeting. On that occasion we met in Nairobi at the house of a brother of his called Kabanda. He said he was sorry about what had happened. He now realised that we were a serious group and that he would like to continue working with us. At the time, I said: 'No problem. But for the time being it would be better to support the democratic process, however flawed, to see how far it goes.'

Now, two years later, we met in the house of Chris Mboijana in Nairobi. Professor Lule admitted again that he had made a mistake in not trying to work with us originally, and that of all the groups in Uganda, ours was the only one which was reliable and on the side of the people. Eventually, after some negotiation, we signed a protocol effecting the merger of the PRA and the UFF into the National Resistance Movement (NRM). Lule really had no forces to speak of, but we were prepared to be flexible and did not insist too much on maintaining our own identity. Apart from his image, Lule had no other contribution to make. However, since some of the Ugandan people would be happy to be identified with him, we were willing to change our identity and create a new body to accommodate him.

Lule was, therefore, designated NRM chairman, while I was to be first vice-chairman and chairman of the High Command of the National Resistance Army (NRA), the new name for the six-month-old army. Moses Kigongo was designated second vice-chairman of the movement. Up to then, I had been chairman of the PRA and Kigongo had been vice-chairman. The rest of the new NRM executive was to be made up of the chairmen of the sub-committees of finance and supplies, politics and diplomacy, publicity and propaganda, and external affairs.

Being a very conservative man, the new chairman of the NRM was worried about my trip to Libya. How would the West look at it? My question to him was this: where is the support from the West? In the end, I was able to convince him that I should undertake the trip to Libya as arranged.

THE LIBYAN CONNECTION

I arrived in Libya after staying in Nairobi for a week. I was accompanied by Matthew Rukikaire and Ruhakana Rugunda. After about two days in Tripoli, we met Colonel Gaddafi, who described the meeting as 'historic'. This was not an exaggeration, considering that I had been one of his principal adversaries only two years previously. He promised to help us and he gave us some money immediately. By August 1981, Gaddafi had managed to smuggle 800 rifles, 45 RPG launchers, some mortars, machine-guns, and 100 anti-tank landmines to a certain point in sub-Saharan Africa. Out of that consignment, the NRA received only 96 rifles (Barrettas and AK-47s), 100 landmines, five GPMGs, eight RPG launchers and a small quantity of ammunition and shells for these weapons. The rest of the weapons were given to the Uganda Freedom Movement (UFM). Because of this group's reckless and incompetent leadership, however, most of the weapons were captured by the UNLA. During 1982, we managed to rescue 220 of the rifles, plus some RPGs, mortars and machine-guns.

Our part of the consignment was smuggled across five African countries by air, and across three by truck. I am really amused whenever I hear accusations and counter-accusations that country 'A' is backing guerrillas fighting to remove the government of country 'B'. A serious movement cannot fail to get arms if it wishes to do so. The surveillance capacity of most African countries is very low as they have no radar, no air defence systems, and no weighbridges at their borders. Above all, the vast majority of them are blessed with semi-literate and corrupt customs and police officials. These facilitate, rather than impede, the smuggling of goods – guns and ammunition included.

It is the 96 rifles, 100 landmines, five GPMGs, eight RPGs and a small quantity of ammunition that constitute the much-talked-about 'massive assistance' given by Libya to the NRA. This relatively small amount of weapons was useful, but not decisive in any way. The mines were particularly useful in blocking the Luwero roads by blowing up trucks. Of course, there are military remedies for mines but Obote's regime had no time to attend to such problems. They were busy drinking and getting involved in business deals, while the Army Chief of Staff, Brigadier David Oyite Ojok, also took the post of chairman of the Coffee Marketing Board. What a circus it was! It was not until 1985, after the overthrow of Tito Okello's regime, that the Libyans sent us two additional consignments of 800 rifles, 800 000 rounds of AK-47 ammunition, and some SAM-47 launchers. Therefore, the NRA was not built up by Libyan support. Rather, it was the capacity of the NRA leadership to provide correct guidance at every stage which enabled the NRA to grow, at the expense of the enemy.

After my successful visit to Libya, I spent a few months travelling between Libya, London and Nairobi. The Libyans attempted to create unity between the various Ugandan opposition groups: ourselves, Dr Andrew Kayiira's UFM, Moses Ali's Uganda National Rescue Front (UNRF), Farouk Minawa's group, and several others. The UNRF had a small presence in West Nile, but they were eventually pushed out of the country into the Sudan. The UFM tried to portray itself as an armed wing of the DP, but they could not organise any coherent activity. The Libyans wanted to create what they thought would be a 'strong' movement. We told the Libyans that in clandestine activities, 'oneness' did not necessarily mean strength and that it could actually create weaknesses. If one group was infiltrated by enemy agents, that sickness would spread to the whole, larger organisation, thereby affecting groups which might have remained secure without the merger. When fighting a national war of liberation, it is crucial to ensure that every group attacks the enemy using their own ways and means, and that efforts are co-ordinated, but not necessarily amalgamated. In the end, we deflected the Libyans from their idea of merging the anti-Obote groups and they merely continued trying to co-ordinate them.

I also made some contacts in London with British politicians such as Lord Carrington, using John Kazzora as a go-between. Among the British ministers was a man called Richard Luce who was the Minister of State for Overseas Development in the Foreign and Commonwealth Office. Soon after the elections in Uganda in December 1980, I had met him at the British High Commission in Kampala. He had been very much in favour of dressing up the elections as a good exercise and had tried to tell me to accept the result. His line was: 'Look here, although politics is important, economics is also important. Won't you concentrate on economic recovery for your country?' I told him that there could be no economic recovery under the kind of regime we were suffering from. But when we made contacts with other British politicians through Kazzora, it seemed they were more willing to listen to our side of the argument.

RETURN TO UGANDA

Eventually, the time came for me to re-cross Lake Victoria. If the outward journey of the previous June had been eventful and hazardous, it was nothing compared with the return journey. We left Kisumu during the afternoon of 6 December 1981. This time we travelled in a fibre-glass boat with a much more powerful engine, our old boat having been permanently 'borrowed' by the smugglers. At first I thought that Lutaya had made some improvements concerning our safety and welfare on the lake. For one thing, there was a hood on the boat, which meant that we were protected from the rain. We travelled fast, as it was getting dark, past Rusinga and Mfangano Islands and onto the open waters of the lake. Relying on the navigational skills of Paddy and Busagwa, we headed for the Ssese Islands. Again, however, Lutaya had only one engine on his boat, and again the engine was gripped by seizures. We drifted on the black waters of Lake Victoria as our marine-engineer boys struggled with the repairs. Nobody had a compass on board, and at one time, when the lone engine was not a problem, we were not sure what direction we were taking. We did not want to end up in Tanzania, which was not a friendly country for us at that time. So we decided to wait for the morning, thereby falling behind our target of reaching the Ugandan shore at Kajjansi by the early hours of the morning.

When morning came, we found ourselves to the east of the Ssese Islands. The boat's engine failed again, but we managed to pull into one of the tiny islands to the east of the main group. I think this time the problem was water in the fuel. We spent the whole of 7 December repairing the boat and it was 6.00 p.m. by the time we got it going again. It almost flew past the islands of Bubeke and Jana heading for Kajjansi. When the engine was working, it was very powerful and what a beautiful sight those islands were against the darkening sky. At exactly 10.00 p.m., midway between Entebbe and Jana, our wonderful boat developed another seizure and all attempts to repair it failed. We drifted in the water for the rest of the night, while the lights of the control tower at Entebbe Airport shone on us every time the rotor turned around. We were in a pretty helpless situation and felt very exposed when daylight came next morning. We felt it was simply a matter of time before we were spotted and picked up by the authorities. The boys kept working on the motor, more for something to do than seriously expecting it to recover. Then suddenly, half-way through the morning, as if by some miracle, the engine fired into life and we felt we might yet be saved capture.

By now it was too late in the day to enter Kajjansi as originally planned, and so we decided to make our way back to Jana Island. The date was now 8 December. Having arrived on Jana, Lutaya left in a canoe to get some clean fuel from Kampala. I stayed with the boatboys and Kutesa on the island until nightfall, still with no sign of Lutaya. At around 10.00 p.m. we decided to hire a canoe, using oars. Although slower, the oarsmen were much more reliable than the engine had been. Finally, at around 2.00 a.m., we arrived at the landing site at Kitubulu, near the place where the Entebbe-Kampala road comes nearest the shoreline between Katabi and Baitababiri, exactly 400 metres from the UNLA's permanent road-block on that road!

We took the precaution of landing about 200 metres to the north of the actual landing site where our boatboys knew a certain family nearby. We paid the boat-boys, walked to the shack belonging to that family and spent the night there. Lutaya appeared the following morning, and at 2.00 p.m. Sam Male came with a car to collect us. The plan was that since there were no roadblocks between the Entebbe area and Kampala, we would drive straight through Kampala and head for the Bombo road, turning off at Kigogwa at mile 14 to rejoin our forces. By the time we got to Kajjansi, however, we found there was a radical change in the situation.

Roadblocks had been set up on all roads in and out of Kajjansi. It seems that the villagers on the island had alerted the authorities that I was in the area so they were specifically looking for a man wearing jeans and canvas shoes – exactly what I was wearing. It was said later that around that time, people who wore jeans and canvas shoes were arrested and harassed because that was thought to be the uni-form of the guerrillas! As I said earlier, however, roadblocks are easy enough to bypass and on this occasion we managed to make our way around them and, after a long and roundabout route, we arrived at mile 14 on the Bombo road as planned.

We rejoined our people at Kigogwa where we found Sam Magara acting as army commander. Before I had left the country in June, I had left Magara in charge of the forces, but I had also given instructions that if Ahmed Seguya should come to the bush during my absence, Magara should hand over the leadership to him. Seguya was senior to all the others present in the bush, having been among the first groups trained in Mozambique in 1971, but he had not been able to join us before we left for the bush in February 1981. All the other senior people were from groups trained in 1976 or 1979. Seguya duly came in shortly after I had left and took over command from Sam Magara, but then he died, apparently because of a longstanding liver problem. He died, in fact, in the present Kisekka Foundation Hospital and his body was embalmed and preserved by Professor Stanley Tumwine, Dr James Makumbi and Dr Lukanga Ndawula. The body was then kept at Mulago Medical School until 30 November 1990 when Ahmed Seguya was finally given a formal burial. This event shows clearly the extent of the co-operation we had from various sectors of society. The Obote regime knew nothing about all this, even though it was happening under their very noses.

Sam Magara had brought two army sections to meet us at Kigogwa, which we reached at 6.00 p.m. on 9 December. We slept soundly that night but were attacked the following morning at around 10.00 a.m. The UNLA tried to encircle the forest where we were, but we managed to find an escape route before they could surround us completely.

I had not taken any effective exercise for six months, having had to remain concealed in hotels in London and Nairobi, since the governments both of the United Kingdom and Kenya had made it clear that my presence in their countries had to be discreet. Therefore, the vigorous movements we had to undertake in the bush to break out of the UNLA's attempted encirclement left me extremely exhausted. I felt more inclined to engage in battle with the UNLA troops than to walk vigorously to get away. However, since our group was small, I heeded my colleagues' advice, in spite of the attendant unpleasant consequences for my legs and chest, weakened from six months' inactivity. It is difficult to exercise properly inside a hotel room. Walking long distances, however, and especially climbing hills, quickly builds up stamina. One develops legs of iron and lungs like the bellows of a blast furnace. There was only one other time that I had ever felt so tired, in the many years of military campaigns that I had experienced. That was in December 1978 when I had climbed the hills of Karagwe, the difference being that in 1978 I had not been under enemy attack. We got out of Kigogwa, however, passed Gomba headquarters and joined our bigger force at Bubaale, where Saleh, Kyaligonza and others were in command.

STRUCTURES AND PRINCIPLES

While I was away, our people had launched a number of operations, using the consignment of arms I had sent, but at the same time a great deal of potentially dangerous confusion had arisen. This had been caused by the lack of proper structures to run our movement and army. Without clearly delineated roles an organisation quickly runs into problems. For instance, who orders operations, and what procedures does he follow in doing so? Who tries cases of indiscipline and what punishment is meted out for what offence?

Before leaving the country, I had gathered the force at Kyererezi and created the six units, as previously mentioned. I had done this for various reasons: to spread operations against the enemy; to ease administration so that the leaders catered for smaller numbers of people; and to enable us to use the tactic of concealment more effectively whenever the need arose. Our numbers were growing fast and the main problem, as we saw it at the time, was lack of guns. By the time I had left in June, our force had grown from the original 30 or so people to about 200, though with only 60 rifles between them. We had lost 13 rifles on 18 April near Bukomero, thus nullifying our gains at Kakiri on 6 April.

During my absence, Magara had mounted operations against police stations and captured more guns which had brought the number up from 60 to about 100. During that period, however, the NRA had grown – it was now 900 strong. The use of landmines in the conflict had badly affected the morale of the poorly led, ill-trained UNLA and, combined with frequent ambushes, had already rendered some parts of Luwero no-go areas for the UNLA troops. The consignment of 96 rifles, 100 mines, eight RPGs, five GPMGs and ammunition I had obtained from Libya, added to the weapons we already had, enabled the comrades to launch vigorous operations that August in Luwero, Matuga and Semuto. They also carried out ambushes and mine-laying operations.

There are, of course, solutions to mines in modern warfare, but the UNLA, led by people of the calibre of Tito Okello and Oyite Ojok, could not find ways of dealing with this mine offensive. Instead, they kept on sending in their poor soldiers to be blown up. Therefore, the period between August and December 1981 was very bad for the government side. It was, however, during an attack on Bukomero in that period that Elly Tumwine lost an eye. The operation was not very well co-ordinated and our people did not manage to overrun the whole detachment completely. It was into that situation that I returned on 9 December 1981.

I saw at once that the main weakness was a lack of appropriate structures to manage our force. These problems were compounded by Magara's attempt to assert his authority over people who are characteristically undisciplined. Distrust had arisen out of contradictions and disagreements over operations, but the main problem had been caused by the execution of a boy called Shaban Kashanku for going to Kampala without permission. The trial had not followed the proper procedures involving all the people concerned, and had therefore caused a lot of fear and suspicion within the rank and file. Some commanders were afraid to go out for operations for fear that they would be 'shot in the back'.

I made a tour of all the units, travelling all the way to Nkrumah in Singo, and visiting Mondlane, Lutta and Kabalega units on the way. Wherever I went, we held leaders' meetings at which there was strong criticism of the wrongs that had taken place. I came back from Singo to hold a meeting in the Lutta unit around Christmas 1981. Christmas was celebrated in the camp by Rev. Bezareli Wamala of Kirema. After Lutta, I went to Mondlane, based in Segirinya forest near Kanyanda. While in London, I had drafted a 'code of conduct' for the NRA, and a Ugandan student there named Edith Nyugunyu had typed it for me. At Kanyanda we adopted this NRA code of conduct and we put in place all the structures that guided us from then on. In fact the army continues to use this same code of conduct today.

The essentials of the code dealt chiefly with the relationship between the freedom-fighters and members of the public, especially the crucial importance of protecting civilians' lives and property. The need for personal discipline amongst combatants, and maintenance of good relationships between officers and men was another important factor highlighted in the code. Political education was to become mandatory in order that cadres and soldiers would understand the purpose of the struggle.

The code also sought to instil leadership qualities in the soldiers by admonishing them to eschew cheap popularity, intrigue and double-talk, tribalism, corruption and liberalism. 'Liberalism' was defined as a situation in which a person in authority knew what was right and what was wrong, but because of his weak leadership, he would not stand firmly on the side of right. The following methods of work were to be used in correcting mistakes within the army: open criticism – holding regular meetings at which all complaints could be heard and settled; and distinguishing between and meting out due punishment for errors which were caused by indiscipline, corruption or subversion. The formation of cliques within the army was strictly forbidden and there was to be no soliciting of information for its own sake. Thus, the principle of 'the need to know' was established. Regular tactics were to be known to all officers, cadres and combatants, but operational matters were restricted only to those who needed to know them.

Later on we added the 'operational code of conduct' to deal with offences on the battlefield, that is, during operations. This code defined the composition and powers of unit tribunals, field court-martials, general court-martials and the offences punishable under that code. The difference between this and the original code of conduct was that punishment would be instant, so that operations could be protected from indiscipline, and lives would not be endangered. In order to make them more alert, the operation commander would first alert all troops that they were now operating under that code. These measures prevented us falling into problems which might have ruined our struggle.

At the top of the structures we adopted at Kanyanda was the 'High Command'. This was made up of myself as chairman, Eriya Kategaya, Sam Magara, Elly Tumwine, Salim Saleh and seven other people, making a total of twelve. They were all drawn from different backgrounds such as Fronasa, the police, the old Uganda Army, Lule's group, the UNLF, and independents. The policy and administration committee comprised all officers in a battalion unit, plus the Regimental Sergeant Major (RSM). This committee was to handle all administration and staff matters like promotions. The disciplinary committee, chaired by the battalion second-in-command, was to act as the court-martial. If a death sentence was passed, it needed the authority of the High Command in order to be carried out. The High Command would advise the chairman on all matters concerning the army. These structures have been little modified and have lasted until today.

They spared the NRA the kinds of problems that have troubled other liberation movements. We also made a differentiation between senior and junior officers, designating them JOI and JOII equivalent to the formal ranks of lieutenant and second lieutenant. We did still continue to have some interpersonal problems amongst commanders, but with some organisational structures in place, such problems could be resolved.

Eriya Kategaya had a particularly important role to play in the struggle, although he never took part in the actual fighting. He was in the bush in Luwero for some months but more as a political than a military leader. Mostly he was doing clandestine work in the town, either in Kampala or in Nairobi. What many people did not realise at the time was that being in the town was in fact more dangerous than fighting in the bush. In the bush, a cadre is free to defend himself, and there is a certain safety in numbers. When doing urban clandestine work, on the other hand, the cadre is really on his or her own and survival depends on total concealment. The contacts that are made may not always be reliable and then cadres are very vulnerable because the contact has information about their identity and movements. If a cadre were found out by the regime, there would be no questions, trial or investigation, simply execution – and thus it was extremely dangerous. That kind of work needs a person with a special kind of courage, patience and stability. Kategaya is just such a man and as such he has always been central to the work we have done over the years.

We had a military training wing by now, and the instructors used our own training manuals, not only for training infantry, but also for training in the use of support weapons. Some of the trainers were from the original group of 28 from Mozambique, but we had also trained many people with the Tanzanians between 1979 and 1981, including 300 officer cadets whom we sent to Monduli Military Academy in Tanzania. During the time of Fronasa, we had not had time to train people in some of the specialised fields, for example signals and artillery. However, officers such as Lt Col. Bunihizi, who came to join us and who had been a signaller in Amin's army, were able to provide such training. When we captured a signal radio, Bunihizi helped us to train other people in its use and that is how we established our signals corps. We used the same methods for building up our artillery expertise. When we were not engaged in battles, we spent most of our time in some sort of training, cleaning the camps, or looking for and preparing food. By the time we had finished finding and cooking the food for the day, it was very often night time. The only recreation we had was singing.

For essential items such as medicines, we would sometimes raid government dispensaries and hospitals. On one occasion, we raided the government hospital in Nakaseke, 15 miles (24 km) south-west of Luwero. We captured a large quantity of medicines and we also took the doctors and other staff along with us. We needed medical personnel to attend to the wounded at the time. In fact, our first doctor, Dr Ronald Batta, came to us a captive in the Nakaseke raid. We gave him the option of going away but he decided to stay and, later on, he became our

Director of Medical Services. Dr Kiiza Besigye also came later as well as many medical assistants, and they carried out all kinds of operations, including removal of bullets, amputation of limbs, and even caesarian sections. Since there were no sterilised conditions in which to carry out operations, they injected patients with antibiotics in order to control the spread of bacteria inside the body.

We used lectures in political education to get people to think in terms of a cohesive movement. We approached this education at two levels. One level was the philosophical approach concerning the way in which society should be governed, but the other was designed to help the people being mobilised to develop a belief in victory. That is important because in spite of an organisation's broad aims, the people may not be sure as to whether these goals are attainable, given the limited means at its disposal. So one must demonstrate, giving examples of how the organisation is going to achieve these broad aims. We would gather *wananchi* in small groups and tell them why we were fighting. This work was not difficult because Obote's regime was so unpopular that as far as the *wananchi* were concerned, it was not a question of whether we should fight or not, it was a question of whether the war was winnable. Therefore, much of our teaching was explaining to the people that our goal was achievable, provided we worked in a systematic manner.

PROBLEMS WITH THE UFM

Although we were not the only ones to have taken up arms against Obote's dictatorship, we operated independently of other groups and, in practice, groups like Dr Kayiira's Uganda Freedom Movement were often more of a hindrance to our struggle than any kind of help in harassing the enemy. For example the UFM would provoke the UNLA, who would then attack them and rout them where they were. The UFM would then flee from their areas, into our 'Luwero Triangle' operational zone, where they would start causing trouble for us by inciting our supporters on a tribal basis.

Matters came to a head in May 1982 when Dr Kayiira tried to attack Lubiri Barracks with the guns that he had secured from Libya. The attack was a complete failure because he had not made adequate preparations. The UNLA captured many of his weapons and dispersed his group, scattering Kayiira troops in all directions. These troops had nowhere to go because they had no firm local base. They had been hiding in Nswangire forest on Mityana Road but they could not go back there because Obote's groops were pursuing them. They drove round and round with the guns they had managed to retain until one of their commanders, Sonko Lutaya, who is now a major in our army, decided to bring the guns to us because he knew that otherwise they would be captured by Obote's people. He brought them to us through Kakiri, coming towards Masulita, 24 miles (38 km) from Kampala. At Ddambwe he turned to the right towards Matuga but there his vehicle got stuck in the mud. I was at Kanyanda when somebody came running to tell us about the guns and I immediately set off with a small force to collect them.

At that time Masulita was peaceful because it was not in our operational zone. Apart from the time we had spent there the previous year on our way to attack Kakiri, Masulita was always a peaceful area. Our operational zone ended at the Danze, a branch of the River Mayanja which faces Karongero. We crossed the Danze in broad daylight, passed a school where some school children saw us, and went and collected the guns. We unloaded them from the UFM vehicle, and took them safely back to our area. It was a rich harvest of more than 200 rifles, mortars and machine guns. This catch brought the total number of our guns to 400, and it was with these 400 guns that we fought most of the war.

Having dispersed Kayiira's group completely, Obote appears to have thought he could do the same to us, and in June 1982 he launched a big offensive against us. By that time, however, we in the NRA were well enough organised to fight off whatever attacks Obote's UNLA forces might launch against us. On this occasion, when the UNLA soldiers came to attack us, we had a terrific battle with them at Bulemezi. By the end of July we had thoroughly defeated this first major offensive against us.

The following month, August 1982, we held a conference with the remnants of the Uganda Freedom Movement. Dr Kayiira tried to argue that we should give him 'his' guns back, but we refused and told him that he had been misusing them. Kayiira and his UFM were, on the one hand, trying to peddle the idea that they were an armed wing of the DP's Baganda supporters, and on the other, saying that the NRA was the armed wing of the UPM and merely represented the people of western Uganda. Their position was essentially tribalist sectarianism and, since we were fighting in Buganda, we had to expose this dangerous line of reasoning. In addition, they argued that we should declare that we were fighting to restore the monarchy in Buganda. Therefore, we invited a large number of local people to listen to our side of the argument.

Addressing a big gathering in Kanyanda, we argued that we were fighting to restore power and sovereignty to all the people of Uganda and that it would be up to the people to decide how they used this freedom. If they wanted to restore the monarchy, that would be up to them, not us. Our mandate was a limited one: to fight to restore freedom, by which we meant that the people should be given the chance to decide on their own destiny, without manipulation. We also pointed out that the Kayiira group were trying to divide the fighting forces and, in doing so, were weakening the struggle against Obote.

In order to expose the opportunism of the Kayiira group, I told the Baganda elders of a Runyankore proverb which goes as follows: 'When you are raising an alarm for food, you do not make a loud noise. However, when you are raising one for war, you should make the loudest noise.' In other words while searching for food you may not want a lot of people around, but when you are preparing for war or for work you need as many hands as you can get. Then I pointed out to the elders that anyone who clamoured for fewer helping hands during a war was not being serious. Indeed, he was an enemy. The peasants understood and started saying: *Omusajja ono si mulungi. Ayagala kulemesa olutalo lwaffe.* ('This man Kayiira is not a good man. He wants us to lose the war against Obote.') In this way, and in that audience, which was 100 per cent Baganda, we were able to defeat this sectarian opportunistic group, which in some fora would claim to be working for the Baganda, and in others for the DP. We defeated them politically, without using any military means.

EVACUATING THE LUWERO TRIANGLE

After defeating the UNLA offensive of June/July 1982, we started attacking Obote's military units, starting with Kakiri in late 1982. The attack was led by Salim Saleh. This was the second time we had attacked this unit during this period, and we also attacked units at Masulita and Sanga. In February 1983 we suffered what was, for us, a major setback. At Bukalabi on 21 February, we lost nine comrades and Saleh, who led the attack, was wounded in both arms. This incident, which we considered a great disaster, shows the small scale of casualties on our side. Because of our successes in the war, the UNLA moved out of their barracks bases and were extensively deployed in encampments in many of the principal trading centres in order to deny us food.

Meanwhile, we had been hoping to get some more arms from outside. I had been given some promises of guns, but the affair had been messed up by the incompetence, rivalry and ideological limitations of some of the members of our external committee. Many of these petty personal rivalries occurred because some people wanted to be seen to be the ones who were doing the most to advance the struggle. Because of this rivalry, lines of contact were disrupted and we could not get delivery of the new guns we needed. Most of our landmines had already been used up and our conduct of the war was becoming very difficult. The number of our soldiers had grown to about 4000 by early 1983 and yet we still only had 400 guns. In other words, we had a ratio of one gun for every ten soldiers. In addition to these problems, there was a civilian population of almost one million in the areas which we controlled. We thus had to use those 400 guns to hold off Obote's army of 40 000 and, in doing so, defend both ourselves and the civilians.

As far back as December 1981, when I returned from abroad, I had proposed that we should encourage the population to leave what we called 'the liberated zones'. By that time, such areas – for example the whole of Nakaseke county, much of Singo county, and parts of Kyaddondo and Busiro counties – were really liberated zones because the Obote government had no influence there. Although we moved about openly, and also had the support of the civilian population, I was nevertheless very apprehensive because I knew that in the event of a determined government offensive, it would be very difficult for us to protect the population and also guard our territory. For these reasons, I had proposed that the civilians should be encouraged to leave the operational areas. Our people, however, had their own interests, such as girlfriends in the area, and my line of argument was defeated in a meeting of the High Command and the NRC.

The counter-argument to mine was that if we told the people to leave, they would think that we had been defeated. I said that these were subjective arguments and that we must argue objectively and truthfully and tell the people as much. My argument was not accepted and I had to withdraw and leave the matter alone. Had my proposal been accepted, we would have been saved many of the difficulties we faced in 1983. The civilian population could have gone over to Obote's side and denounced us as 'bandits'. This would have relieved us of what became a major responsibility and would have left the liberated zones thinly populated and relatively easy to defend. The area known as the Luwero Triangle covered the whole of Luwero District and adjoining parts of Mpigi and Mukono Districts.

There were three main advantages to evacuating the Luwero Triangle zone, quite apart from removing the people from the battlefield. Firstly, it would allow us to concentrate our forces for offensive operations against the enemy, instead of being forced to scatter our few rifles to try and protect the population, which we would not be able to do effectively because we could not stop the UNLA from penetrating the Luwero Triangle. By the use of mines and ambushes, we could deny the UNLA supplies and force them to withdraw, but in the meantime they would have shot as many civilians as they could find – which is what they did. Their hostility to the civilian population was due to the very reactionary UPC prejudice against Baganda and Bantu in general. It was also due to the ideological backwardness of the UNLA leadership. They did not know that in order to win the war against us, they had to win over the people to their side.

Secondly, a depopulated Luwero Triangle would starve the enemy of information. Although the people supported us and were reluctant to give information about us to the enemy, Obote's thugs could always extract it through torture. Finally, a less populated operational zone would reduce the need for the supply of food and medicines. Too many people in an operational area could lead to the collapse of the struggle because of the problems entailed in looking after them, even before one started tackling the problems of actually fighting the war.

I did succeed in persuading some Bahima people in the Lukoola area to move with their cattle up to Gomba, which was not in the war zone. But if the *wananchi* had left the Luwero Triangle *en masse* and then denounced us, I am sure Obote would have been happy. He could have said that the people had grown tired of the 'bandits', as he used to call us, and that they had managed to escape. At that time Obote was weak, so had the people gone, I do not think he would have punished them for having lived in 'bandit areas' for so many months. He would instead, have put them on television and been grateful for what he would have regarded as a political propaganda coup against us. It would have helped us a great deal later if our people had appreciated my line of reasoning.

ATTACKS, COUNTER-ATTACKS AND PROBLEMS OF FOOD SUPPLY

In March 1983, when Obote launched another major offensive, we faced a lot of problems. For a start, the UNLA had gathered its forces from all over the country for its biggest offensive yet. Originally, we had had to contend with the central brigade, which was based at Bombo. When they had not managed to suppress us in 1981–2, they realised they were facing a serious problem and so this time they reinforced the central brigade with troops from the other three brigades based in the north, west and east of the country. They started by using artillery, which, fortunately, is not very effective against a guerrilla army since guerrillas do not concentrate in any one position. They also used helicopters, not so much for fire action, but for spotting and dropping supplies.

Although the UNLA assault was militarily futile, it caused a lot of inconvenience. I had to order the population to withdraw from the Bulemezi area near Kampala, into Singo, the northern end of the Luwero Triangle, where they were very crowded and there was almost no food. At the same time, our army was bogged down in operations to defend the population, instead of launching offensives to capture more arms, which was still our main objective.

In May 1983, in an attempt to increase our guns, and also to destabilise Obote's offensive against us, I led an expedition to attack Kabamba for the second time, our original attempt having more or less aborted in February 1981. We travelled from Bulemezi to a place about nine miles (15 km) from Kabamba, which meant that we had covered a distance of almost 200 miles (320 km). When we arrived near Kabamba, however, we had problems of food shortages and some of the young soldiers had become rather undisciplined. I was no longer sure that we would not be detected because there had been some delays on the way and some of our boys had run away. I therefore called off the expedition, even though we were just nine miles away from Kabamba. We had to turn back because I could not afford to make any mistakes. There were about 1500 of us, all moving together.

Moving such a large force of not-so-well-trained or well-fed people is not easy, especially at night. If you put two metres between one soldier and the next, 1500 people will stretch to a distance of about three kilometres. Secondly, after crossing a visible obstacle, like a stream, the people in front are supposed to slow down until the last commander, through a courier running alongside the convoy, confirms that the last person has crossed. Ideally, each soldier should stay awake and keep in touch with the soldier in front of him. If all these things happen, then the column can move to its objective successfully and in time. In theory, a column could travel up to 30 miles (48 km) in a night although a distance of 18 miles (28 km) is more realistic. Seldom, however, do such things go smoothly.

Because of exhaustion and sometimes hunger, a soldier might doze off, even while he is still walking. Then the soldier in front of him will increase the distance between the two, thus breaking the pattern and the rhythm of the column. When the soldier who has been sleeping on his feet finally wakes up, he will hurry and try to catch up with the people in front. In his anxiety he may sometimes take a wrong turn. The soldiers behind him will follow him in the same direction. The column has been cut and this will only be noticed after some time has elapsed. The group ahead will stop and begin a search for the lost group. A delay of an hour or two is likely to occur before the column can be reconnected and the advance resumed.

Another major problem for such long columns was food, especially if the distance was great. Ordinarily, we ate cassava and other bulky foods, but for long distances we had to get dry foods, such as dried maize (*emberenge*) and dried meat. While dry maize grain was an adequate food, we had to eat it cooked. It took a long time to prepare and could lead to exposure during attempts to collect firewood, as well as from the smoke of the fire itself. Moreover, since the soldiers did not have good enough bags for carrying the maize, some of the grain might spill, leaving a trail for the enemy to follow. We had to remind the soldiers constantly of these dangers. Failure to address the food supply situation on a long march may result in soldiers running away or uprooting *wananchi's* cassava or sugar cane. The latter occurred when we were returning from the aborted march on Kabamba Barracks.

Just south of the Kassanda-Myanzi road the soldiers descended on the sugar plantation of a *mwananchi* called Kalanzi. I, in turn, descended on them with my stick, beating whomever I came across clutching pieces of sugar cane. After about 30 minutes, I was able to restore order. Nevertheless, those who escaped my attention successfully munched their loot and proceeded to spit the cane all along the route, leaving a trail that the enemy could easily have followed. Fortunately for us, by that time Obote's soldiers were not very eager to fight us.

Ideally, what we needed on such a long journey was dry food that could be eaten without the need for further cooking. Regular armies use dry rations – tinned meat, tinned fish, tinned beans and hard biscuits – none of which need to be cooked. This saves time and maintains concealment because there are no cooking fires to generate smoke and attract the enemy. During the march to and from Kabamba, we had bought dry maize, boiled it, and tied it into small bundles for each soldier to carry his own ration. We estimated that it would take us six days to our destination, but because of poor discipline during the night marches, the journey took much longer. Furthermore, the dry, boiled food went bad and many soldiers either ate more than their share or spilt quantities of it.

On 1 June 1983, soon after our return from Kabamba, Julius Chihandae and Stanley Muhangi attacked Kiboga and captured a few guns but we could not hold off the enemy offensive effectively while we still had that huge civilian population with us. Around June, therefore, the evacuation proposal that my colleagues had rejected in 1982 now had to be accepted, although it was now more difficult for the people to withdraw. Nevertheless, we told them that except for people who were specifically known for their activities in supporting our cause, the rest should hand themselves over to the authorities. We had no food left, so it was absolutely imperative that they should go. For much of June and July 1983 we were busy evacuating the civilian population from Luwero and by the end of the year the whole of the area was depopulated.

Without the civilian population, our fighting work was very much easier, although we now had a more serious problem, that of food scarcity. With fewer mouths to feed, however, we managed to survive somehow. The main hardships at this time were lack of food and medicines. In September 1983, while we were in the Ngoma area, we ran out of starch foodstuffs. We tried to plant our own cassava but Obote's army came and cut down the crops because we did not have enough forces and ammunition to fight pitched battles defending our territory and our crops. One such major battle would have finished all our ammunition and the war would have been lost. In fact, we lost one of our prominent political leaders, Sekitoleko, at Bulamba in Ngoma where we had established a production unit growing food for our forces.

Unable to grow enough of our own food, we depended on using our clandestine contacts to buy food from areas which were on the periphery of our operational zones, areas which the enemy thought were completely under its control. These were Buruli, Katwe-Kanjiri and Kyanda. This process involved people travelling long distances of up to 40 miles (65 km) there and 40 miles back again searching for food. They would sometimes be attacked on the way and have to drop the food as they fled. The Bahima people of Ngoma and Wakyato rescued the NRA by giving us a total of 21 000 head of cattle which sustained us between September 1983 and June 1984.

The arrangement was for the peasants to give us their cows on loan, and we promised to repay them after the war. This arrangement had two advantages. One was that the NRA would get food to sustain it, for a period at least. The cows were certainly more convenient than crops because they could be moved around, although they also left large tracks which the enemy could easily trace. The solution for this was to ambush the enemy as they followed our tracks. Although the need to defend our food supplies forced us to expend ammunition, it was easier to defend the cattle since that would entail fighting mobile battles, not static ones, as would have been necessary when defending crops. In fact, we ate the last of these cows after our attack on Hoima on 30 June 1984.

EXTENDING THE OPERATIONAL ZONE

Sometime in 1982, we had formed what we called the First Mobile Force, commanded by Fred Rwigyema and Salim Saleh. The idea was that this force should launch offensive operations, while the zonal forces guarded and defended our zones. In addition I created a mobile battalion comprised of one armed company and three unarmed ones. This mobile battalion was directly under my command and concentrated on carrying out national operations.

By the middle of 1983, the number of our guns had grown to between 500 and 600, although we were still acquiring them the hard way, by capturing them from the enemy. Apart from the Kagogo incident in 1981 where we had lost guns to the Tanzanians, we very rarely lost guns to the enemy. Our casualties were also low, especially in comparison to the enemy. The reason why we had few casualties was because of meticulous preparation by the leadership and the commanders.

There were two types of operation, national and zonal. Major, national, offensive operations could only be authorised and ordered by myself, as chairman of the High Command. These entailed attacking enemy barracks, encampments or other defended localities. It is difficult and dangerous to attack the enemy while he is behind his defences, but easier when he is on the move. The enemy on the move is not dug in, and is not protected by trenches. Because of the difficulties of attacking an entrenched enemy, it was decided that such attacks could only be undertaken when I was satisfied that it would be absolutely safe or that any loss on our side would be minimal.

Zonal operations, on the other hand, were carried out under a zonal commander. They entailed repulsing enemy attacks against our camps, launching ambushes on enemy units and laying landmines within his zone. A zonal commander could liquidate enemy infiltrators and defend himself and his units without necessarily making prior contact with the High Command.

I would say that our meticulous planning was a very important factor in winning the war. Had we suffered many casualties and lost many arms, the outcome would undoubtedly have been different because we would have lost hope in victory. A certain amount of damage is sustainable. The most dangerous thing would have been for our soldiers to despair and think that the war could not be won.

After the abortive attack on Kabamba, one of our forces attacked Kiboga on 30 June 1983 and captured 30 guns. Then on 3 July, Fred Rwigyema, Saleh and Joram Mugume attacked Luwero. They killed a good number of soldiers and captured about 24 rifles. Although we lost three comrades at Kiboga and four at Luwero, our losses were very small in comparison to those of the enemy. We also carried out successful ambushes at Kigweri in Ngoma, capturing 30 rifles and at Nabisojjo where we killed a lot of soldiers and captured some more rifles. The ambush at Kigweri was carried out by Muhangi, Karuhanga and Sabata, and the one at Nabisojjo by Peter Kerim. During this time we lost some close and valuable comrades: Emmy Ekyaruhanga was killed at Sambwe near Ndejje, Tumushabe at Mugoogo, and Kakwezi at Luwero.

Before the March 1983 offensive, my headquarters had been at Semuto, near the border between Luwero and Mpigi Districts. When the offensive commenced, I withdrew north-west, with the bulk of the population, to Singo (now Kiboga District). After evacuating most of the population, in July 1983, I moved my headquarters back to Luwero District at Ngoma. At the same time I maintained a small force behind Obote's lines all the way to Matuga, just 12 miles (20 km) from Kampala.

156

By the second half of 1983, the range of our six zonal forces had been extended considerably. Abdel Nasser had been renamed the Task Force and its job was to carry out urban operations around Kampala. Mondlane controlled the area around Kalasa and Makulubita; Lutta controlled the area of Kikandwa and Semuto; and Kabalega controlled the areas of Kapeka and Kikubanimba. Nkrumah was in the Lukoola area and there was also a unit patrolling the Ngoma zone. Mwanga unit controlled the Wabusana area, that is Kikyusa: in other words, we had crossed the Gulu Road. Having beaten off Obote's major offensive of 1983, we were now on the right-hand side of the road as one goes to Gulu from Kampala, and were operating towards Bugerere and as far as the River Sezibwa. The Mobile Force had by this time grown into the Mobile Brigade and was active in this extension of our zone of operations.

Chapter 12

FIGHTING OBOTE (3)
[1984–6]

MASINDI AND ITS AFTERMATH

I had been reconnoitring Masindi Barracks since 1982 and by September 1983 I believed we had enough information to enable us to attack it. I had intended to lead the expedition myself, but at that time my liver had become enlarged because of an amoebic infection and so I sent Elly Tumwine in my place. On the way, however, the expedition encountered a small force of UNLA soldiers and they exchanged fire. Realising they had been exposed, our people called off the attack and returned to base.

We made a fresh assessment of our plan and by early February 1984 I decided we had sufficiently good intelligence information on it to launch a fresh attack. Over the previous two years, I had sent several groups to reconnoitre Masindi. A man named Kaka had worked there as a grass cutter and had a network of informants there. He gave us intelligence about the layout and activities of the barracks by day. This was useful, but since we wanted to attack at dawn, it did not give us a picture of what the barracks would be like at that hour. I therefore sent two other men: Stanley Muhangi, an army officer who has since died, and John Mugume, now in the military police. They went to the barracks at night to monitor what went on. One of them waited for a group of soldiers and joined their line from the bush, mingling with them. When they reached the barracks and dispersed, each going to his house, our soldier went and sat near one of the flats. He was able to sit there the whole night because the barracks was not properly lit and there was also no check on the side where they had entered. The only checking was at the quarter-guard.

In addition, inside the barracks there was only a small guard outside the armoury. This was a serious weakness from their point of view. If an enemy can get near the armoury, and there is only a small guard outside, the attackers will simply force the guard to flee by firing at them. Our soldier waitcd until dawn and came back to report that the only guards were at the quarter-guard and the armoury. This was good news for us. It would have been more dangerous if they had posted groups a kilometre or so away which would have exposed our advance and alerted the people in the barracks to go on the defensive.

I authorised Salim Saleh to lead the expedition, using the Mobile Brigade. I very much wanted to go myself, but I had to stay behind because I did not want to alert the population about our plans. Although the local people were on our side, their excitement over such an operation was another of our problems. In order to protect the Masindi operation, therefore, I had to remain behind and concoct a complicated story, telling the *wananchi* that the force which was going to Masindi was going to help people cross over to Buruli through Kyanamira. I added that we wanted this operation to be carried out very quickly so that we would be able to concentrate on fighting the war.

I briefed Saleh and he left with a force of 700 fighters, 375 of them armed and the rest going as 'commandos'. Since July 1983, we had withdrawn our main forces to the Ngoma-Wakyato peninsula, a large slice of territory surrounded on three sides by rivers – the Mayanja, the Lugogo and the Kafu – leaving an entrance through Butalangwa. When Obote had pressed his offensive of 1983, we used many of the river crossings to counter his moves. We inflicted damage on the enemy at the battles of Kasozi, Nyakashagazi, Birima, Kyabalango, Kitindo, Nyabishojwa and Kyakamunyweere, in addition to earlier battles at Kalongelo, Dambwe, Busemba and Kikubanimba.

When the enemy discovered our use of the river crossings, they decided to use the rivers to besiege us and deny us food. Therefore, in order to go to Masindi, one had to avoid several enemy detachments at Buhanku, Bulyamishenyi and Biduku. In particular, our large force of 700 had to cross two kilometres from the Buhanku UNLA detachment on the River Mayanja, enter Singo, cross the River Kafu, enter Masindi District, and then undertake day and night marches in order to reach and attack Masindi Barracks 60 hours later – and all without arousing the suspicion of the enemy! In the event, they were able to move swiftly across the open ground at night, helped by the low level of the grass which had recently been burnt.

The attack was launched at dawn on 20 February 1984 and it was a complete success. We captured 765 rifles, our biggest booty to date, along with machine-guns and ammunition. We had used only 375 armed men in the attack although we had in all a force of 1400. I had remained behind with 700 armed fighters as a back-up force. As soon as Saleh communicated to me that he had succeeded in getting inside Masindi Barracks, I left with my group of 700 men and we met up with his force at the River Kafu. On the way back, we were attacked two or three times by the enemy trying to make us drop our booty, but we repulsed them and returned safely to Ngoma.

After Masindi, we were able to increase the number of guns to 150 for each of the Mobile Brigade's five battalions of 300 men. The Brigade now had a total of 750 guns, while the zonal forces had about 60 guns each. Masindi was definitely a turning point in the war, because it finally ended the offensive which Obote had started in March 1983 and which had lasted nearly a year. Previously, we had merely made it impossible for the enemy to achieve their objectives. In the attack on Masindi, we had not only bypassed the enemy by making an extremely complicated river crossing, without losing a single soldier, but we actually made a strategic gain against them. We had been meticulous in our planning and that is why we succeeded.

Obote, who had recently lost one of his more competent commanders, Major-General Ojok, who had been killed in a helicopter crash in December 1983, now launched a number of wild, unfocused offensives, to very little effect. His forces were sometimes able to use aerial surveillance to spot the cattle we depended on for food, and in this way to trace our movements, but even then it was not easy for them to attack us.

After Masindi, we concentrated on more training to improve the quality of our troops. Then, on 1 June 1984, I led a group to attack Hoima. We captured more guns again and this time we also raided the local bank. We ordered the bank manager to give us as much money as we could carry. We needed the money to help us buy things from the peasants, otherwise we would be in trouble. Loaded with guns and cash, we returned to our areas, having travelled more than 300 miles (480 km).

On our way back from Hoima, we learned that Obote had launched another offensive in the areas of Matuga and Singo. This, Obote's third major offensive, was led by John Ogole using 5000 soldiers. Although slightly more organised than previous offensives, it used more or less the same manner of attack. The enemy flooded the area with several units and dug in. Well-defended units like these were dangerous to attack and, in any case, they would yield us no spare guns, so, wherever possible, we ignored them, preferring to bypass their positions and attack the areas behind them.

It was at about this time, towards the end of 1984, that we started exploring the possibility of talks with some of Obote's commanders. It was becoming clear to us that Obote would soon be defeated and we wanted to speed up the peace process in order to shorten the period of suffering which the population had already undergone. Contacts were initiated by one of our officers, Sam Katabarwa, who had been on the NRM external committee in Nairobi. One of Obote's people had contacted him there, proposing that the two sides should talk in order to end the war. Katabarwa crossed Lake Victoria by boat to where I was in the bush and told me that the Obote people had made contact. He mentioned the name of the person who had made contact, whom I also knew. Katabarwa was eager to follow up the contact, but I warned him that these people were crooks and were not to be trusted. I suggested that if any talking was to be done, it was best done outside, say in Europe, not in Kampala. But the poor man was convinced by his friend, an army officer who had trained with him at Monduli Military Academy in Tanzania. He insisted that he could make some progress and I made the mistake of not overruling him. Katabarwa went ahead to Kampala where he was betrayed, arrested and murdered in November 1984. With his death, our delicate line of contact with Muwango and Okello was broken. Up to now I have not been able to identify who betrayed him.

KABAMBA III, JANUARY 1985

Meanwhile, we had been planning for a long time to make a third attempt at attacking Kabamba. We travelled again with a large group. There was always a tension in our planning between the need for concealment and the need to take a large enough attacking force for the task. In order to carry the arms and ammunition we captured, we needed to send a large number of people, so the balance was always a delicate one. This time again we decided we needed a sizeable force.

Towards the end of December 1984, we crossed the River Mayanja at Sebuguzi. At this point the river is divided into two by a narrow strip of land which provides a useful 'resting point' halfway across the river. On this occasion, however, the current in both halves of the river was flowing very swiftly and it took us until 2.00 a.m. to get the whole force across. We had planned to reach Kyamusisi before dawn, but we had only travelled as far as Kiryowa by morning. There we were spotted by some UPC people, who promptly reported us to the authorities at Mityana. Faced with this problem, I decided to trick Obote's men. I again split our force into two groups of about 700 people each and put Saleh in charge of one section so that he could move as rapidly as possible to attack Kabamba. The rest remained with me.

Our job was to loiter around the areas of Kyamusisi and Bukomero so that the enemy would have no idea of our true intentions. Kabamba was to the west of Kyamusisi, so my group turned northwards, conspicuously passing through Bukomero, only three kilometres from enemy positions. The enemy panicked in their camps because they did not know what we were up to. We camped at a place near Muyanje and later on moved to Kembogo.

I established my base at Kembogo around 28 or 29 December, and Obote's forces attacked us unsuccessfully. Having repulsed them, we moved from Kembogo to Kagaali. I was trying to give Saleh time to reach Kabamba. After separating from us at Kyamusisi on Christmas Eve of 1984, Saleh had tried to lead his 700 men across the Kasanda-Myanzi and Mubende-Kampala roads during the hours of darkness. However, his column became split after the first crossing and he had to go into hiding for the whole of the following day. He crossed the Mubende-Kampala road that night, spent the daylight hours of the following day at Wamala and eventually got to Kyahi. There he got in touch with a girl called Jane Komugisha, who was our contact in the Mawogola area.

This young lady had procured food beforehand at our request, and she fed Saleh's force. This time Saleh followed the northern bank of the River Katonga, going through Bubanda, and his force attacked Kabamba on New Year's Day

1985. They succeeded in overrunning the barracks, a feat which we had first attempted four years previously, at the very beginning of our armed struggle. On this third attempt, Obote's soldiers fled at the sight of our force. One man tried to repeat what the Tanzanian corporal had done in 1981 by entering the underground armoury in order to deny us entry. This time, however, we were better prepared. A landmine was pushed in, electrically detonated, and killed the poor fellow. Fortunately, the ammunition inside did not explode and we reaped a rich harvest indeed – between 500 and 600 rifles and a great deal of ammunition.

Saleh sent me a message around 3.00 p.m. on the afternoon of that day, 1 January 1985, while I was still waiting with my force at Kagaali, in Singo. The message informed me that they had successfully attacked Kabamba, captured a large haul of arms and beaten off counter-attacks from government soldiers coming from Mubende. We decided to travel during the day instead of at night, so as to link up with them as soon as possible. We left early on 2 January, crossed the Kampala-Hoima road near Lwamata and climbed the Bulenga hills. While scaling these hills, I fainted because of acute dehydration. I dosed myself with rehydration salts and we continued on our journey.

We left Kyamusisi at around midnight, passed through Bukuya and headed for Ntwetwe where we arrived in the evening of 3 January. We did not enter Ntwetwe itself because a UNLA detachment was there, but we stayed about four miles (six kilometres) away. The next day we followed the Butologo road but lost our bearings during the night in the steep hills of that area. The next morning we resumed our march, reaching a place known as Nkondo, on the Nalweyo-Kakumiro road. After resting at Nkondo for a few hours, we resumed our march up to Kasambya *gombolola* headquarters. We spent the night there and the following day Saleh contacted us by radio to inform us that he was near Birembo Primary School. We lost radio contact with Saleh for sometime after that, but when we were in touch again, he told me that he was moving towards Bugangaizi. Eventually we met in a valley near Birembo. I decided we should move back towards Birembo Primary School, which is on higher ground, and we stayed there for a day or so.

Meanwhile, the UNLA force led by Ogole was desperately chasing us, trying to make us jettison our equipment and on 8 January, when we were about to start moving, he attacked us at Birembo with artillery and Katyusha rockets. We managed to repulse him, but we lost five of our boys in the process. We moved away during the night and by morning we were far away. That night we reached the Nalweyo-Kakumiro road and rested for a while. After we had eaten, we continued and reached Nkooko in the middle of the following day. The soldiers were hungry so we had to procure some maize to eat. We moved on and after crossing the River Mpongwe, we set up camp, cooked and ate.

The following day, 10 January, as we crossed the Hoima-Bukwiri road, we were again attacked by Ogole's soldiers. We repulsed them and captured more guns and ammunition. This really was a windfall. We moved the whole of that day up to a place called Rwamagari, crossed the Hoima road and re-entered our normal operational zone. In the ten days since 1 January, we had successfully travelled a distance of more than 100 miles (160 km) through enemy territory, across particularly difficult terrain. Salim Saleh's group had travelled even further and had successfully taken possession of more than 500 rifles and plenty of ammunition. It was indeed a famous victory.

Although we were now back in our own Nkrumah zone, Ogole would not give up chasing us. He went into Bulemezi to try to trap us there. When we got to Kikandwa, he was there ready to attack us but we repulsed him. We found that our people had moved to a place called Kikoko. We had had difficulty in contacting them on the radio, because they had gone off air for some reason. As we were moving out at night in a very long column, we were detected and shelled with Katyushas and 120mm mortars. I was very worried that the boys would drop our weapons. Ogole's people were at Kirema School and also at Namirembe as we were just emerging from Kikandwa forest and they started shelling us. It was a very close shave indeed. At night, while they shelled our column of more than 1500 troops, we crossed at Kabere and Mijinje and headed for Kikooko to link up with our people, who were under Fred Rwigyema's command. We reached them safely, distributed the guns and our victory was complete.

Ogole, however, persisted and tried to follow us. We fought with him on several occasions, once at Mataba swamp near Karege where a battle took place. His column was finally beaten back by our Third Battalion, commanded by Patrick Lumumba.

On getting back into Nkrumah zone after Kabamba, I reorganised the forces there. We started by creating more fully armed battalions of 300 guns each. It is true that the normal size for a battalion is between 500 and 700 guns, but 300 guns was a very big achievement for us. It meant that within each battalion we could now have four companies of 75 guns each. If one recalls that when we attacked Masindi in February 1984, we only had 75 guns to a battalion, one can see how far we had advanced within a year. The 1st Mobile Battalion was commanded by Pecos Kutesa, the 3rd was under Lumumba, the 5th was led by Steven Kashaka, the 7th by Matayo Kyaligonza, and the 9th by Julius Chihandae. I also created one more battalion, the 11th, under Chefe Ali. We had thus established six battalions of 300 guns each, which meant that we had 1800 guns in total and there were other guns for training wings. Moreover, each of the battalions was given a zone. The 9th Battalion was in control of Nkrumah zone; the 7th Battalion controlled Kiwanguzi and Gulu road; and the 11th was held in reserve. The 1st, 3rd and 5th Battalions now made up the Mobile Brigade, which meant that the Brigade now had a total of 900 guns.

OPENING THE SECOND FRONT

After our victory at Kabamba, I decided to open a second front against Obote. The opening of a second front had been discussed as early as 1983 when we had moved from Bulemezi to Singo. Because we had been under pressure from Obote's major offensive of that year, some commanders had agitated for the opening of a second front then. At that time, however, I had insisted that a second front was premature. It would have meant diverting some forces from action on the central front, and yet we did not have any to spare. In 1983, I had argued that we should first extract the last ounce of benefit from our presence in the central sector. I had plans to attack Masindi, Kabamba, Nakasongola and other barracks. I thus discouraged the opening of a second front until we had fulfilled our major tasks in the central sector.

By the beginning of 1985 we had made a lot of headway. We had scored a triumph at Masindi in February 1984; and we had successfully attacked Kabamba on New Year's Day 1985. I felt we now had enough guns to open that long-awaited second front. Therefore, I gave orders that we should open a new front line in the Rwenzori Mountains of western Uganda, and I detailed Fred Rwigyema, commander of the 11th Battalion, to lead the forces to the west, taking along all the non-fighting staff, all the sick, all the casualties, and all the elderly people who had been with us in the bush.

While preparations were under way for the expedition to the west, I decided it was time for me to launch a diplomatic offensive outside the country. I had discussed with my comrades the fact that the Obote regime could not last much longer. If we were not careful, however, it was going to disintegrate without us having the capacity to control the country; and that would be very dangerous. I convinced my colleagues that it was time I went out to do some diplomatic work in the knowledge of the imminent and certain collapse of Obote's government. This was in order to avoid a power vacuum after Obote's fall, where indecision would endanger the country even further. I left on 12 March 1985 for Sweden and arrived on the 29th after a long and hazardous journey, again across Lake Victoria. My wife, Janet, had been in Sweden with the children since late 1983. They had had a very difficult time in exile in Nairobi because they had no money, but they were now comfortable as the Swedish government was looking after them.

Meanwhile, Fred Rwigyema left with his group on 30 March. It was a very long journey requiring much heroic perseverance, not only from the soldiers, but also from the civilians. We did not lose any people along the route, however, and that was in itself quite an achievement. The convoy was guarded by two battalions – the 5th and the 11th. The Mobile Brigade remained with two battalions in central Uganda. The 9th Battalion was in the Nkrumah area, the 7th was near Kampala in the Kiwanguzi area, east of the Gulu road towards the River Sezibwa.

THE FALL OF THE OBOTE REGIME

With the opening of the second front, Obote's forces were completely overstretched. As usual, Obote was putting out a tissue of lies to the effect that we were running away to Zaire. But reality soon began to dawn on him when he realised the implications of our opening another front. He tried to salvage the situation by deploying a new brigade commander for his forces in the western region, but the poor man, Obot, was promptly killed by our forces before he could even take up his command. With the offensive which Ogole had launched in November 1984 already defeated by our successful attack in Kabamba, the second front was an additional nail in the coffin of the UNLA. Ogole, however, would not give up. He pressed on with the remnants of his Special Brigade which had been created for this purpose, and at Kembogo, in Singo, on 21 June, he tried to attack our Mobile Brigade, commanded by Salim Saleh. In that battle, the Mobile Brigade inflicted a major defeat on the remnants of Ogole's forces. Ogole himself was in command and when his forces were routed, this brought to an end his military effort in the central sector.

At around the same time, our forces in the west attacked Rubona Prison, where UNLA forces had been stationed. This was another great victory for our side in the course of which the enemy lost 66 soldiers. At Kembogo they had lost 49 and these two defeats sparked off a mutiny in Obote's army. It became clear to everybody that the UNLA was defeated and could not cope with the assault from our offensive.

The mutinous mood in the UNLA spread and, unfortunately, fights broke out on a tribal basis. I tried to co-ordinate with the mutinous elements in the UNLA but it was not easy from abroad. I had even gone to the extent of meeting Paulo Muwanga in Germany in June. We met at the Koblenz Military Hospital where he was receiving medical treatment. I told him that the NRM might look favourably at redeeming his past mistakes if he would co-operate in the expeditious removal of Obote, as that would minimise the blood-letting that had gone on for so long. He told me that he was working closely with Tito and Bazilio Okello but I emphasised that, because of their past behaviour, we could not accept a situation where their group played the principal role in reshaping the politics of Uganda. We would permit them, however, to play a supportive role to the NRM's drive to remove Obote. Muwanga was trying to rely on the Acholi faction led by the Okellos. Obote, on the other hand, relied on the Langi, under Ogole, as well as a scattering of other groups, including Captain Robert Namiti, a brigade commander in Mbarara, and Chris Rwakasiisi, Minister of State in charge of security in the Office of the President.

There was a dichotomy of interests within the UNLA-UPC factions which wanted to remove Obote. The ordinary soldiers, especially the Acholis, wanted to remove Obote so that they could reach a peace settlement with the NRA. However, their leaders, later supported by opportunists from the civilian sector, hoped to pre-empt the NRA victory by removing Obote and replacing him with a coalition of forces led by the Acholi of UNLA. They imagined that they could invite the NRA to be co-opted onto this reactionary grouping. Of course, we could not accept this at all. We insisted on being the major force, because our programme was more far-reaching and our record was untainted. Although later events were shaped by these basic motivations, the forces opposed to Obote were somewhat ill-disciplined, and it was not easy to co-operate with them. In July, the commander of the UNLA forces in the west, a man named Okwera, opened contacts with our people in Fort Portal. Unfortunately, he died before the collapse of the regime, on his way to Karuma to try to establish contact with Bazilio Okello.

When the *coup* occurred on 27 July 1985, it was no surprise to us. If anything, it had come about partly as a result of our co-ordination with people within the UNLA. Unfortunately, as soon as Bazilio Okello and his group made statements on Radio Uganda in Kampala announcing that Obote's regime had been overthrown, they abandoned the contacts they had made with us and teamed up with all sorts of opportunists to try and isolate the NRA. Meanwhile, Obote quickly left the country, this time making his way to Zambia where the government offered him sanctuary.

FIGHTING THE OKELLO REGIME

At the time of Okello's *coup*, I was in Sweden and I immediately established telephone contact with some of the key people involved in these manoeuvres. Very soon it became clear that they wanted to form an administration unilaterally. This would not only isolate the NRA, but also fight it later on. We warned them that in that case they would lose.

In early August, I came down to Nairobi from Sweden. We had managed to smuggle a military radio out, but I also kept in touch with my colleagues by telephone. At the same time I contacted Bazilio and Tito Okello and Paulo Muwanga, but in spite of my appeals, they went ahead and formed an administration. Their plan was clear: they were co-ordinating with foreign powers in order to set the stage for isolating the NRA, and eventually attacking and defeating us by military means. Of course, they were day-dreaming, but they would not be advised. Several friendly countries, including Tanzania and Kenya, tried to mediate, but the new Ugandan authorities made it very difficult for any meaningful negotiations to take place. They were also prepared, in their attempts to isolate us, to make an open alliance with former Amin soldiers. Amin himself was said to be in contact with the new regime.

Having seen the trend, we decided to go on the offensive. We arranged for 800 000 rounds of ammunition and 800 rifles to be parachuted over our area in Ngoma using Ilyushin 76 planes – the only significant support we received from Libya. On 24 August our forces attacked four detachments in the central sector at Matuga, Kiboga, Busunju and Luwero. In the west we attacked Fort Portal and Kasese, disarming the units stationed there. We pointed out that this was just a warning and that if they did not co-operate, we would go even further. They did not co-operate and instead went on feverishly preparing for war, airlifting more soldiers from northern Uganda to Entebbe and stationing them in Kampala, Mbarara and Mubende. On 12 September, we launched another offensive, this time aiming at controlling the west and south-west – that is, Bunyoro, Ankole, Kigezi, Masaka and parts of Mubende. Leading the Mobile Brigade from the Luwero area, Saleh attacked Mubende and overran it. Our forces operating in the west, under Fred Rwigyema and Julius Chihandae, advanced from Fort Portal and Kasese, passed through Kamwenge and attacked Mbarara, but they made some mistakes and were repulsed. We lost 45 of our soldiers in that encounter, an unusually high level of casualties for our operations.

Having been repulsed from Mbarara, our forces did not withdraw completely but established themselves around mile 17 on the Mbarara-Masaka road. From there they mounted a siege of Mbarara Barracks, to which the UNLA soldiers of the district had retreated, and blocked the route for any reinforcements which might try and come through the town. Our forces dominated Nyamitanga, Ruharo and Rwabusheeri, while 3000 UNLA soldiers remained inside the barracks. Tito Okello sent a relief column from Masaka, but this was repulsed by our soldiers at Kibega, near Sanga. The column then tried to establish itself at a place called Rwebiteete, on the Mbarara-Lyantonde road, but Saleh's forces, having overwhelmed Mubende, advanced through Fort Portal and, moving through Kamwenge, Ibanda and Rushere, routed the UNLA group at Rwebiteete and carried the attack through to the garrison at Masaka. They did not manage to overrun the Masaka garrison, however, as the perimeter fence was extensively mined. Saleh's forces quickly encircled the government garrison at Masaka, taking advantage of the high ground which Tito Okello's soldiers had neglected to defend, and the sieges of Masaka and Mbarara were begun.

Meanwhile, I had decided to return to Uganda. I came through Tanzania, going to Dar es Salaam to see Dr Nyerere, who was then on the verge of retirement. He had initially supported the idea of dialogue with the new regime in Kampala, but when the Okellos included some of Amin's men as ministers, Nyerere became hostile towards them. Okello's position was weak and in order to marshal support he was prepared to bring in anybody, including Amin's people. That had antagonised Nyerere and the Tanzanian president became more friendly towards us. After my meeting with Nyerere, I travelled by way of Bukoba and rejoined our forces outside Masaka on 15 September, just after the siege had begun. It was the first time I had been in Uganda since leaving for Sweden in March. I reorganised the besieging forces. Patrick Lumumba commanded the 3rd Battalion in laying siege to Masaka town, the 1st Battalion under Pecos Kutesa and Fred Mugisha and the 5th Battalion under Kashaka and Kashillingi blocked the Katonga river crossings. Having sealed off approaches from north of the Katonga, we were able to clear most of the south and south-west of the country of enemy soldiers except for those in Masaka and Mbarara. Besieging Mbarara were the 11th Battalion under Chefe Ali, and the 9th under Chihandae. The 7th Battalion under Kyaligonza and Stanley Muhangi was laying ambushes in the Katende area. The overall commander of the operation was Salim Saleh.

On many occasions in the months that followed, Okello's forces tried to relieve the garrisons from across the River Katonga, but each time they were repulsed. In fact, throughout the two sieges, which lasted some three months, they failed to get a single drop of additional supplies through to the beleaguered towns and conditions became very bad for the troops stuck inside the barracks. Indeed, when one of their commanders died during the Masaka siege, they had no way of burying him and we had to make special arrangements with the Red Cross to get the body out.

During this time, I established my headquarters at Rwenge near Mbirizi, on the edge of the Katonga valley, about 20 miles (32 km) north of Masaka. I travelled several times to Nairobi for the peace talks, going through Rwanda. For the first time since 1981 I was able to travel into and out of Uganda by air rather than canoes and boats across the treacherous Lake Victoria.

The battles of Katonga and Masaka were vitally important because it was at Katonga that we really destroyed the UNLA forces. This made our eventual assault on Kampala much easier. While fighting at Katonga, we decided to carry out a huge recruitment exercise. We recruited nearly 9000 soldiers whom we put through a crash training programme at Buhweju, Semliki and other places, and passed them out in December. We increased the size of our forces by adding new battalions: the 13th under Ivan Koreta, the 15th under Samson Mande, the 19th under Peter Kerim, and the 21st under Benon Tumukunde. These battalions were bigger than the usual size of a battalion, each consisting of more than 1000 soldiers. We had debated the issue of whether to create normal-sized battalions or to have fewer over-sized ones. We decided on over-sized battalions because we did not have enough experienced commanders who could lead such forces independently.

THE NAIROBI PEACE TALKS

In the meantime, during the battle of Katonga, we had been engaged in peace talks in Nairobi which were chaired by President Daniel arap Moi of Kenya. A lot of effort was put into the peace talks, but the Tito Okello government was simply not the type of regime which could solve the fundamental problems of Uganda. Many people in its army were tainted with bad records from the past. The politicians who had been co-opted into the new government were opportunists and could not exert any influence on the UNLA, whose soldiers continued to massacre people even while the peace talks were taking place, notably at Kabasanda near Mpigi and in Luwero and Kasala.

The Okello regime offered to include us in their government by giving us a ministry, as if that had been our problem all along. We refused to accept that and insisted on a power structure in which we would have some influence, and which would guarantee that our programme could be implemented. The Okellos' sole priority was to remain in power, supported by a gang of criminals who could loot, kill, and inflict any harm on the public, as long as they did not interfere with the so-called government. That was exactly how Amin's regime had operated. The

Okellos announced, for instance, that all the many crimes that had been committed by people who were now in power should be 'forgiven' and a new chapter started. For our part, we said that people should be answerable for crimes they had committed, otherwise the new government would have no credibility. We also said that we should henceforth be very strict in the areas we controlled, and that anyone who committed a crime should be punished.

On 10 December, Masaka surrendered to our forces and this defeat put pressure on Okello. A week later he agreed to sign a compromise deal which guaranteed us equal status in a provisional government. However, even while we signed the agreement which stipulated that we had 50 per cent of the seats on the ruling 'Supreme Council', we knew that the provisions would not work so long as the Okellos were motivated by power and nobody was fully in control of the army. The UNLA's massacres of civilians continued even after we had signed the peace accord and we knew that we had no option but to continue with the war against them. Following the fall of Masaka, we concentrated our forces around Mbarara and that town also surrendered peacefully at the beginning of January 1986.

THE FINAL ASSAULT

On 15 January, I chaired a meeting of combat commanders and we resolved to move on Kampala, starting on the 17th. After the meeting, I went through Kabamba and Mubende to inspect the forces on the western front which had not moved up to Hoima. From Hoima, I came through Luwero and arrived at Kibibi in time to see the departure of the Seventh Battalion troops who were going to attack Kabasanda. After our forces had accepted the surrender of the enemy forces in Masaka, they crossed the Katonga river, went through Buwama and established themselves at Kampiringisa forest, just off the Masaka road, about 30 miles (48 km) south-west of Kampala. At the same time, other forces established a western line of defence from Kabibi, north through Mpenja to Mityana. By 17 January our forces had moved up to Buloba on the Mityana road, just ten miles from Kampala city centre, while on the north-west flank they were at Kakiri, 15 miles (28 km) from Kampala on the Hoima road. On the Bombo road they were in the bush just opposite Bombo town, about 20 miles (32 km) north of the capital.

When we launched the offensive on the 17th, our initial task was to capture and overwhelm the enemy at Kampiringisa, Kabasanda, Buloba and Bukasa and so advance our front line on the western and south-western front. The offensive went very well on almost all sectors, although there were some slight delays on the Kampiringisa side, where the Fifth Battalion experienced a few problems.

By the evening of that day, our forces were established at Busega swamp in the western suburbs of Kampala, just four miles from the city centre, while the 5th Battalion, having finally taken Kampiringisa, were advancing along Masaka road towards Mpigi. The offensive continued until the enemy was forced to withdraw from Mpigi town and then the 5th Battalion came up to join the main force at

Busega swamp. The plan now was for the 1st and 3rd Battalions to cross at Busega and the 7th Battalion to cross from the Mityana road side. This meant that we would have three battalions moving up to the Natete sector. The 11th Battalion, which had taken part in the siege of Mbarara, were now free to cross to Nansana and attack Nakulabye, aiming for Kololo Summit View. Meanwhile, the 5th Battalion were to advance along the Mpigi-Entebbe road, take Kasanje and block the Kampala-Entebbe road in order to cut off the enemy forces in Entebbe.

The final attack on Kampala started on 24 January. I was chairing a meeting of commanders at Mpigi Town Hall, 23 miles (37 km) from Kampala, when I received information that the forces at Busega had crossed without opposition, which was a surprise to us. Immediately, we decided to exploit this advantage and I moved my headquarters nearer Kampala, to Nabbingo, 10 miles (16 km) from the capital. By the evening of the 24th, our forces had swept across Busega swamp into the area of Rubaga, Natete, and there were others in the area of Nakulabye. Meanwhile, on the south the 5th Battalion, led by Ahmed Kashillingi, had blocked the Kampala-Entebbe road at Kisubi.

The following day, 25 January, our forces attacked Lubiri and Makindye Barracks. The fight for Lubiri Barracks was very bitter: the struggle went on the whole day and, as night fell, the barracks had still not been taken. At around 9.00 p.m., however, I heard that our soldiers had entered Lubiri and that the enemy had fled. This had been the work of the 1st Battalion, led by Pecos Kutesa and Fred Mugisha, and the 3rd Battalion led by Patrick Lumumba. The 7th Battalion, under the command of Matayo Kyaligonza and Stanley Muhangi, attacked Makindye Barracks, while Chefe Ali's 11th Battalion overran the Nakulabye area and cleared the Makerere side.

On the morning of the 26th, I moved up to Republic House. This building had been the palace of the king of Buganda when he had been the non-executive President of Uganda in the first years after independence. It had been taken over by the army in 1966 and turned into the Ministry of Defence. We had captured it the previous day and so it was from there that I co-ordinated the movement of our battalions through the final hours of our assault on the capital. The battles in the areas of Bakuli and Makindye were still in progress. By 1.00 p.m. the battle had moved to Parliament Avenue. Kutesa had been transferred to headquarters, so Fred Mugisha was in command during the heaviest fighting on that sector. By 3.00 p.m. they had captured the Radio Uganda building. Meanwhile, Chefe Ali's 11th Battalion moved through Kamwokya and attacked Kololo Summit View, forcing a large enemy force to withdraw. It had been commanded by Lt Col. Odwor who had been opposing us in the bush for many years. He had led the forces which had fought us in Luwero and he had also been in command at Mubende when Saleh's forces attacked Kabamba on 1 January 1985. Ever since that time, the poor man had been in constant opposition to us until the 11th Battalion finally forced him to withdraw from Summit View. He was eventually killed at Corner Kilak in January 1987 when he became part of the counter-revolutionary insurgency armed opposition which had started in 1986.

Meanwhile, there was still work to do at Kamwokya, Summit View, Kampala Road, Nakasero and the area around Radio Uganda. The 3rd Battalion was in reserve under my command at Republic House. We received information that a problem had developed along the Entebbe Road. The 5th Battalion had been disorganised by an enemy force of about 1000 men which had been in Entebbe. They broke through the 5th Battalion lines and started advancing on Kampala while we were still busy fighting in the centre of the city. This was a worrying moment because we really did not have enough forces to counter this attack. The only force we had in reserve was the 3rd Battalion. It was a reasonably strong force but it was our only remaining battalion. I had earlier tried to raise a force to block the Mukono road but I had not been very successful. I had only managed to raise four companies which I had sent, under Namara Katabarwa, to reinforce Ivan Koreta's 13th Battalion on the Bombo road. They had become bogged down there and so I had been unable to get them transferred to Mukono road.

The breakthrough by the enemy force on the Entebbe road was, therefore, quite worrying. They had broken through our troops in the Kisubi area and, passing through Kajjansi, were advancing on Kampala. I deployed the 3rd Battalion under Lumumba to confront them, but nightfall was already approaching. The 3rd Battalion met the enemy just behind a church in Najjanankumbi, a small township about three miles from Kampala. Our forces opened fire on them and halted their advance, but we could not see clearly what they were up to as it was getting dark. Fortunately, however, the 7th Battalion in Makindye overran the barracks and thus became available as a reserve force. I became a little more relaxed, and I reorganised the battalion around the Kibuye roundabout. At around 10.00 p.m. I heard from Saleh, who had gone to support Lumumba's 3rd Battalion, that the whole of the UNLA Entebbe force of 900 had surrendered. With this surrender the battle for Kampala was really over.

The announcement that the NRA had taken Kampala was made the following day, 27 January. With the fall of Kampala, the enemy had been forced into two directions – to the Jinja-Soroti road and the Masindi-Gulu road. We could now concentrate our forces to deal the enemy decisive blows, unlike in the past when we had had to scatter our forces. We were now in charge of matters in the capital.

SWEARING-IN AND AFTER

On 27 January 1986 I held a meeting at Lubiri, to which I called some of the few commanders who were available and some members of the NRC to draft a proclamation for the formation of a new government. Even in this we were faced with tremendous problems: no telephones were working, there was no electricity, and Radio Uganda was not on the air. Indeed, we had to bring in our own bush transmitter to use instead! We did not manage to get anything working until the 29th, which is the day when I was sworn in as President.

A huge crowd turned out for the swearing-in, which took place in front of the Parliament Building. Since I am not a very excitable person, the main emotion I remember feeling on that occasion was an immense sense of relief – at last we were going to be able to have a government not paralysed by indecision and excessive compromise (which is the kind that would have been produced by the Nairobi Peace Accord). Now we could have a government that could give leadership and direction. While we were still fighting in the bush, we had drawn up the Ten-Point Programme for implementation in government (see Appendix). Now was our opportunity to put this into practice.

In my address to the nation, I made three major points. First, I explained that this change of government was a fundamental revolution and not a 'mere change of guard': our thinking was radically different from previous regimes which had been sectarian and neo-colonial, presiding over an economy which was not properly integrated. Secondly, I assured the nation that henceforth the people of Uganda would be in charge of their country's governance; and thirdly, I declared that the security of person and property was a basic right for citizens, and not a favour given by a regime.

Immediately after the swearing-in, I had to go the same day to Goma, in Zaire, to attend a meeting which President Mobutu had called. His motive for inviting us was not entirely clear. Perhaps he was worried by the force of example – the people of Uganda overthrowing the established order by a popular revolution. He may have wished to appear to be a patron of the changes that were going on. I myself was not entirely confident of President Mobutu's acceptance of our regime, but, though mainly concerned with our own internal problems, I recognised that I must keep on good terms with our neighbours, so I drove straight from the swearing-in ceremony to the airport for the flight to Goma.

It was a short, courtesy meeting and I was soon back in Uganda for we still had to carry on fighting in the east and in the north of the country. The forces of the 1st, 7th and 11th Battalions all proceeded eastwards where they managed to enter Jinja town without much opposition. They then proceeded to Tororo. The 13th and 19th Battalions took the Nakasongola-Karuma route. The 21st had remained in Kasese because at that time there was still a danger of Zaire intervening in the war against us. At the River Manafa the 11th Battalion was attacked by Kilama, who was trying to reorganise the remnants of the defeated army in order to recapture Tororo. Their attack was repulsed, however, and the 11th Battalion entered Mbale. Kilama committed many atrocities in Mbale town as he was withdrawing his forces and leaving for Kachumbala. After Mbale the 11th Battalion pursued his troops to Kachumbala and there were some further encounters around Atutur Hospital. I was worried about a possible counter-attack at Awuja Bridge, which traverses a large swamp just south of Soroti town. There was a counter-attack by Kilama, but this was repulsed.

I visited our forces in Dokolo, from where they went to Lira town, in which there was no fighting. They then advanced north to Kitgum. On the Karuma Falls sector, there was heavy fighting: the enemy attacked our forces at Kigumba, but the attack was repulsed. There was also heavy fighting at a place called Ngimu on the south side of the Karuma Falls. The defeat of the enemy there enabled our forces to cross the Karuma Bridge and head towards Gulu.

Other than this resistance by what was left of Okello's forces, the NRA was well received, not only in Kampala, but also in the east and north because of universal relief at the removal of the Okello clique. In south-western Uganda and Busoga, people regarded the Okellos as a remnant of the hated Obote regime, and were glad to see them removed. In Teso and Lango, which had been pro-UPC, the undisciplined soldiers of the Okello group, prompted by tribalism and a brand of primitive Catholicism, had started a vengeance campaign against former UPC supporters, with the result that here, too, the people were relieved by our victory.

It was only in the Acholi area that we detected real fear of the NRA. We encountered some resistance to the south of Gulu town, at a place called Bobi, which our forces eventually overcame, and after which there was very little fighting in that area. When our forces reached Gulu town itself, however, they found it deserted. This was because Bazilio Okello had been telling people in Acholi that they were going to be punished by the 'southerners' for the crimes they had committed in Luwero. Therefore, the people of Gulu first sent an old woman, obviously regarded as expendable, to test the water. When she was well treated by our soldiers, other civilians followed suit.

As for West Nile, although some ex-Amin soldiers tried to organise resistance against us, the population refused to support them and the *wananchi* sent a delegation through Zaire to tell us that there would be no fighting in the Arua area and that all the soldiers of the defeated armies would surrender peacefully to the NRA, which is exactly what happened. After that there was peace in the whole of the northern region until the bandits started their activities in August 1986.

Chapter 13

THE RECONSTRUCTION OF UGANDA

[1986–96]

BUILDING A NEW NATIONAL ARMY

For a long time, we had realised that once we came to power it would be necessary to do away with the old colonial-style army which had been recruited along sectarian lines and manipulated by unscrupulous politicians and dictators. Therefore, immediately after the fall of Kampala we started organising a new national army.

By the time we entered Kampala, we had something like 20 000 soldiers under our command, grouped in a small number of oversized battalions, since we were short of good commanders. Even 20 normal-sized battalions, however, would not have been enough to control the whole country, especially with its history of insecurity and sectarianism. We needed trained manpower quickly and we decided to utilise the existing trained manpower to consolidate security in the country. Thus we took a positive decision to incorporate soldiers from other forces into the NRA. There were two reasons for this. Firstly, these soldiers were already trained, and although they had been widely misused in the country, we saw the problem as one of leadership, not the soldiers themselves. At the same time, we were aware that incorporating these young men into our new national army would help build confidence among the population in the regions that they came from. For these two reasons we decided to absorb them.

The creation of new battalions was a steady process, continuing even while our military drive towards the north was still going on. The last battalion we had created before entering Kampala was the 21st, in Kasese. For some time we had had a small force on Mt Elgon, trying to open another front against Obote. After the fall of Mbale, they came down from Mt Elgon and we formed them into a new battalion known as the 23rd. Later, we created the 25th Battalion out of the UNLA forces which surrendered in Mbarara and Masaka. We went on building our army slowly, forming the 27th from the Fedemo forces under Nkwanga, and using the forces from Soroti to create the 29th Battalion. With some other UNLA soldiers we formed two more battalions, the 31st and 33rd. From Kayiira's UFM we formed the 35th Battalion, although later on this was disbanded because it misbehaved in Namukora. We formed two further battalions from the FUNA forces and from Moses Ali's UNRF. In this way, by the time we finished chasing the enemy out of the country, we had formed several battalions from personnel who had formerly been opposed to us. The incorporation policy was made possible by our non-sectarian line. Initially, we even left the battalions under their original commanders. The only requirement was that they should be under national command. This was an interesting and unusual model that could be followed by comrades elsewhere battling with similar problems.

In order to build a new national army like ours, however, it is essential, first of all, to clarify the ideology of the armed forces and establish a firm code of conduct that will be respected and adhered to. Thus, you must first of all ask yourself the question: 'Where does our strength come from?' If you call yourself an army and you want to defend the country and its borders, or to defend a system, what will give you the strength to do so? An army *per se* is nothing because it cannot fight without fresh recruits and without economic means. Therefore, an army uprooted from the people is a weak army. Previous armies in Uganda were brutal because they came from the colonial system. Their strength did not come from the community but from their status as auxiliaries of an alien force. If you want to defend the country and the system, relying on the people to give you the fresh manpower you need, how can you afford to antagonise them, and at the same time achieve your mission?

The ideological realisation of where your fundamental interests lie is crucial if the mission is to succeed. Even if fairness, even-handedness and altruism are forgotten, given the mission of defending the country, using internal resources, there is no alternative but to make sure harmonious relations exist with the population. Previous armies in Uganda were brutal because they did not owe their existence to the people – that is why they deluded themselves that they could get away with their crimes against the population. Of course, in the end, we proved to them that the people were the ultimate deciders of their country's fate. Once this is realised, the rest is a question of discipline in order to keep in close harmony with your basic goals.

Therefore, anybody who acts in a manner which antagonises the basic interests of the army has to be removed from power. An army must adhere to a strict code of conduct, which itself comes from the understanding of its basic mission. Then it is easy to enforce such a code, because enforcement is in the interest of the army and the country, and a commander can thus be as harsh as necessary in order to achieve that. Once this is understood, even within the army itself, strict discipline is not resented. Thus success depends upon a clear understanding of the mission, both by civilians and soldiers, and upon ideological and organisational discipline.

Recruitment into the armed forces since those early years of the NRM has been based on recommendations from local village councils and committees who must vouch for a recruit's character and personal discipline. In this way, the recruiting team would only be concerned with health and physical fitness, because the ideological and psychological factors had already been taken care of.

The army which we have now created in Uganda is governed very closely by the concept of collective responsibility. Consultation takes place through policy and administration committees at all levels so that responsibility is shared and there is the benefit of contribution by everybody, even on matters of discipline and promotions, which can be particularly sensitive issues. The Army Council is like the army's parliament and is attended by all battalion, brigade and division commanders, and all heads of department at headquarters. Then there is a smaller group composed of division commanders, headquarters department heads, the army commander, the Chief of Staff, and the President, who is chairman of the High Command. This principle of collective leadership democratises military input so that decisions are not only obeyed in mechanical fashion, but are also respected because they are understood.

For instance, between 1992 and 1995 we were able to retire 50 000 soldiers in circumstances where there was a serious problem of unemployment, and where discharged soldiers might not be able to get another job. We were able to carry out this exercise without any problem because the army accepted and understood the reasons why this had to be done. We called the Army Council and explained that if we were to maintain such a big force indefinitely, the welfare of everybody would deteriorate, and, at the same time, our combat effectiveness would decline because we would not be able to afford to buy new equipment. All the decisions that were taken on this issue were shared. This exercise of retrenchment in the army was unique in Africa because elsewhere people who have had to take similar actions did so only with the help of external backing. So the control bodies of the Ugandan army are now as democratic as they can be in any army. Indeed, some foreigners have begun to show interest in our methods and actions because ideas, not resources, seem to be the big problem in Africa.

PROBLEMS IN 1986

When the National Resistance Movement came to power in 1986, the problems facing the country were immense. First and most urgently, we had to contend with threats to our security from rebellion and lawlessness in the north beginning in August 1986. Secondly, we had to plan and implement the economic reconstruction of Uganda from the state of near-bankruptcy to which it had been brought by two decades of neglect and mismanagement, and all this with the infrastructure, especially roads, in a state of almost complete collapse. At the same time, we owed it to the people of Uganda to restore to them some level of democratic participation, of which they had been deprived since the early 1960s.

INSECURITY IN NORTHERN UGANDA

There have been two security problems in the north since 1986. One was the counter-attack by the defeated army with the aim of recapturing power, launched in August 1986. The other was the Karamojong cattle-raiding which had been a longstanding problem.

By March 1986, we had secured control in the north and the remnants of the army of Obote and Okello who had not surrendered – about 10 000 of them altogether – fled into the Sudan. These former UNLA soldiers were disarmed on entering the Sudan, but among them were elements who had ambitions to reassert themselves in Uganda. In the meantime, there was total peace in the north between March and August 1986.

On 19 August, a Sudanese army officer called Lt Col. Clement, who was a Christian southerner, but working for the Arab authorities in Khartoum, summoned together these Ugandan ex-soldiers who had been staying in camps near Parajok in southern Sudan and proceeded to rearm them. It appears that the Sudanese army wanted to establish a quisling regime in neighbouring Uganda in order to help it cope with its own internal southern Sudanese insurgency from the SPLA (the Sudanese People's Liberation Army). They formed a battalion from these Ugandan ex-soldiers and moved them south to Nimule, a small town on the Sudanese side of the border with Uganda. Their aim was to cross the border and capture Bibia, a small town directly opposite Nimule. They intended to take the district headquarters of Gulu next and then move on to Kampala. They thought they were at a wedding party, but they had sorely miscalculated the strength and determination of the NRA. They were defeated on the spot at Bibia where they lost about 200 men. Although they were defeated in a conventional attack, the ex-UNLA soldiers did not return to Sudan because they had experienced the pressures of hunger in the camps from a serious shortage of food. After being defeated at Bibia, they dispersed into the bush where they caused us many problems. At one time their numbers swelled to about 50 000, with 10 000 pieces of equipment.

At first we decided to operate defensively because, in spite of their defeat at Bibia, the rebels still seemed determined to fight. Keeping to the bush and away from the main roads, they continually attacked the townships of the north. Gulu was attacked twice, Kitgum twice and Lira once. When they failed to capture any of the administrative centres of the north, for reasons known only to them, the rebels decided to come to Kampala. This was poor leadership. A woman named Alice Lakwena took advantage of their desperation. Assuming the role of their spiritual leader, she told them that she had medicine which could protect them and stop bullets from penetrating their bodies. They made a long trek through the bush, fighting as they came, and attacked Soroti. At the time we, too, were suffering from the same weaknesses. We had no technological advantage in the form of armoured cars, tanks or helicopters. We did not even have superiority of numbers, for they by then had 50 000 men or more. That is why the fighting dragged on. All we had in our favour was better discipline, leadership and organisation.

It was purely tribal opportunism that brought such numbers to their side. You could not say that they were fighting to bring resources to the north, other than by way of looting and corruption, for social corruption had widely taken root in the region. Under previous regimes, the soldiers, most of whom came from the north, had been free to loot civilian property. Whenever they looted such things, for example corrugated iron roofing sheets, they would take them to their homes, and their parents would not ask where they obtained them, in spite of the fact that one could easily tell the difference between a new iron sheet and one that had been previously nailed to someone else's roof. In this way, the whole community in Acholi and Lango had become involved in the plundering of Uganda for themselves. In other words, the reason why those rebels in the north, organised on a tribal basis, were fighting for control of the national government, was that the NRM as a government had stopped them from looting.

When the rebels got as far south as Busoga, the population there was very hostile, and it was easy for us to destroy them there. In the north, however, it was not so easy, for every time we attacked them, they would go back to the bush and because of our poor mobility, we could not quickly re-establish contact with them. In January 1987, they managed to overrun one of our units at Kilak, on the main road between Kitgum and Lira. Success went to their heads and, thinking they had succeeded in defeating us altogether, they stayed there on the main road for three days. This gave us time to organise a brigade-size force and surround them. We destroyed quite a number of them and captured more than 1300 rifles in the one operation. Lakwena deserted her 'army' at this point and fled into Kenya. Even after that, however, they still continued with their attacks, in groups, in the remoter areas of Uganda, which again put us on the defensive.

Although the NRA was clearly a superior force, we lacked the sophisticated technology to finish the conflict. When we received co-operation from civilians, however, this compensated for our lack of mobility and matters turned in our favour. In particular, when civilians helped us with reconnaissance, we were able to move around in vehicles since the rebels did not have any landmines to stop us. Once we were able to move quickly and surround the rebels, we defeated them in a number of battles at Mutelele and Ntelelo. As an effective force, they had been completely destroyed and a few remnants returned to the north. During 1987 we received some helicopters from the Soviet Union, for which we quickly trained some pilots. From then on, our reconnaissance was quick and mobility good. The remnants of the bandits began to avoid attacking our army and turned on the civilian population instead, attacking and mutilating them simply because the civilians supported us.

We developed a formula whereby we had two types of forces. The zonal forces would stay in a zone permanently, and the mobile forces could move up in support at any place. That combination was a very difficult one for the bandits to deal with because it meant that every area was covered. There was a residential force in each zone and as soon as a bandit force arrived in it, this was immediately challenged by a local force, whereas, previously, a group of bandits might have been free to rampage for several hours before we managed to rush in a force to deal with it. In the end, civilians gave us the same support in the north as we had in the east because of the atrocities committed by the bandits. At this point we ordered them to surrender, but in spite of realising that they were losing the conflict they refused. Since many of them had committed crimes, even in their own home areas, they feared reprisals from the local civilians. The only solution, as they saw it, was to commit more crimes.

The other problem that we had to contend with was cattle-raiding by the Karamojong. This was a serious problem at the time because while the army was busy with the insurgency, from 1986 to 1989, we did not have enough forces to deal simultaneously with the cattle-raiding. As a result Karamojong cattle-raiding intensified, especially in Teso. The Karamojong had acquired a very large number of guns during the 1978/79 war to drive out Amin, and they had simply kept these, which they now used for cattle-raiding. In 1987–8, when we acquired helicopters, we managed to put a stop to this practice because we had mobility, and a person driving away cattle is very conspicuous from the air. By then, however, much of the damage had been done. In little more than six months, virtually all the cattle in Teso, Acholi and Lango had been stolen.

A further security factor which we had to tackle in the north was the question of the people of West Nile. This problem dated back to the defeat of Amin's army in 1979. At the time it was only Amin's soldiers who left the country. The civilians in West Nile stayed where they were because they saw that the Tanzanian army did not seek revenge against them. In June 1980, however, the Tanzanian army withdrew from West Nile, leaving behind the UNLA under the command of Oyite Ojok. Then the fears of the West Nilers returned because they knew that Amin had committed many crimes against the UNLA, who were badly led by officers and politicians who could not restrain them. In August 1980 the remnants of Amin's army invaded West Nile from the direction of Sudan and Zaire. Immediately, the poorly led UNLA unleashed a reign of terror on the civilian population, most of whom fled across the border, ending up in refugee camps in Sudan and Zaire. The population of West Nile at the beginning of 1980 had been 600 000: about 500 000 of them fled, 300 000 into Sudan and 200 000 into Zaire.

While these refugees were in the camps, Amin's soldiers treated them as a useful political base, intimidating them to prevent them from returning to Uganda, by telling them they would be killed if they went back. After 1986 we sent our agents to go and speak with them, to reassure them and to persuade them to return. Eventually they agreed, but then the UNHCR, who had been in charge of the camps, tried to complicate the issue with logistics. They argued that one truck carries 30 people, so to repatriate half-a-million people you needed 17 000 trucks. Therefore the project was impossible. It would take 17 years to bring back all those people. I asked, 'When they went, did they go in lorries? Let them come back the way they went.' The area where they were was not so very far away – for example Yeye is only 46 miles from the Ugandan border. If the people walked at an average of five miles a day, they would be there in ten days. So we told the people to come, and they came.

ECONOMIC PROBLEMS

The economic situation we inherited was extremely difficult. The infrastructure of the country, especially the roads, had almost totally collapsed. Most of the country was inaccessible and, in any case, there was a critical shortage of trucks for transporting goods from place to place. Large numbers of trucks had been either destroyed or stolen by the withdrawing armies of former regimes. The whole communications network – roads, railways and telephone services – was in a terrible state of disrepair. Utilities, such as water and power supply, had severely deteriorated. The power station was producing only 60 megawatts of electricity, and we were tied by a 1955 agreement with the British to supply Kenya with 30 megawatts of electricity. No new station had been built since 1956 and even the existing one had not been maintained. Manufacturing plants were either closed or operating at very low rates of capacity. As a result, there was a total lack of basic consumer goods such as sugar, soap and paraffin. Goods were being smuggled into and out of the country, and sold on the parallel ('black') market. The economy had become completely informal and speculative and bringing it back to function in the formal sector was clearly going to be a very big battle indeed.

At the end of 1985, official foreign exchange reserves were down to only US$24m, equivalent to about three weeks' imports of goods and services, and net foreign reserves were negative, to the tune of US$254m. Throughout 1986, inflation was very high and output remained constrained by the lack of infrastructure, imported raw materials and spare parts. For the same reason, the country could not take full advantage of the high coffee export price.

Clearly, we needed some outside help and we began the year 1986 debating among ourselves and with the International Monetary Fund and the World Bank on how best to tackle these problems, but we did not reach an agreement until 1987. We had to resolve some conceptual problems because many of the people we spoke to were structural economists concerned with restructuring the economy in a physical manner, such as building roads, factories and so on. I think where the IMF helped us was in making us realise the importance of macro-economic tools, such as letting prices find their own level. This was something that many of our people did not understand at first. They wanted to concentrate on producing goods rather than spending time working on macro-economic stimuli. They did not realise that if you have the stimulus of free pricing, then it will be easy to produce the sugar in large quantities and release the government from involvement in producing and pricing consumer goods. So we spent that year sorting out those conceptual problems within the cabinet and the caucuses of the movement, and between ourselves and the World Bank. When we internalised the means of stimulating growth, then we were able to move forward and we signed our first framework paper in mid-1987.

The Privatisation Debate

A number of radical theorists, for example some lecturers at Makerere University, accused us of having betrayed our principles and selling out to Western ideology. However, our answer was that when we had studied the inflows and outflows into the economy, we saw that there was no other way in which we could stimulate resources. These people assumed that the outflows out of the country would be more than the inflows, which is not necessarily the case, because dividends cannot be more than the total investment into an enterprise. The second flaw in the 'selling out' argument was that its advocates overestimated the altruism of people and underestimated their selfishness. They thought that people would work devotedly for what they did not own personally. We were able to show the radical wing that it was actually more patriotic to privatise the economy than to leave large chunks of it in the public sector.

Privatising is a method which will tap the energies of people to cause economic growth, while keeping the economy in public hands will cause its decline. So who is more patriotic – the one who builds up the economy, or the one who runs it down? The confusion was caused by the belief that the nationalisers were more patriotic because they argued that foreign companies were taking out more than they were bringing in. People who thought like this, however, had not analysed properly the dynamics of the situation.

For our part, the moment we were sure that the pro-nationalisation debate was misconceived, it was very easy for us to explain it to the public. We were able to remove the privatisation and free-market debate from the realm of ideology and show that it was part of the actual tactics of building the economy. There had been a 'disengagement' theory which had argued that we could not build a modern economy unless we disengaged from foreign control which was sucking out more money than it was bringing in. For instance, even in the 1960s, the Asians whom Amin had expelled in 1972 were building the economy more than the parastatals were doing. Many of these arguments had been based on emotion rather than empirical evidence. We took the view that it was best to study a matter of detail and if it was in our national interest, to go ahead with it. We did not adopt market economics as a consequence of pressure, but because we were convinced it was the correct thing to do for our country. If we had not been convinced, we would not have accepted it.

It took a long time for the idea of privatisation to become accepted and it was widely debated in the press and other media. In April 1993, I presented a statement to the National Resistance Council, the equivalent then of our parliament, urging them to recognise the sense behind privatisation, and also on the return to Ugandan Asians of the properties expropriated from them by Idi Amin in 1972. I gave them the example of a textile factory in Jinja called Nytil, which was due to be sold off to private entrepreneurs. The factory had an installed capacity of 37 million linear metres of textile, but at that time was producing only 21 million. Meanwhile, the government had borrowed more than US$32m on behalf of the factory. The factory had never made a profit and the government had, therefore, never received any dividends on its investment. I reasoned that if the factory was to become fully operational and thus capable of making a profit, there would be many advantages including providing a market for the raw cotton produced by peasants, as well as for utilities such as water, electricity and telephones. The factory would provide labour for workers, and the government would also collect taxes from the business. I added that all these benefits would accrue to our country whether the factory was owned by a Ugandan, a European or an Asian. Gradually, as the benefits of privatisation have become self-evident, the idea has become fully accepted by the politicians and the people.

Since 1987, our economic priorities have remained the same because we have concentrated on macro-economic stabilisation, that is, stabilising the exchange rate and interest rates, increasing the tax portion of GDP, liberalising prices, and creating a free market by removing marketing monopolies. The fundamental point of liberalisation is that we have shifted the emphasis from the bureaucrat to the producer. For instance, we have reduced the bureaucrat's power to license and we have removed the control of foreign currency from the bureaucrats and given it to the exporter who earns it.

The economy has responded very well to these liberalising and stabilising policies. The growth rate has climbed from negative growth in 1985 and 2 per cent per annum in 1986 to 10 per cent in 1995, while inflation has dropped to 5 per cent from 240 per cent in 1986. In 1986, foreign exchange inflows amounted to only US$500 million, but we now get an inflow of US$1.4 billion, including exports and private remittances. Since 1991, we have licensed 1837 new enterprises, which have the capacity to create more than 100 000 new jobs.

Eliminating Rural Poverty

The problem of rural poverty is a threefold one. The first problem is infrastructure. Once one has adopted a free-market economy, whereby private entrepreneurs will be the main actors, it follows logically that the next priority is roads, to allow people to move up and down the country in pursuit of their economic activities and, in the process, develop the country. If there are no adequate roads, then it is difficult to produce goods for sale. Unfortunately, in our case, the appropriate ministries did not follow up this issue quickly. Instead, they focused their energies and resources on research, on setting up various poverty relief programmes, such as PAPSCA (Poverty Alleviation Programme for the Social Costs of Adjustment), and generally scattering money in inappropriate directions.

It is only quite recently, since about 1994, that I have intervened and pointed out their errors. My view is that these ministries are wasting resources. We have agreed that we are going to develop our country through private efforts, where the free price factor is the main stimulus. Therefore, all the bureaucrats need to do is to ensure that people can communicate physically. For instance, our officials would equate telephone communication with physical communication by road. You would, therefore, find money being put into telephones before opening up roads. Telephones are indeed an important form of communication, but what is the point of somebody being able to speak on a first-class telephone line, telling people elsewhere that he is not able to come to see them, or to bring his goods to sell to them, because there is no road? Before we talk about poverty alleviation and other such things, we should talk about the movement of goods and services. If people are able to sell their goods and services, they will be able not only to alleviate their own poverty, but to eliminate it completely through their own efforts.

The second problem to be tackled if one is to eliminate rural poverty is the whole economic policy framework which was established during the colonial days, when the only commercial crops were those needed by the colonial industries. The people were not producing crops which were beneficial to them, they were producing for factories in Manchester and other industrial centres in Britain and the developed world. Therefore, production in colonial times was not really market-oriented for a family to produce what would give it maximum returns. For instance, Uganda produces 9.5 million metric tonnes of bananas per year, but they are never exported.

Unfortunately, because of the turmoil and poor leadership, this state of affairs has persisted. Until recently, some people were still parroting slogans about the vital need for the country to grow cotton and coffee, and so on. Then we asked: 'What is the purpose of production? Is it to produce raw materials for somebody else's factory or it is to solve your own family's financial problems?' The colonial policy framework was really wrong, and, indeed, even before independence there was some quiet resistance to it. The marketing boards had monopolies for the marketing of cash crops such as coffee and cotton, but they were so inefficient that farmers were discouraged from expanding their production.

Through our new approach to economic policy, we have now dealt with these irrationalities and encouraged people to recognise that the main purpose of production is the solution to their own financial problems. We have, therefore, advised people to survey the market and if the price of a particular crop goes down, they should switch to another one. In other words, they should receive maximum returns from their plots of land. The source of poverty in this respect has been small-scale farmers producing low-value crops on a small scale and being unable to balance their household budgets as a result. I think eventually the rural economy will crystallise into two forms of production. People with small pieces of land will produce more and more high-value crops, plus their own food crops, whereas medium- and large-scale farmers will produce low-value crops, but on a large scale.

The third aspect of the rural poverty problem was the conceptual confusion that persisted as to who should play what role in the economy. If somebody does not have enough money to meet his needs, he blames the government: 'I am poor and it is the fault of the government.' In recent years I have been going round the country clarifying matters for the people by defining who is supposed to do what. I do this mostly by using local imagery in order to illustrate the concepts. I have been using the example of *olubimbi* or *ogrugyezi*, words in our local languages meaning the piece of land marked out of a farm for an individual to cultivate with his hoe. In the army, the equivalent would be the arc of fire one is supposed to cover. It is the role of the government to ensure peace and to build the infrastructure such as constructing roads because these problems are too large for private people to solve. Once the government has done that, then the individual must do his part, which is to use his land optimally to get enough income for his household.

Another image I use is *okulembeka*, which is tapping rainwater running off the roof to use in the home. The imagery here is that it is possible for God to make rain but if the individual does not take the trouble to tap the water to use in his own house, it is not up to God to do it for him. This sort of imagery has helped the people to realise that if there are money-making possibilities in the country, the individual must take the trouble to look for avenues to tap the money into his household in order to balance his needs with his income. This is because people have simply been producing goods or crops without tabulating the household requirements and the money they need to offset those needs. The focal point is the household and if its income is boosted, poverty will be eliminated and development will be sustainable. If you build a PAPSCA school and claim to have 'alleviated poverty', but the people in the area have no money to pay the school fees for their children, how will this alleviate poverty in a sustainable way?

During my rural teaching sessions, therefore, which I normally carry out at the headquarters of every county I visit, I use an illustration of three columns on a blackboard. The first column is for household needs, the second is family assets, including physical assets, as well as non-physical ones such as education, and the third is to work out how to use what is in column two to offset the requirements of column one. I have been teaching like this for a long time, but more intensively in the recent past, because we have now put some of the infrastructure in place. Originally, when there were no good roads anywhere in the country, you could not tell people to use roads to tap money where there was none. Although there are some areas which are still remote and cut off by lack of infrastructure, there is no good reason why many areas in the country should not now do better economically.

According to my demarcation of roles, government has taken on an extra role, not normally its work, which is to prop up the financially weak through a revolving loan fund of 'seed money', known as *Entandikwa*, meaning a beginning or a start. The money is provided by the central government and controlled at the county level, which is also usually the average size of a constituency. When the scheme started in 1994, every constituency received 30 million shillings, equivalent to US$30 000, making the total for the whole country about US$6m dollars. We shall keep adding to the revolving fund so that more people have access to the money, which is lent out to individuals or small groups at concessionary rates.

REGIONAL INTEGRATION

In the 1960s, there were two aspects of the East African Community (EAC). One was the commonly owned services such as the railways, the airlines, the harbours, and the postal and telecommunication services. The second aspect was the common market. The EAC broke down because of underdevelopment: there was no indigenous big business lobby that needed this market, and therefore, nobody to appreciate the need for such a large market. In addition, the community was hampered by the incapacity of the politicians to project their vision into the future; in other words, to be able to see what was not yet on the ground. In fact, outsiders such as the British were more pro-EAC than our local politicians, because British companies could see the importance of a large regional market.

However, I think the situation is beginning to change, because we are beginning to have manufacturers in Uganda and Kenya who now need this market. Certainly, the East African common market will come back on the agenda. With the expansion of the economy, the jointly owned services will not be as important as they were in the 1960s because even private people can buy their own aircraft. What is crucial is the market – the rules that govern that market and the ease with which people can do business. There is no regime which will be able to avoid the reality of the need for large, integrated markets. COMESA (the Common Market for East and Southern Africa), which is the EAC on a bigger scale, is still rather more theoretical than real, again because of a lack of reasonable roads across the area covered by the organisation. There are no roads between Kenya and Ethiopia, although Ethiopia is a very big market, nor are there roads between Uganda and Zaire, and none worth mentioning between Tanzania and Mozambique.

In the southern African region, the economies of some countries depend on exporting goods outside Africa, for instance those who export minerals. These countries do not see very easily the value of a regional market. There is talk of SADC (the Southern African Development Community) developing along these lines, and some people who favour this cite ephemeral factors such as instability in Somalia, chaos in the Sudan, and so on. However, these are temporary factors. We are designing a strategy for the future, not for the unsatisfactory present. Also, like the East African Community in the 1970s, these countries do not yet have a strong business lobby which appreciates a strong regional market. That is why they are still hazy in their concept of regional integration and they do not see the value of a regional market for exporting what is produced. Because of that, some people in SADC have been talking of creating COMESA-North and COMESA-South.

For our part, however, we are very firm that one COMESA, which includes South Africa, is the correct strategy to adopt.

One other problem is that most African countries (contrary to what the West will have us believe) are still underpopulated. East Africa is a very large area, almost the size of Western Europe, but Uganda, Kenya, Tanzania, Rwanda and Burundi, all together have a population of only 90 million, less than that of Germany, which itself is geographically not very much larger than Uganda. The small population postpones crises because you have large, underutilised resources which are used on a subsistence level. There is an inherent crisis in such a situation, but it does not reach explosion point.

The third problem which faced us in 1986, that of restoring democracy to Uganda was, in some ways, the most intractable. In the final chapter of this book I describe how we brought this about, and the culmination of the process in the recent presidential and parliamentary elections of May and June 1996.

Chapter 14

BUILDING A DEMOCRATIC FUTURE

THE CAUSES OF UGANDA'S POLITICAL CRISIS

In my view, between 1962 and 1966 the political crisis of Uganda was characterised by two related problems – sectarianism and socio-economic underdevelopment. Uganda, and most other countries in black Africa, are still pre-industrial societies and they must be handled as such. Societies at this stage of development tend to have vertical polarisations based mainly on tribe and ethnicity. Even when polarisations in underdeveloped societies are horizontal, they are sectarian by religion, as has been the case in Uganda. This means that people support someone because he belongs to their group, not because he puts forward the right policies. That delays the process of discovery of the truth and by the time the people wake up to the situation, many things have gone wrong or passed us by.

To take one example, Idi Amin should have been sacked from the army in 1960. The Governor-General of Uganda at the time, Sir Walter Coutts, recommended that this should be done because Amin had committed atrocities in northern Kenya where he had been taking part in an operation in the King's African Rifles. (These atrocities including cutting off people's private parts.) However, since Amin originated from northern Uganda, Obote's zone of the country, and in those days Obote was already scheming to use tribal groupings, he glossed over Amin's crimes and left him in the army. As I have shown earlier in this book, pre-capitalist polarisations based on identity rather than rationality can be extremely injurious to a country.

Sectarianism is a consequence of an incomplete social metamorphosis. In other countries, society has been changing continually – initially in Europe from a two-class society of feudal lords and peasants and, by 1789, a four-class society of feudalists, the bourgeoisie (or middle class), the proletariat (urban working class), and the remnants of the peasant class. Now Europe is again basically a two-class society, of the middle and working class. In the United Kingdom, the middle class, made up of professionals and businessmen, makes up 52 per cent of the population, the working class makes up 46 per cent, and the upper class 2 per cent. Therefore, in its metamorphosis society in Europe has gone through several stages in order to reach its present state, just as a butterfly or a cockroach does. The insect's first form of life is an egg, which develops into a larva, then a pupa, after which it matures into a fully-fledged butterfly or cockroach.

The problem with Africa is that not only has its society not metamorphosed, it has actually regressed. When the British explorer seeking the source of the Nile, John Hannington Speke, came to Uganda in 1862, many of the societies here had three classes – a feudal class, an artisan class and a peasant class. Both the feudal and artisan classes were wiped out and Uganda effectively regressed into becoming an almost exclusively peasant society. The situation now is that 92 per cent of the population are peasants.

So who are the peasants and how do they live? Peasants are, very largely, illiterate people who depend on subsistence farming, as opposed to specialisation and exchange, the crucial factors which bring about modernisation, efficiency and the flow of business. But if people are frozen in their subsistence activities, effectively trying to be jacks of all trades and masters of none, the economy cannot grow and society cannot develop. At present, our people grow their own food; they are their own carpenters, their own masons, even their own doctors. The process of displacing the subsistence economy will mean producing for profit. Once an exchange is created, there is full monetisation of the economy.

Lack of education also means lack of entrepreneurship and, therefore, lack of savings. In Uganda, and in Africa as a whole, a large proportion of the population is deficient in enterprise, deficient in savings, possesses no special skills and has nothing to exchange. The effect is to produce countries with a very small tax base. This is no small matter, but a major structural problem. The situation has very serious implications for the continent and it must be addressed and reversed. I think the most extreme blow to sectarianism is to monetise the whole economy, which will undermine the subsistence existence of most Africans. It will mean that people are free to produce, and free to exchange what they produce. Then they will be able to value one another, and have a common interest in stability.

A commodity relationship between one area and another will, in time, undermine sectarianism. For instance, my father does not sell his milk to his tribesmen – he sells it to other people outside his area. He has discovered that his customers are even more important to him than his tribesmen, who do not buy his milk because they produce their own. Therefore, ethnicity and sectarianism, in my view, are short-term problems caused by a failure to identify the real interests of the people. It is a failure of leaders since they have not created an atmosphere where ordinary people can discover their real interests. Ugandans did not know the implications of sectarianism until we pointed out to them that modern societies are no longer based on primitive agriculture, which is only suitable for subsistence. They are built on technology, industries and large-scale production.

Large-scale production, however, implies big markets, which leads to integrating large population groups which can form the market which will make a country's industrial production viable and competitive. A leader should show the people that those who emphasise ethnicity are messengers of perpetual backwardness. This process of undermining a sectarian mentality of 'my tribe, my religion' is linked with the process of modernisation and overcoming underdevelopment. When subsistence farming is undermined and the exchange of commodities is introduced, there will be more efficiency and, in time, savings, which will in turn result in investible capital. Eventually, the society will be transformed and modernised. The moment that process takes place, one's tribe or religion cease to be of much consequence.

Given all these problems, the least we could do would be to ensure democracy so that the people can at least discuss these problems. First of all, colonialism disenfranchised Ugandans. Then towards the end of the colonial period, an attempt was made at re-enfranchising the people. But what did Obote do in 1966 to add to the country's already serious problems of sectarianism and socio-economic underdevelopment? He disenfranchised Ugandans again by suspending the constitution and declaring a one-party state. If the constitution was that bad, the people of Uganda, not just one man, should have voted to get rid of it.

The over-centralisation of power in the 1960s was another major problem. At least during colonial times the tribal areas were quite autonomous, although they were not able to do anything much in terms of development, apart from growing cash crops for the colonial economy. Obote concentrated all the power from the districts to the central government under the pretext that decision-making would be quicker and more effective, but this only served to entrench his dictatorship further. Since 1986, that power has been restored and the districts now have control over all their affairs except defence, the currency, foreign policy, the major trunk roads and the railways. This was provided for under the Decentralisation Statute (1993) and was confirmed in the new constitution of 1995.

LOCAL GOVERNMENT THROUGH RESISTANCE COUNCILS

Originally, when we started the bush war in 1981, we had secret committees of volunteers who banded together as support groups for the fighters, to mobilise food, recruits and intelligence information. From 1982, beginning in the liberated zone near Semuto, we started holding elections to these committees and formalising them as local 'Resistance Councils' (RCs). Their brief was extended to controlling crime and to general administration in their areas. After our victory in 1986, we spread the concept and practice of Resistance Councils throughout the country, and the people responded very positively to it. In that first year or so, while our army was dealing with security problems, our political cadres were going round the whole country, explaining our mission and advising the people at the village level on the setting up of their own Resistance Councils.

The Resistance Council system started at village level, known as RC1. All the adult people of a village, that is the electors, formed a Resistance Council from which they elected their committee of nine, to run the local affairs of the village on a day-to-day basis. Each member of the committee had a specific field of duty. In the beginning we did not use a secret ballot for these local RC elections, we just asked people to line up behind the candidates of their choice. People were very happy with this for the simple reason that it eliminated cheating – which goes to show how much the practice of elections had been perverted in the past. Secondly, these elections were not on the basis of parties. Many people do not understand our aversion to political parties, but it is because of the history of sectarianism which these parties fostered in our society, mainly on the basis of religion. It was a great relief for the people to choose an individual for his merit rather than choosing an individual because of his religion. Hatred and disharmony had always accompanied this polarisation on the basis of religion. For these reasons the system of RCs which we established from village level upwards was very popular. In addition, it gave people power over their own affairs in their locality. Over the years, and especially since 1993, we have added new roles to the range of responsibilities of local councils. They vet recruits into the army and police, they have judicial powers to decide on some civil cases, and they have been made responsible for a broad range of development in their areas, such as building clinics, dispensaries and schools.

At other levels the RC system was built upon a pyramid-like structure. Above the RC1 came the Parish Resistance Council, RC2. All the committees of nine from all the villages in a parish formed the RC2 Resistance Council, and it was from this council that the RC2 Resistance Committee was elected. The system was replicated through the sub-county, RC3, level, to the county, RC4, and on to the district, RC5, level. Under the new constitution these resistance councils have been renamed, and are now Local Councils (LCs) 1–5.

At the beginning, there were some difficulties with the RCs at the lower levels because they were not properly funded. Their function then was really only identifying problems and petitioning national leaders. The Decentralisation Statute of 1993 gave the RCs power over civil servants by giving them supervisory powers as well as money. At the district level there are now district service committees which are responsible for the appointment and discipline of civil servants.

For funds, the local councils share the money that had previously gone directly to the district and central government coffers. There are about 800 sub-counties in Uganda and they usually cover a radius of four miles (six km) and have about 20 000 inhabitants each. Whereas previously, when taxes were collected at the sub-county (*gombolola*) level, all the money was taken away by district and central government, now 50 per cent of it is left at that administrative level to cater for their activities. A further 10 per cent of the money is taken to the higher county level and the rest goes to the district level. This is a new measure.

WOMEN

One of the policies the NRM is proud to have initiated is that of bringing women into the mainstream of the country's governance. Women constitute more than half of the country's population and carry out most of the work in the major economic sector, that is agriculture. In spite of this, however, for a long time, they were relegated to the periphery of political activities. The NRM has created opportunities for women which were aimed at redressing this historical imbalance. Women are represented at all levels of government from LC1 up to Parliament and they have successfully competed with men in constituency elections. In addition, through the policy of affirmative action, there is a woman in Parliament representing each district. Our parliament has about 50 women members, the second highest number in Africa after South Africa.

As a result of this policy initiative, the new constitution provides for a special quota for women in Article 180 2(b) by which a minimum of one third of all seats on local councils must be reserved for women. Thus, by deliberately involving women at all levels of governance, such as the cabinet, Parliament and the judiciary, we have demonstrated that they can play a very effective role in the country. When we initiated the *Entantikwa* credit scheme, 30 per cent of those funds were earmarked for women and youth.

As far as education is concerned, the tendency in most homes in Uganda has, for a long time, been that where a choice has to be made between educating a girl or a boy, it is mostly the girl who loses out. Because of this bias, very few girls reach post-primary levels of education. It is against this background that my government decided to give preferential treatment to girls entering state universities by adding 1.5 extra points to their marks. This is intended to redress the existing imbalance between the numbers of girls and boys who reach university. I am proud that our policy of bringing women to the fore has been enshrined in the new constitution. In addition to Article 180 2(b) referred to above, Article 33 provides that women shall have the right to equal treatment with men, and to affirmative action for the purpose of redressing the imbalances created by history, tradition or custom.

There were some complaints that the women and youth councils which we put in place have not been fully functional because of lack of money. That is true, but some people were saying that the NRM did not really care about their welfare. According to these people, appointing a few women to high posts is not a solution. However, I told the people two stories about some of our chiefs in the past. One story is from Ankole and the other is from Buganda but their message is the same.

The story from Ankole concerns a king, who had a subject who did a distinguished service for him, and the king asked his subject how he could reward him. He said to the king: 'Your Majesty, I don't want any gift from you. All I want is that when we are in a public place you should just call me by my name.' The king was baffled and asked the *mwananchi* how that could help him. He replied: 'Your Majesty, it will help me very much because if the king calls me by my name in front of so many people, everybody will wonder who I am and they will all come to me and help me.' The story from Buganda is similar, again involving a subject who had done some distinguished service for a king and whom the king wished to reward. The subject said to the king: 'Whenever we are in public, I want you to call me to your side and whisper something to me, even if you don't actually say anything to me.' This is what we did for the youth and the women. By appointing a woman Vice-President we singled out women and whispered something to them to give them prominence and confidence.

EXTENSION OF THE INTERIM PERIOD OF GOVERNMENT, 1989

When we came to power in 1986 the NRM formed the National Resistance Council (NRC) as our national governing body. Legal Notice No. 1 of 1986 (Proclamation 1) had provided as follows: 'The National Resistance Movement Government shall be an interim government and shall hold office for a period not exceeding four years from the date of this Proclamation [which] shall be deemed to have come into force on the 26th day of January, 1986.' This meant that the interim period was due to end on 25 January 1990.

In 1989 we expanded the National Resistance Council through indirect elections. We had to use indirect elections because of logistics – we did not have enough money or vehicles to mount a full national ballot, and most of the roads were still largely impassable. Because of these constraints, we could not have carried out a secret-ballot election. Therefore, we used an indirect system of elections, drawing representatives from the Resistance Council pyramid. We thus acquired a new, legal and legitimate body of national government. Originally we had said that the group which took power in 1986 would be in government for four years, and we kept that promise: before the end of the four years, a new group had come in. The expanded NRC of 1989 was not the same as the old one of January 1986. Although it had some of the original members, it had changed its character with the addition of new forces, some of them actually hostile to the NRM. Indeed, some groups that remained within the movement did not necessarily support all of our programmes. However, in the new NRC there were always more people supporting us than against.

On 24 October 1989, I presented a statement to the National Executive Committee (NEC) of the NRC stating that the NRM had had two main objectives for the interim period:

1. Reasonable rehabilitation of the country's collapsed infrastructure and of the economy as a whole;
2. Laying a firm foundation and preparing the ground for security, political stability and orderly succession of political authority. This included the development of a national army, the development of an adequate police force, development of an efficient and respected judiciary, and, above all, evolution of a nationally acceptable and respected national constitution.

In spite of the considerable successes we had achieved up to that point, however, it was clear that these set programmes had somewhat lagged behind their time schedule. I enumerated our successes as being the following:

1. The reversal of an annual economic decline at the rate of 2.6 per cent per annum between 1973 and 1986. This decline had now been replaced by a rate of growth of 7.2 per cent in the 1988–9 financial year;
2. Building a democratic mass political movement in most of the country, culminating in the constitution of the NRC and NEC;
3. Restoration of Uganda's respectability abroad;
4. The re-establishment of peace and the rule of law in most parts of the country;
5. Ending the massive refugee problem. (Uganda had been the fourth largest exporter of refugees in the world.)
6. Building – in record time – a national army capable of maintaining internal peace and defending the country's borders.

Our schedule had lagged behind because the resurgence of insecurity in the north and north-east of the country had led to a breakdown of civil administration in those areas and necessitated diversion of efforts and resources from the rehabilitation programme. Also, in spite of increased internal effort, there had been a decline in the prices of our major export crops, which had led to a sharp deterioration of external earnings. Coupled with the other factors, this was a critical setback in the achievement of our set objectives. For instance, the government's capacity to acquire the necessary logistics, such as opening up roads and acquiring vehicles for holding a genuine election on the basis of one-man one-vote, was severely limited.

It was, therefore, clear that the magnitude of the primary problems in the interim period had been underestimated. The level of socio-economic decay had reached a higher level than we had realised at first. Furthermore, the effectiveness of the Civil Service in implementing our programme had been grossly overestimated. I therefore recommended, and the NEC agreed, that the interim period be extended to complete the work we had started. I proposed that a clear timetable be worked out on the basis of the uncompleted tasks so that the population could be assured of continued progress. These measures would help close the openings for speculation about the direction and intentions of the National Resistance Movement.

DEVISING A NEW CONSTITUTION

The Constitutional Commission, which was established by statute in 1988, was chaired by a High Court judge, Justice Benjamin Odoki, and composed of 21 people, ten of whom, including the chairman, were lawyers. They were appointed by me as the President in consultation with the Minister for Constitutional Affairs.

They were selected because they represented the broad spectrum of opinions in the country. Some were identified with the idea of a movement structure of governance, some were from the old political parties, some were from the monarchist groups, and some were from the churches.

The assignment of the Commission, which started work in February 1989, was to find out how the people of Uganda wanted to be governed. There was a questionnaire containing the various topics which they knew to be topical, such as: 'Would you like to be governed from the region, the district or from the central government? Would you like traditional leaders to be reinstated? Would you like political parties to be brought back or to wait for a period for this?' First the commissioners travelled all over the country and held seminars educating people about their mission, and later on they went back with the questionnaires. Anybody could pick up a questionnaire and answer it. Then the parish councillors were called to discuss the issues raised and they passed a resolution which was recorded by the commissioners.

I think the final report was quite representative of the people's views because on some of the crucial points such as whether or not political parties should become fully operational or not, I knew the opinion in the country to be against parties, and this is what the report showed. In fact, the commissioners watered down what the people wanted – the people did not want the return of parties for a very long time – but the Commission compromised on a return to party activity five years from the first elections held under the new constitution. Therefore, the Commission was a temporising force as far as some local and international political thinking was concerned. They gravitated more to international thinking, especially on political parties, rather than reflecting the views of the people themselves.

The Constitutional Commission recommended that a new Constituent Assembly, elected by national, secret and direct ballot, should be the body to approve the contents of a new constitution for the country. Accordingly, elections were held for the Constituent Assembly (CA) in March 1994.

In my opening speech to the Constituent Assembly I said this:

> We must ensure that our political institutions spring from our social structure. If we are to develop, we must evolve institutional models which will liberate us from our backwardness. We must modernise our societies and lay the foundation for industrialisation. We cannot modernise, industrialise or develop without creating an appropriate institutional framework within which to work. It is the historic responsibility of this Constituent Assembly to set our country on the path to development and prosperity.

It was only in Buganda that there were pressures from the traditional groups for a federal arrangement between their area and the central government. By *federo*, as it was called, its advocates really meant provincialism because, otherwise, the same powers which they wanted under a federal structure were already provided for at the district level. Many people prefer power at the district level because it brings

194

decision-making nearer to the population. I think the *federo* group were seeking tribal solidarity, in other words to use the eight districts in the Buganda area to pressurise the central government into doing things not only for the area as a whole, but for different social interest groups. If they were really interested in giving power to their people, the devolution of power to the districts had already provided for that. However, out of 70 or so delegates from Buganda to the CA, 50 were against the *federo* idea.

Another issue of importance in the CA debates was whether or not we should have political parties. We in the NRM argued that there are no healthy grounds for party political polarisation in Uganda at this time because of the absence of social classes. In Western democracies, parties have usually been founded on some sort of class basis – parties for the middle class, parties for the workers, and so on. On what basis would parties in Uganda be formed, since Ugandans are overwhelmingly of one class, peasants? The polarisation one is likely to get in Uganda and countries like it is vertical polarisation – tribe A will join party A, tribe B party B, and so on. They will all be sectarian. What is crucial for Uganda now is for us to have a system that ensures democratic participation until such time as we get, through economic development, especially industrialisation, the crystallisation of socio-economic groups upon which we can then base healthy political parties. The CA voted overwhelmingly not to have political parties at this stage and to put the matter to a referendum in the year 2000.

On the question of how issues are decided on in parliament in a no-party system, it was decided that the members should vote as individuals, according to their own judgement of the issue – what is called a 'free vote' in a multi-party system. Some motions come from the individual members of parliament and others come from within government and are presented to parliament for their consideration and approval. The advantage of this system is that the members of parliament divide differently on different issues. There is more objectivity because people have to consider matters on their own merits as each issue comes up. There are thus no permanent, built-in, unhealthy fissures which would be a danger to our society and which have led to terrible consequences in the past.

Western democracies criticise our system of government, but we ignore them. Their opinion is not our concern and they themselves are not perfect. They do not even research the Ugandan situation properly, but would just have their own system imposed on Uganda. I consider it arrogant to say that the whole world must be managed the same way both in substance and form. I have advised these critics that the substance of democracy is essentially the same – governance by the population, but the forms must be different, depending on different situations. I have given them the example of water, H_2O: the formula remains the same whether it is liquid, solid or vapour. You have to choose the form of water that will suit or serve your purpose. An ice cube will be useful for your thirst but not your bath! Likewise, the form of democracy should be in accordance with local circumstances.

The Constituent Assembly approved the new constitution in 1995 and it was promulgated on 8 October. The date for the country's first direct presidential elections was set for 9 May 1996. I was opposed by Paul Ssemogerere, a former DP politician who formed an unofficial alliance with the UPC group, to be their combined candidate, although, of course, in theory, no party political campaigning was allowed under the terms of the constitution. Another candidate, Mohammed Mayanja, also stood for President in the election. Although I was campaigning as an individual, I had been leading the movement for 26 years. Therefore, the success of the NRM and my success were intertwined.

MODERNISING UGANDA

In my election manifesto and during the whole campaign, I emphasised the fact that, all along, the mission of the NRM has been to modernise Uganda by reactivating the process that had been frozen by colonialism.

Therefore, throughout the campaign, I explained to the voters that the main problem facing African countries at this historic moment is the fact that they have not benefited from the great leap forward by the human race in Europe and North America in the area of scientific knowledge and, consequently, the metamorphosis of society from a feudal to a largely middle-class one. In Europe, North America, Japan and, more recently, in South East Asia, man has been able to free himself of two age-old bottlenecks to the realisation of his full human worth. These are, firstly, domination of man by nature, which has been the biggest problem. I am here referring to the floods, droughts, diseases and pestilences, slow means of locomotion, impenetrable forests, vector insects – all of which in the previous centuries had made it difficult for people to live a prosperous life. The second bottleneck is oppression of man by man in the form of feudalism, slavery, colonialism, neo-colonialism, imperialism and fascism. Up to today, many parts of Africa are still suffering from these two major constraints which people in other continents have overcome.

Therefore, when we talk of modernisation, we mean the elimination of these two constraints from Africa. The way to achieve this is through a combination of industrialisation and democracy. Thus, firstly, instead of man relying on muscle power to solve his problems, he should rely on machines, chemicals, harnessing the power of natural forces such as the wind, water and the sun, in order to improve his welfare and make life easier for himself. He should be able to improve his housing conditions and nutrition, control diseases and find quicker means of locomotion in the form of air, rail, steam, water and road transport.

The second point is that the African man must control his destiny through democratic means. Only recently, we have been battling with the effects of a military coup in Burundi. When other parts of the world have long forgotten such undemocratic phenomena, here in Africa it has been a regular occurrence and the main form of government for the last 30 or 40 years – more Africans have lived under military dictatorships during that period than have lived under their own freely elected governments. In fact, this phenomenon of usurpation of power by minority cliques nullifies the whole idea of independence. It is meaningless to say that we are independent when we are controlled by small groups of people, just as we were in colonial times. What difference does it make if we are controlled by a small group of locals instead of being controlled by a small group of foreigners? Therefore, in order to modernise Africa, we should depend on industrial power rather than human or animal muscle; and we must let all sovereignty reside in the hands of the citizens of the country.

When it comes to a detailed examination of the industrialisation process, we have to find means of interlinking the different sectors of the economy. You cannot have industries unless you have raw materials for them. These raw materials come from agriculture, from forests, from minerals and, in the case of Uganda, from freshwater resources. Therefore, you cannot meaningfully talk of integrated industrialisation without modernising these sectors of the economy. In agriculture, you must get rid of the present subsistence economy, because in that situation a peasant tries to be a jack of all trades and ends up being master of none. He tries to build his own house, collect his water from the well; cultivate all the food he eats; look after his own cows; and become an informal teaching instructor for his children. This means that he is over-stretched; he does not specialise and cannot, therefore, become an expert in any one of these fields. He touches on everything but cannot do anything in detail or depth.

Modernising Agriculture

Therefore, modernising agriculture means introducing specialisation and exchange. Farmers must specialise in growing two or three crops or engage in other lucrative agricultural activities. Then, they will be able to exchange their products with other people in the economy. Alongside this specialisation must come the monetisation of the rural agricultural economy so that money becomes the nexus between one producer and another in the rural areas, and also between them and the producers in the urban areas. Thus farmers should engage in a limited range of specialised activities, sell to the market, earn money, and so be able to buy the other goods they need from shopkeepers and market operators. This, of course, implies improving agricultural techniques, whether aided by chemicals, machines such as tractors, relying on organic means of fertilisation, or improved feeds. It also means that agriculture becomes completely commercial, with farmers producing what is profitable for them.

In the case of Uganda, we have had the problem of the colonial legacy in agriculture. During colonial times, agriculture was not for the benefit of the farmer – it was designed to benefit colonial industries. Farmers produced low-value raw materials on a small scale and were, therefore, earning peanuts from their labour and produce. They could neither benefit from high prices per unit nor from large-scale production. Of course, the colonial industries benefited immensely because the aggregate of a large number of semi-slave peasant farmers produced huge amounts of raw materials. Uganda, at present, is ranked number five in the whole world in the amount of coffee it exports (between 3.5 million and 4 million bags per annum). This is in spite of the fact that much of this coffee is produced by small-scale farmers who did not get much out of their labour until recently, when we introduced clonal coffee, whose yield is three times higher.

In the case of cotton, which is currently grown in many parts of Uganda, the annual yield per acre, using the available techniques, is only about 200 kilograms. Until recently the price was 400 shillings (40 US cents) per kilogram. Since land is already fragmented because of archaic inheritance practices, the average household landholding in some parts of Uganda is about three acres. With this amount, they can set aside only about an acre for cash crops, and use the other two acres for food crops and shelter. For a whole year, therefore, if a farmer concentrates on growing cotton, he will earn only 80 000 shillings (US$80). This is a family consisting of between 10 and 20 people, all depending on US$80 per year. Even if there were only 10 people, which would be a small extended family by our standards, this would mean that the per capita income of such a rural household would be no more than US$8. Therefore, the miserable US$270 per capita income, which is the national average, only comes about when you aggregate the eight dollars per person per head of the rural farmers with the US$200 million of an industrialist such as Madhvani. At the lower end of the economic scale, therefore, there are really poor people – poor not because of the land, or the overall economic situation in the country; but because of the backward farming practices that we inherited from colonial times.

Therefore, when I talk of modernising agriculture, I mean ensuring that the farmers are taught how to use their land optimally. They should produce food crops for their own consumption and any other crops that will bring them maximum returns from the market. These are crops such as spices, special nuts, special fruits, and medicinal plants that are in high demand from industries. By extension, the modernisation of agriculture also involves campaigning against land fragmentation. It means that we have to have two types of agriculture: the agriculture that is useful to people with less than 10 acres of land, who should engage in growing food crops and high-value cash crops; and another that is useful to medium, large-scale and plantation farmers, who have no problem because they are more flexible. They can either grow large quantities of low-value crops such as maize, cotton and bananas and make huge profits because of economies of scale, or they can put some of their land under high-value crops and the rest of the land under forestry, and they will still earn a lot of money. This approach will completely change the Ugandan countryside. Instead of the present scrubland and thorn bushes, in future we hope to see well-organised small-scale production or large-scale production with a lot of planted forests and commercially viable agricultural plots.

Developing Mineral Wealth

In order to have industries, you need raw materials, and these are derived not only from agricultural produce but also from minerals, forests and freshwater resources. Therefore, those three sectors also need to be developed. Uganda has a huge deposit of iron ore estimated at 50 million metric tonnes, in Muko, in the Kabale area; we also have some other deposits of the magnetite type of iron ore in the Tororo area, estimated at 30 million metric tonnes, and four million metric tonnes in the Busumbu area in Mbale; we have 230 million metric tonnes of phosphate rock; we have gold; and there are some traces of oil in the Rift Valley in western Uganda. All these need to be developed so that they can be used to support the economy. The development of iron ore deposits, in particular, are vital for the large-scale construction activities now taking place. At the moment, much of this construction is supported by recycled scrap iron which is enough to last only five years. The phosphate rock is sufficient to make fertilisers for the whole of the East African agricultural economy, including sulphuric acid for industries. The whole of this mineral sector should be developed to support the modernisation of our country.

EDUCATION

In order to have modern industries and modern agriculture, and manpower for the service sectors such as tourism, banking and insurance, we need educated manpower. Uganda has a reasonable pool of such manpower, but it is only 'reasonable' now because of the low level of development. As soon as the economy moves into the full employment of factors of production, into the more optimal use of our vast natural resources, the present pool of educated manpower will simply not be enough. Already previous training programmes have been shown to be deficient. Take the example of medical doctors – Uganda was amongst the first countries in Africa to train doctors. The medical school started producing doctors in 1923 but, since then, we have produced only about 2500 over a period of 60 years, to cover a current population of nearly 20 million people.

In order to exploit raw materials such as minerals, you need trained manpower. Uganda's training programmes, both in colonial times and since independence, have been characterised by two factors. First of all, they are not training enough people and, secondly, much of the training is not relevant to the development needs of the country. If we go back to the example of doctors, 500 of the 2500 we trained were non-Ugandans – they included Kenyans and Tanzanians initially, and later Zambians and southern Sudanese. So the true figure of Ugandan doctors trained is only about 2000. Additionally, the first trainees from the medical school are now very old, and many of them have died. Even assuming that all the 2000 Ugandan doctors who trained at Makerere University since 1923 were still alive and working in Uganda, the doctor-patient ratio would be 1:10 000 (compared with the doctor-patient ratio in Europe of 1:1500). However, the situation is much worse than that because, owing to the numerous problems which the country has experienced, many of the 2000 Ugandan doctors who are still alive are not working in Uganda.

This example graphically illustrates that, even at its best, and eliminating all other intervening factors, the training of manpower in Uganda has been inadequate for the country's needs. Therefore, we need to train on a massive scale. We need to introduce mass education instead of the elitest system which has hitherto been characteristic of our educational pattern. We must send all our children to school. It is estimated that, at present, there are 3.82 million children of primary-school age, of whom only 2.68 million (70 per cent) actually attend school. Our task is to ensure that this figure rises to 100 per cent school attendance in this age group. The NRM intends to design a system of education which is cheap to fund. We shall do this, first of all, by greatly reducing the number of boarding schools, which have been given emphasis since colonial times. As soon as day schools are promoted rather than boarding schools, expenditure is concentrated on classrooms, libraries, laboratories and the training of teachers. This would cut down the indulgence in non-scholarly expenses such as feeding and accommodation, which consume so much money. The rest of the costs, such as uniforms and scholastic materials can be provided by the parents or guardians. If we concentrate on these aspects of education, this will be a viable package which will enable millions more children to attend school at a lower cost than at present.

PRESIDENTIAL ELECTIONS

Politicking in a free atmosphere was a new experience in Uganda and we had travelled a hard road to get this far. In my view, the post-independence history of Uganda can be divided into three parts. The first, from 1962 to 1966, I call the era of confusion and ideological bankruptcy. The British had tried to introduce their bourgeois liberal democracy to Uganda, as they had tried in all their other colonies. This bourgeois democracy was based on a multi-party system. The incongruous factor was that the political parties of Europe had evolved over several centuries, out of the socially differentiated forces of capitalism. It is the complete absence of such social and political evolution in our continent that has caused so many problems for Africa since independence.

As soon as political parties were introduced, they became sectarian, based on ethnicity and religion. Thus, in Uganda, the Democratic Party was for Catholics, the UPC was the party for Protestants, and the Kabaka Yekka the party for Baganda Protestants. It is for this reason that I call the 1962–66 period the era of ideological confusion. If you are engaged in a battle, violent or peaceful, you must first of all define who the enemy is, who the friend is, and why you characterise them as such. These parties misdefined the enemy both for themselves and for their followers. For them, the enemy was not the colonial system that had caused

Africa to miss out on the great human revolution from pre-capitalist to capitalist modes of production; the enemy was their neighbour, who happened to be of a different religion or tribe. A friend was someone who belonged to the same religious denomination irrespective of his or her qualities – whether good or bad, pro- or anti-peasant. This was the greatest form of idological obscurantism, because it completely obscured reality, and thus the understanding of the numerous social and economic issues that had to be dealt with.

The second type of governance that Uganda experienced since independence was dicatorship – by Obote between 1966 and 1971; by Amin between 1971 and 1979; by Obote again between 1980 and 1985; and by the Okellos, briefly, from July 1985 to January 1986. During this period, all the pretences and the farcical arrangements of the pseudo-liberal order were thrown away and Uganda was ruled by brute force of the worst kind. People, including women and children, were killed indiscriminately, if they were perceived as belonging to the enemy side – which meant the other religion or the other tribe, or anybody who threatened your business or social interests. Under this type of governance, approximately 800 000 Ugandans were killed in the 20 years between 1966 and 1986. In the area of Luwero, the results of this criminality have been preserved: there are 30 mass graves and each holds an average of 2000 skulls. This gives us a figure of about 70 000 skulls in this area alone, a figure which does not include those people who were buried directly by their relatives. All these people were victims of the primitive dictatorships that engulfed Uganda as soon as the pseudo-liberal democracy collapsed.

The third type of governance has been the liberation phase, where elements of the intelligentsia and the peasants organised a massive liberation movement, first of all quietly under Idi Amin, but more openly and independently since 1981. This eventually resulted in the defeat of the dictatorships.

Therefore, the politicking in a free atmosphere which we experienced in the election campaigns of 1996 could not escape the effects of these three types of governance on the people of Uganda. As usual, foreign observers and critics of our democratic process failed to appreciate this. They were engaged in their own stereotypical and mediocre understanding of the situation. According to them, the people of Uganda were extremely hungry for political parties, and as soon as they got a free vote, they would vote for them. There is even an element of racism in this perception because it seems some people think that Africans are not able to know what is good and bad for them, even when the bad is presented in the most outrageous form.

This irritating paternalism on the part of some of our foreign friends put us under great pressure to do what they thought was desirable. Indeed, quite a number of our own intellectuals, trained in the colonial tradition of not thinking for themselves but instead imbibing whatever others tell them, also fell victim to this paternalism. Thus, the campaigns for the elections of 1996 took place against a background of tremendous external pressure to 'keep up with the Joneses' in

Africa, in other words, to adopt multi-partyism as our political system. Our own feeling, however, was that we should 'keep down with the Joneses', because we also happened to have our own Joneses here who were more relevant to our own particular political interests.

In spite of the interference of the international community, and pressure from international and local-enclave media, we, in the National Resistance Movement, were absolutely sure that our people did not want parties at this moment in our history. On account of our work over many decades, I was confident that most of our people would not fall prey to religious or tribal sectarianism, and that the NRM would win by at least a two-thirds majority, whatever the machinations of the opposite camp. I was also convinced that if we managed to blunt the effect of some of those machinations, we would gain around 75 per cent of the vote or more. Campaigning, therefore, centred on the issue of whether to continue the liberation process – erasing the effects of the past dictatorships, sectarianism and subservience to foreign interests – or not.

We were given 39 days in which to campaign, from 29 March to 7 May 1996. Since the NRM had achieved tremendous progress in the previous ten years, it was not difficult to campaign, although external observers did not realise this. The difficulty for the opposition was not so much our use of state machinery, as they kept saying in the press – in fact, our use of state machinery is very inefficient. The NRM never uses the radio or newspapers for its own causes; if anything the radio and the newspapers are used more by the opposition than by us. The problem for the opposition lay in the work the NRM had done over the ten years since 1986.

Firstly, we had brought peace, security and respect for human rights, especially in the elimination of extra-judicial killings. Secondly, we had repaired some of the infrastructure, especially roads. Thirdly, we had rehabilitated industries, and there was now an abundance of consumer goods which in the pre-NRM days used to be called 'essential commodities'. In those bad old days, Dr Moses Apiliga used to be euphemistically called the 'Minister of Supplies' when, in fact, he should have been more appropriately called the 'Minister of Shortages'. This also applies to one presidential aspirant who did not make it to the nomination, Dr Adonia Tiberondwa, who, for a long time, was 'Minister of Industry' at a time when there were no industries to be minister of. These three major achievements of the NRM were not easy to bypass, however hard the opposition tried.

In fact, there were only two real problems faced by the movement during the election campaign. Firstly, many young people had grown up during the time of the NRM, and took its achievements for granted. A new young voter of 21 in 1996 would only have been an 11-year-old child in 1986, and not very concerned with the shortages his or her parents had had to cope with at that time. Such a person would be more worried by new issues such as high educational costs and lack of employment for new graduates from the university. He or she would not be worried by the elementaries which the NRM government had had the unpleasant task of dealing with. Therefore, the apathy that comes with success posed a major problem, especially in respect of the younger voters. Among the older voters, although there was no problem of apathy – many of them were very firmly behind the movement – there was, ironically, the most susceptibility to the old sectarian thinking. While the new voters did not have the sectarian inclinations of their parents, they were taking the movement's success for granted.

The second problem we had to contend with was largely due to the poor quality of much of the NRM cadreship. While the NRM had scored many successes, these had not been translated into higher incomes for the three or four million rural households. Therefore, the opposition tried to nullify the NRM's achievements by simply concentrating on those areas which the movement had not yet reached in its programme of reconstruction. The movement had started the journey of reconstruction from mile zero; it was now at mile eight; the destination was mile ten; and the opposition concentrated their fire on the two miles that were still to be covered. They said 'This movement is useless because it has not covered the last two miles.' Our defence of our record was to point out to the public that we had covered the eight miles over the ten years we had been in power and, therefore, we only had two more to go. These were basically the battle positions.

As far as the campaign itself was concerned, the only issue I was not sure of was the effect of the anti-NRM ingrates in some areas of Buganda. In fact, this region has benefited most from the work of the NRM. We saved the people of Buganda from the humiliations and persecutions imposed on them by the regimes of Amin and Obote. All the infrastructure reconstruction that has taken place has favoured the region – the roads radiating out from Kampala to Gayaza, Mubende, Luwero, Gulu and Busunju, the power projects and the huge expansion of Kampala itself. The problem of Buganda, however, has always been poor leadership. Quite a number of the Baganda leaders decided to oppose the NRM, thinking that the movement would fail through a combination of their own activities and those of other sectarian groups throughout the rest of the country. I knew that this would not cause the NRM to lose the election, but I was concerned that the movement should not perform poorly in the areas around the capital, because this might have caused apprehension amongst our supporters in other parts of the country.

Therefore, I decided to start my campaign in the areas of Buganda where I knew that support was guaranteed because of our previous work. My first rallies were in the Luwero Triangle, starting with Nakasongola and Wobulenzi on 29 March, and going on to Nakaseke, Bamunanika and Bombo the next day. In order to fulfil our campaign schedule, we had to have three or four rallies a day and some of them had to be held early in the morning. This created a problem because in rural areas, where the population is quite sparse, it is not easy to raise huge crowds at around 10.00 a.m. This was the case at Nakasongola where there was a crowd of only 15 000 people. In fact, when we were leaving the rally people were still arriving to hear me speak. One member of my staff approached me, worried that a crowd of only 15 000 would not be good enough for our overall image in the country. However, I told her that this had been caused by the sparseness of the population in that area and that the situation would improve as we went along. This concern about numbers had arisen because the main opposition camp had waged psychological warfare against my own people by mobilising a large crowd, ferrying people from different parts of the country to Kololo Airstrip for the presidential nomination day on 27 March.

A hot debate ensued as to which candidate had drawn a larger crowd at Kololo on that day. I was sure that our crowd had been bigger because we had not ferried many people to Kampala, apart from the leaders from the various districts, and yet large numbers had gathered. Nevertheless, some of my supporters developed an obsession with large crowds, in an attempt to wage psychological counter-warfare against our opponents. After the first rally at Nakasongola, the crowds increased as we went into more populated areas. The crowds at Wobulenzi and Bamunanika were big, the one at Kikamulo was medium-sized, and, as we progressed towards Mukono, they became very large indeed. The first really massive crowd was at Kasawo in Nakifuma county and there were equally huge ones at Kangulumira and Mukono town.

In Uganda, the science of estimating crowds is not well developed. I think this is due to the fact that since there was no history of democracy in the country, neither the police nor the newspapers have any experience in estimating the size of crowds. I, however, devised a simple technique of my own which I think other people could usefully borrow. When I went back to State House in Nakasero, I measured one square metre on the floor in one of our rooms. I stood in that square metre space with my wife and one of our daughters and I found that, although we three are not of inconsiderable size, there was still room for three more adults of the same size as ourselves in the space. I thus concluded that you can squeeze six adults of more than average size into a single square metre. Thereafter, it became easy for me to estimate the size of crowds from the space they occupied, although I kept my formula to myself. I was amused by the inaccurate estimates of the police and the newspapers and all those other people who never bother to do research but just give out their own prejudices as facts.

Using my technique, I would estimate the crowds I saw in Kasawo, Kangulumira and Mukono town at not less than 100 000 people each. In other areas such as Mbale, Nyenga, Nkonkonjeru and Lugazi town the crowds would be of the magnitude of between 30 000 and 40 000 people. The crowds in Mpigi town, Buwama, Masaka town, Bukomansimbi and at Nkumba university – all in the Buganda area – would have been in the region of 100 000. In the western region, at places like Mbarara, Bushenyi, Kabale and Rukungiri, the crowds were between 100 000 and 150 000 people. In eastern Uganda, at the rallies at Mbale, Pallisa and Iganga, the crowds were equally massive. At Kololo, on the last day of the campaign, I would estimate the crowd as at least half-a-million people. The size of Kololo Airstrip from Heroes' Corner up to Wampewo Avenue, and from the embankment on Upper Kololo Terrace down to the public utilities, measures about 150 000 square metres. If you multiply that size by six people, you will get the figure of 900 000. This calculation proves my formula correct, because the crowd covered only about three-quarters of Kololo Airstrip.

During these rallies, I discovered that one factor which the politicians and public servants did not appreciate was that, with such massive crowds of people, it is very dangerous to begin the rally with a lot of formalities. The principal character whom the crowd came to see should immediately start speaking. When he does not, the crowd surges forward to try and catch a glimpse of him and this can result in people being crushed to death in the stampede. On a number of occasions, I had to take over the running of the rallies from the election officials because I could see that their methods were a recipe for disaster. In fact, it is a miracle that we did not have people crushed to death. Instead of speaking into microphones, out of sight of the crowd, there should always be a prominent platform where the speakers can be seen by everyone. The other major danger I saw in these crowds was the children, who are not tall enough to compete with adults for space. When people are running alongside the vehicle or the convoy of the principal, there is a danger that a small child could be knocked down and crushed by the vehicle. This was a constant nightmare for me. Our security personnel need to learn how to manage such large crowds.

Throughout the whole of my election campaign, my wife, Janet Kataaha Museveni, was always by my side, and I greatly appreciated her support.

USING IMAGERY TO COMMUNICATE

One problem all leaders face is communication – the ability to convey their vision to their audience. In the case of Uganda, and possibly in other parts of the continent, this problem is compounded because black Africa is composed of numerous tribes, each one speaking its own language or dialect. Owing to the bankruptcy of the colonial system and of the pre-colonial African rulers, as well as the post-colonial African political elite, there is always a tendency to exaggerate the differences among these dialects.

Essentially, in the whole of Africa there are six or so different language groups: (a) the Bantu languages, spoken by approximately 200 million people in central, eastern and southern Africa, from Cameroon to Kenya and from Uganda to South Africa; (b) the Cushitic languages, spoken mainly in southern Ethiopia by the Oromos, the Somali and some groups in northern Sudan such as the Buija and the Hadendawa; (c) the Semitic languages, spoken by the Amhara and Tigray peoples in Ethiopia and Eritrea; (d) Arabic, spoken in northern Sudan, Egypt and the Mahgreb; (e) the West African languages such as Ibo and Yoruba of southern Nigeria, and the languages of Benin, Togo, Ghana, southern Mali and as far west as Senegal; and (f) the Nilotic and Sudanic languages spoken in southern Sudan, northern Uganda, south-eastern Ethiopia and parts of Kenya.

In Uganda, we have four of these language groups – Bantu in west, central and much of eastern Uganda; the Nilotic languages in north-central Uganda; the

Cushitic languages in north-eastern Uganda; and the Sudanic languages in north-western Uganda. By far the largest set of dialects are found in the Bantu language group, spoken by about three-quarters of the Ugandan population. These dialects are mostly mutually intelligible, if one cares to master one of them very well and then listen carefully to the others. This is how I have been able to listen to and understand the Bantu dialects other than my own.

The problem of communication is even more difficult in Uganda than in other African countries, partly because of the diversity of languages and partly because many Ugandans have not mastered well even their own mother tongues and will, therefore, certainly not be able to understand other sister dialects. When it comes to campaigning, it is a sad story. There are political agitators trying to get messages across to the peasantry, without succeeding, by mixing English with some of the local languages. The consequence has been complete lack of communication between the leaders and the led. As I explained at the beginning of this book, I was lucky in that I grew up in a completely traditional family. I was able to master, in great detail, my mother dialect, Runyankore, which happens to be one of the most ancient in this area. Runyankore has links with all the Bantu dialects of the interlacustrine area – that is Buganda, western and eastern Uganda, eastern Zaire, Rwanda, Burundi, north-western Tanzania, the Mara region of Tanzania – and even as far afield as Zambia, especially the Bemba language. Owing to my deep knowledge of Runyankore, I have been able to follow all the speeches in all the Bantu areas of Uganda. This is a great advantage, if one bears in mind that the Bantu-speakers are the great majority of the population of Uganda.

Using my wealth of knowledge of both Runyankore and the culture of the rural peasantry (which is quite similar in all parts of Uganda, Bantu or non-Bantu), I was able to think up images that would convey my message clearly to the *wananchi*. The first issue I helped to convey to the public through imagery was the whole question of power and the quest for political power. Since independence, the main notion of many of the political leaders in Uganda has been that being in power is a privilege. This was a phrase coined by Godfrey Binaisa, one of the post-Amin leaders, who talked of 'falling into things' – *okugwa mubintu* – which in essence meant that those who were lucky enough to be in power had become rich overnight. I do not need to belabour the negative connotations such an idea conveys. That is why there is such a mad rush for people to get into power, regardless of what they plan to do there. Everybody had developed the idea that being in government was a privilege, not a service to society. I had, therefore, to think about this prevailing attitude and find a way of conveying my ideas to the public.

My own feeling towards power is that it is the farthest thing from privilege one can experience. It is taxing; it diverts you from your own more lucrative activities (if you are thinking of making money) and it exposes the leader to endless risks, especially in a country such as Uganda where politics took a very violent turn. Therefore, being in power, as far as I am concerned, has been one endless story of sacrifice. Ever since 1966, when I and my comrades started opposing Obote's dictatorship, we have never rested. From 1966 to 1970, we were engaged in active student politics, including our journey to Mozambique; the whole of 1970 was spent in fighting local battles against the ranchers in western Uganda; between 1971 and 1979 we were involved in a most brutal struggle against Idi Amin in which many of my personal friends died; we endured two years of instability and insecurity between 1979 and 1981; the time between 1981 and 1985 consisted of a most horrendous war in the Luwero area; and ever since 1986 we have been engaged in battling against one criminal group after another, as well as coping with the endless intrigues of the unarmed politicians.

To call such a contribution a privilege is an insult. There is a real danger that, if those who perceive being in power as a privilege actually succeed in becoming the dominant force in government, we shall be back to square one. Obviously, those who do not understand the primary purpose of being in government in a Third World country will not govern successfully. It may be that in the developed countries, where most issues are already sorted out, it could be a privilege to be in government, but in an underdeveloped country it is, if anything, a tremendous sacrifice.

I had to think of a way of conveying all this to the public, and I thought of *orubengo*, a traditional grinding stone. These are granite blocks which are very heavy – an ordinary *rubengo* would weigh between 50 and 80 kilograms. Apart from the weight, a *rubengo* is also very compact, and yet it is a useful tool to have in a home, for if you do not have one, you will have nowhere to grind your millet and your family will have nothing to eat. This image was easy for everyone to understand. In traditional rural Ugandan society a family would periodically move home to a new site. Then all the family's possessions would need to be carried physically, by members of the family. The question now was: is the carrier of the *rubengo* being accorded a privilege, a punishment or a duty? It surely could not be a privilege to have to carry such a weight and in the end eat the same share as the rest of the family. On the other hand, it could not be called a punishment either, because you are part of the family yourself. If the family does not have the *rubengo* and, therefore, cannot grind its millet, nobody will have any food. A *rubengo*-carrier is, therefore, doing nothing more than carrying out an assignment. It is a heavy one, but a necessary one, which somebody has to do. This image helped the people understand quite clearly my concept of leadership in a country like Uganda.

The other image I used during the campaign was *okulembeka*, an idea I had been using for some years during my teaching sessions in connection with the sharing of responsibilities in the country. The opposition, in its contemptibly opportunistic way, campaigned by condemning the government totally, without giving it due praise where it had succeeded. Obviously, the NRM government had succeeded in many areas. It had brought peace to most of the country; it had repaired the infrastructure; it had attracted industries; inflation had been controlled; the foreign exchange inflows to the country had reached US$1.4 billion compared to US$500 million in 1986; and Kampala had grown by 100 per cent over the ten years. In spite of all this, the opposition could stand up and say: 'This government has done nothing!' Then they would cite household poverty, which was still a reality, as proof that the NRM had done nothing.

The question of lingering household poverty was partly due to the weakness of our own NRM leaders, many of whom are no different from the other opportunistic politicians: they simply want to be in power and use it for no other purpose than serving their own interests. These kinds of people put us in a dilemma. On the one hand, since we are engaged in constitutional governance, we need the support of such people; we need their votes in Parliament and elsewhere. On the other hand, in a sense they are no different from the opposition. The dilemma arises because we do not want to antagonise or undermine them, but they are not doing a satisfactory job for the movement either. It is, therefore, true that if we had had more conscientious NRM supporters, we could have done more over the ten years in respect of erradicating poverty, just as we did in the areas of repairing roads and in macro-economic stabilisation. In spite of these achievements, however, the opposition persisted in saying that the NRM had done nothing.

I had to think of a way to extricate the movement from this quagmire created by opportunists on two fronts – the internal opportunists within the movement and the opposition outside. I recalled the image of *okulembeka*, an image extracted from rural life where indoor piped water is unknown. We used to tap rainwater from corrugated iron roofs into containers. We would put a funnel made from the bark of a banana tree (*orugogo*), about a metre long, in the direction of the water falling from the roof, and this would channel it into a container. This technique is called *okulembeka* in Luganda, *okutangiriza* in western Uganda, *jolo pii* in Acholi, and in the Cushitic languages it is called *akiwoun ngakipi*. This image brings out the sharing of responsibilities between the individual and the government: God brings the rain onto the roof of the house, but if the occupant does not bother to trap it and put it into a container, the house will remain without water, in spite of the rain having fallen right on the rooftop. In other words, there are things the government can do to end poverty in the rural areas, but there are others which must be done by the individual. However, what I had to cover up in order to protect our inefficient NRM politicians was the fact that one function of leadership in a backward country is precisely to teach the people a means of tapping wealth, because they do not know how to do it on their own. I have, therefore, given notice to our colleagues that this time round there will be no cover-up. We shall denounce people who do not perform and disassociate ourselves from them.

This imagery helped me tremendously to explain these issues to the people. In fact, I had started using it before the start of the election campaign period because I had anticipated this problem, bearing in mind what the opportunistic politicians were saying in the newspapers. By the time of the campaign, I had immunised the public against the poison of the opposition.

Another good example using local imagery was in connection with my battle against unprincipled compromises. The opposition, and some sections of the church, had taken the line that we should negotiate with the bandits, who have done so much damage to the population in northern Uganda. We have fought many wars and we have become reconciled with many people who were opposed to us in the past. However, we do this carefully, always making a distinction between the misleaders and the misled, and also between opposition – even armed opposition – on the one hand, and criminality on the other. When rebels attack the army and kill soldiers, that is very bad. It is treasonable and can be punished by death. However, even in such a case, if there is an opportunity, we can achieve reconciliation, because we reason that the fellow who engaged in these acts was acting out of political confusion, yet clearly in search of political power. If, however, somebody rapes a woman, or kills a peasant who has no power, one cannot say that this fellow is killing because he is in search of political power. He is killing because he is a criminal – the people he is killing and raping do not possess power. It was crucial, therefore, that we convey our concern to the public about the position of the opposition.

I thought of the image of *olumbugu,* which is a very vicious weed grass, called couch grass, that invades gardens. A small piece of its underground stem will very quickly grow into a mass of fibrous tissues if it gets the slightest chance of attaching itself to the soil. Once it is in the garden, getting rid of it is a very difficult task. When I told the public that those who wanted to negotiate with bandits were reintroducing olumbugu where we had already cleared the garden, the message was very clear, and received most enthusiastically. A combination of these images dealt devastating blows to the opposition. I have no doubt that these images increased our support by anything up to 20 per cent, because they clarified people's perceptions of the problems.

MOBILISING THROUGH *KAKUYEGE*

Apart from communicating one's message, in a campaign the techniques of organisation are crucial. Whom do you mobilise, why and how? the opposition had concentrated on some urban elements who had lived like parasites on the state of Uganda, especially since the collapse of democracy during Idi Amin's regime. These parasites included the *mafuta mingi,* who had received businesses stolen from the Asians expelled during Amin's time; speculators who made exorbitant profits, taking advantage of the shortages of commodities; retrenched civil servants who did not care whether Uganda collapsed or not, as long as they stayed on the payroll of a bloated civil service that was doing nothing except increasing the country's problems; and the political elites of former regimes who sat like vultures making merry over the carcases of cows killed by an epidemic. These political elites used to get chits to obtain scarce commodities from the few operational industries, which they would then sell at exorbitant prices, making huge profits. It did not matter to them that the money they were extorting from the public was valueless because of the high levels of inflation. These types of people formed the constituency of the opposition during the election. Once in a while, they would make common cause with some lecturers from the universities who had also come up during the period of the collapse and whose understanding of the dynamics of production and distribution in an economy was deficient. The position of this constellation of forces could be summarised as follows: they wanted reward without work; remuneration without effort.

I had been thinking of another image of a lonely mother who was living alone with her eight-month-old baby. The mother died, and since they were living alone, and since the baby did not know what death was, it continued suckling its dead mother's breast until two days later, when some people came and rescued it. This was the attitude of some of the groups I have talked about. They did not seem to know that their mother, Uganda, though not actually dead, had gone into deep coma. Yet it was from the same comatose Uganda that they were demanding a living wage; they were demanding *entandikwa*; roads immediately; they were demanding everything without any effort on their part. We, on the other hand, took a different line. We knew that what was required now was to revive this mother of ours slowly, up to the point when she would be able to sustain us.

Therefore, having perceived these parasitic constituencies, which were natural allies of the opposition, we decided to mobilise our own natural constituencies. Among them were the peasants who, above all, treasured peace and the absence of persecution from the state, which had been the hallmark of the previous regimes. They appreciated the non-sectarian rural harmony we had introduced into the countryside under the NRM system which had got rid of the old political parties. Our natural constituencies also included the businessmen – the real producers who have factories and farms, and who knew that the NRM were the only people who could guarantee order and security in the country to enable them to carry on with their economic activities. To some extent, we also had links with the industrial workers because their industries similarly depended on the stability we had brought.

How do you mobilise peasants? The social structure in a typical village, such as Rushere in Nyabushozi county, is roughly as follows. There is a small group of university graduates who come from a village but who never go back there until election time. Since they have not been in constant contact with the people, they cite sectarian positions in order to get support which they do not deserve. There are normally about ten such people in a typical village. The second group may have, educationally, reached upper secondary school or 'A' level. There may be about 30 or 40 people in this group. They know how to read and write, they can communicate in English and they are normally the natural leaders of an area. Owing to bad ideological influences, some of these people are among those who want quick riches without work. Others, however, are steady farmers and rural businessmen, and many of them supported us because of the stability the NRM has brought. The third group in the village are the ones with little or no schooling and they are the majority in the rural areas.

In our mobilisation, therefore, we concentrated on these three groups. First of all, we had to mobilise some of the university graduates, because without them we would not have been able to win a majority in Parliament, which transacts business in English. Unfortunately, many Ugandans are barred from Parliament because of the foreign language we use. We needed these graduates as parliamentary candidates for whom we could canvass support in the rural areas.

We also had to mobilise the middle group of secondary-school-educated people because they form a link for us with the third category, the peasants, and they provide the leadership at the district council and lower local council level. However, we also had to have a direct relationship with the peasants, not only working through the first and second group of the village structure. So we sent out cadres directly answerable either to myself or to the National Task Force, which was specifically set up for the election. These cadres would be in direct contact with the peasants, especially in central, eastern and western Uganda. It was because of this thorough work that we had such huge majorities in many areas. In other parts of the country, for example northern Uganda, where we were not able to establish such a thorough network, the results were very different from those in the rest of the country. We called this method of mobilisation *kakuyege*. Enkuyege are very small ants which operate in huge numbers. Once they invade an area, they are able to cover a large piece of ground, penetrating through every crevice in the grass.

THE PROBLEM OF NORTHERN UGANDA

During the presidential election campaign, my candidature was very popular throughout the country, as the results eventually showed, except for the areas of Gulu and Kitgum, and there were also rather small rallies in the counties of Terego, Madi Okollo and Aringa in the West Nile region. When I asked my campaigners about this in West Nile, they told me that there had been intimidation. That could have been the case, but I also suspected that, owing to the history of this part of the country, there may have been genuine anti-NRM feeling in some of those areas of West Nile. In the case of the Acholi area – that is Gulu and Kitgum districts – and, to some extent, West Nile, this stemmed from colonial times. The colonialists marginalised some parts of the country, including northern Uganda. Instead of introducing commercial agriculture there, as they did in Buganda, they just kept the area as a reservoir for cheap labour for the plantations in the south of the country, and also as a source of recruits for the army. The people in the area did not get into the habit of generating wealth through cash-crop production.

Whenever I go to the north, I always hear the cliché that the north was once prosperous and that it has declined in the last ten years. I have never shared this opinion. I do not think the north has ever been prosperous at any time. It is true that in the last ten years there has been more human suffering than before, but to say that the area has ever been prosperous is to tell a lie. Whenever I visit areas such as Zirobwe and Kibinge in Masaka, there is evidence that there was prosperity in the past because there are iron-roofed houses and even some tile-roofed ones which have since declined. In the north, there is no evidence of past prosperity. The houses are all grass huts, and there are no permanent crops. Therefore, what anybody who is interested in the north should say is that the area has never been developed. However, there was security before – people were not being killed by bandits. They were just living in their villages, producing some cotton and tobacco from which they were getting very poor returns. What has deteriorated in the north is security rather than prosperity.

This implies that the colonialists did the most damage by keeping the area backward. When Uganda became independent, the politicians, who came into government, were themselves mainly from the north and never had the vision to identify, let alone correct, the bottleneck factors which had kept the area backward. Instead, they encouraged our people there to flock into government with or without qualifications, thereby removing them further and further away from productive activities. Many Acholi soldiers who fought in the Second World War never retired from the army as those from Buganda and other areas did. One can contrast those Acholi soldiers whom we know, for instance, with Benedicto Kiwanuka, who was also a soldier in the Second World War. When he returned, he left the army and went to South Africa where he gained a law degree. By 1960, he was a practising lawyer, and was able to become the first Chief Minister of Uganda in 1961. His counterparts, however, never improved their educational level, until many of them were either killed in the ensuing upheavals or left the army when the old armies were disbanded by successive revolutions.

This is the source of the problem of the north. The people have not been trained, except recently in our times, to know where wealth comes from. Many people in the north believed that wealth came from government service as soldiers, as civil servants after independence, or as plantation workers. The resentment in the north, therefore, is really due to the fact that our government made it categorically clear that we shall develop Uganda through agriculture, industrial production, or the growth of the services sector. The role of the bureaucracy is minimal in our scheme of thinking.

One reason why African countries in general have remained marginalised all this time is that they have continued to be bureaucratic states. Our emphasis is to develop the private sector, because we know that is the only sector which can develop our country sustainably, efficiently and cheaply. It is this individual entrepreneurial spirit that is lacking in northern Uganda. Those people who were used to government handouts because they were members of UPC, or because they were in the army or the intelligence services, feel completely lost now that the approach is totally different. This is why you hear talk of the north being marginalised. In fact, if one looks at government expenditure on infrastructure, more attention has been paid to the north than to the south. The northern districts received road development before many districts in the south.

These problems, of course, were compounded by the insecurity which itself was linked to the factors I have just outlined. The bandits are all, in one way or another, linked to the old regimes. The Kony bandits came out of the Lakwena-Odong Latek group, remnants of the UNLA who fled into the Sudan in 1986 after we defeated them. The Juma Oris group operating in the West Nile region is directly linked to Idi Amin – Juma Oris was a protege of Amin. The role of northern politicians in the history of Uganda since independence has further added to the problems. Since the army was dominated by people from the north, and since the first Prime Minister, Milton Obote, came from the north, and was of the opportunist bent I have described previously, he could not resist misusing the army in order to keep himself in power. Since the army itself was not well trained and had a colonial mentality, it engaged in numerous anti-people activities, including mass killings of Ugandans. This made the northern politicians and their army very much hated in other parts of the country. For the army, murder had become a way of life. They would kill people, and take their cars and other property: and they believed that was how government should be run.

When the NRA defeated them, they thought we had deprived them of their rights. This is manifested in the Kony legacy – Kony still thinks it his right to kill people who do not agree with him. He learnt this from the UNLA, who learned it from the original Uganda Army. I was, therefore, not surprised by the lack of support in some parts of the north, because we had not had time to address all these issues, nor did we have strong cadres who could undermine the legacy of the old anti-NRM politics of the region.

However, I knew that even without much support from those areas, we would still win the elections. Indeed, in spite of the vicious propaganda of the opposition, we still received support in some northern districts, although it was not as overwhelming as in the south. In Moyo and Nebbi districts, the movement won an overall majority. In some constitutencies in Arua district, we got a reasonable number of votes, and even in Lira and Kitgum I won about 10 per cent of the votes cast. In the Lango area, although the opposition won, I gained 16 per cent. In Kwania county, for instance, I got 13 000 votes and in Maruzi I got 7000. Therefore, even in the worst times of misinformation, there was still support for the movement in the north.

Of course, when we refer to 'the north', many people do not think of Karamoja, where we had almost 100 per cent support for the movement. Therefore, the whole question of the 'northern problem' is overdramatised. It was a big problem in the history of Uganda because people from there were being used by colonialism and by the dictatorships but, with the rise to power of patriotic forces, a basis has been created to integrate the north politically with the rest of the country.

On the issue of security, I refuse to negotiate with the bandits, not because they are armed opponents of the government, but because they are criminals. If they were merely armed opponents they would be committing treason and that would be a crime against the state. What Kony's bandits are doing is not only a crime against the state: it is a crime against the population. They kill peasants, who have nothing to do with state power; they kill young people or kidnap them to make them cannon fodder; they rape women; they marry girls by force; and they spread AIDS in the north. These are crimes against humanity on a massive scale. I find it completely distasteful that people do not with one voice condemn these crimes of Kony and his bandits.

LOOKING AHEAD

The people of Uganda clearly showed their approval of the achievements of our movement, support for the principles we have stood for over the past ten years and, in particular, rejection of the system of party politics, when they elected me President for a five-year term with 75 per cent of the vote. In the parliamentary elections which followed, in June, supporters of the movement won about 85 per cent of the seats which were contested.

The mission of the movement hereafter is to effect the modernisation of Uganda. I know people are worried about some rivalries amongst individuals who all belong to the movement. These are a problem but they are not the main issue facing Uganda now. The main problem is the underdevelopment of the rural economy. Any politician who does not relate vigorously to this basic requirement for transforming and modernising Uganda should not be regarded as a movement person – whatever he or she says. The target I have set for the movement leaders is for them to ensure that the rural economy is transformed to the extent that the return per acre per annum is not less than one million shillings (US$1000).

In our system of government we have divided up responsibilities. The Prime Minister carries out the day-to-day government administration. This has been a deliberate strategy so that, with time, the President has become more or less a guarantor of security. His job as Head of State is to keep the army under good management and to ensure that there is no disturbance of the peace. Cabinet meetings are chaired by the Vice-President and the Prime Minister, except when there are very major decisions, such as new policy measures, to be taken. Examples of this include the adoption of the policy that would lead to the election of the Constituent Assembly; the privatisation policy; and the decision to allow the Asians whom Amin had expelled to return and reclaim their property. For these, and other major political decisions, I chair the cabinet myself.

Otherwise, apart from security, my job is mainly political. I receive delegations, meet tribal chiefs and try to keep these and all the other people united. I am always mobilising people around the country, and I do not do much paperwork. This is because most of the major decisions are already in place. There is not much to be done about these, except to have them understood by the public. In this we are different from developed Western countries. A president of Uganda has to be a combination of security chief, political commissar and economic consultant – all fused together in one personality.

Now that I have been returned to office as President in the elections of May 1996, I have a number of major objectives for the years ahead.

1. I want to consolidate what my government has already achieved, especially expanding the rate at which we can attract investment, so that we can build more factories and fully tap the resources and money to help people. This will allow people to get a good education and the capacity to earn income for their homes.
2. We must now focus on the rural households, which are the majority, so that their economic activities are metamorphosed from subsistence farming to farming for the market, which will enable them to save for their immediate financial needs and to invest in bettering their family's position in the future.
3. My third objective is to achieve closer East African co-operation. We should work for this, and even form an East African union government or a federation of East Africa which shares some activities such as defence and foreign affairs. There would be an improvement in efficiency if we shared some of these things. An East African currency, for example, would create an internationally powerful market.

A good number of these objectives can be realised in the coming years. We have already attracted investors. They will continue to come and rural incomes will definitely increase. All the other stimuli are in place, except that there is still a need to provide more roads. We have free trade, liberalisation, and a convertible currency. As for regional integration, even if nothing has happened in the near future, I shall have stated my position and it will be up to subsequent generations to follow it up.

Looking further ahead, I am optimistic about Uganda's future. Our present line of progressive development might get delayed along the way, but I do not anticipate any serious breakdown as happened in the past, unless we get confused political groups in charge. They might delay the industrialisation and economic liberalisation process, but the fundamental principles are now in place. There are now people of presidential calibre and capacity who can take over when I retire, and I shall be among the first to back them. By that time, I am confident that Uganda's modernisation process will have taken root and the mission of the movement for which we have struggled for 30 years will have been achieved.

THE TEN-POINT PROGRAMME OF THE NATIONAL RESISTANCE MOVEMENT

BACKGROUND

Over the five years of the protracted liberation struggle (from February 1981 to January 1986), the National Resistance Movement, together with the High Command and Senior Officers of the National Resistance Army, under the chairmanship of Yoweri Kaguta Museveni, worked out proposals for a political programme. This formed the basis for a nationwide coalition of political and social forces which could usher in a better future for the long-suffering people of Uganda. This programme is popularly known as the Ten-Point Programme of the National Resistance Movement.

THE TEN POINTS

Point No. 1   Restoration of democracy

Point No. 2   Restoration of security of person and property

Point No. 3   Consolidation of national unity and elimination of all forms of sectarianism

Point No. 4   Defending and consolidating national independence

Point No. 5   Building an independent, integrated and self-sustaining national economy

Point No. 6   Restoration and improvement of social services and rehabilitation of war-ravaged areas

Point No. 7   Elimination of corruption and misuse of power

Point No. 8   Redressing errors that have resulted in the dislocation of some sections of the population

Point No. 9   Co-operation with other African countries

Point No. 10   Following an economic strategy of a mixed economy

GLOSSARY

APC	–	armoured personnel carrier
CA	–	Constituent Assembly
CP	–	Conservative Party
DP	–	Democratic Party
Fedemo	–	Federal Democratic Movement
Frelimo	–	Front for the Liberation of Mozambique
FUNA	–	Former Uganda National Army
GPMG	–	general purpose machine gun
KM	–	Kikoosi Maalum
KY	–	Kabaka Yekka
NCC	–	National Consultative Council
NCO	–	non-commissioned officer
NEC	–	National Executive Council
NRA	–	National Resistance Army
NRC	–	National Resistance Council
NRM	–	National Resistance Movement
PRA	–	Popular Resistance Army
RCs	–	Resistance Councils and Committees
RPG	–	rocket-propelled grenade
SADC	–	Southern African Development Community
SMG	–	sub-machine gun
TANU	–	Tanzania African National Union
TPDF	–	Tanzania People's Defence Forces
UFF	–	Uganda Freedom Fighters
UFM	–	Uganda Freedom Movement
UNLA	–	Uganda National Liberation Army
UNLF	–	Uganda National Liberation Front
UNRF	–	Uganda National Rescue Front
UPC	–	Uganda People's Congress
UPM	–	Uganda Patriotic Movement
USARF	–	University Students' African Revolutionary Front
bayaye	–	lumpen proletariat
kiyaaye	–	lumpen proletariat culture
mwananchi	–	citizen/local person
shamba	–	garden
wananchi	–	citizens/local people

INDEX